The **I** of the
TIGER

The Athlete Identity
& Remedying Sport's Greatest Conflicts

Kimberly Carducci

Everything Athletes

everythingathletes.com

Book Design by Matthew Revert

Edited by Mohamad Al-Hakim, Ph.D

First printing edition 2021.

ISBN: 978-1-7376801-2-3

Dedicated to the future version of You

CONTENTS

PREFACE

My athlete identity was ruining my life. I retired from collegiate swimming a decade ago, yet my intense drive toward perfectionist ideals plagued me in adulthood. I was stuck in a never-ending hamster wheel of desiring more, faster, stronger, smarter, prettier, nicer, happier, better, better, better, better, BETTER. I was burning bright, burning fast, and burning out.

Ultimately, my extreme behavior led to a heartbreaking pitfall hurting the person I loved the most, detailed in Chapter 2. Enough was enough. I needed to understand why I was the way I was. My personality traits, such as my relentless competitive nature, perfectionist attitude and lack of compassion, were reinforced over 15 years as an elite athlete. Those traits needed to be examined, understood, and delicately resolved as I was on the fast-track to a lifetime of unhappiness. A lifetime of perpetual critiques. So, I decided to sit down and write a book. This book.

I researched psychology principles, observed the most elite athletes of our time, reviewed my own life experiences, and attempted to unravel what it means to be an athlete. If you're reading this, I'm glad you have this book in your hands, but I wrote this for myself. I embarked on this project because there wasn't anything out there to help me unpack, decipher, and understand the athlete identity. Therapy had not worked. There was no YouTube series to follow. There wasn't anything I could find about the modern athlete journey that made sense of it all. This book is what I wish I had when I was 21.

Survivor wrote the song, The Eye of the Tiger, for the 1976 movie Rocky, one of the most popular sports films ever made. In it, Sylvester Stallone plays an amateur Italian-American boxer who, by a stroke of luck, gets the opportunity to fight the heavyweight boxing world champion, Apollo Creed. It's a story of underdog versus long-standing champion. It's a story of unwavering dedication. It's a story of becoming the best you can be. It's a story of the thrill of the fight. It's a story of being an athlete.

However, there is so much more to an athlete than favorable physical attributes and a desire to win. *The I of the Tiger* submerges us into the total identity behind the fighter, the "I" of the tiger. We're here to examine everything that accompanies being an athlete and how that affects our lives, both during and post-sport. We're here to make sense of being an athlete in our modern world.

What's inside?

In this book we are going to take out our magnifying glass and dive deep into the sports gauntlet. As athletes, we are going to unravel the many layers, fears, insecurities, complexities, and other characteristics comprising the athlete identity. We will look at how competition influences us, how we build an inflated sense of ego based on our physical capabilities, how injury and retirement deflate our sense of worth, why we might equate defeat with death, and everything that comes with being a fierce competitor. Once we define the central features of the athlete identity and understand our attachment to those, we will then delve deeper into the toughest events athletes face - defeat, injury, and retirement - and how the heck we get through them. Like a game, the book is divided in two halves consisting of four quarters.

First Half: Athlete Identity

The first half of the book is semi-autobiographical focusing on my athletic career and my own journey through the road of victory, defeat, injury and eventual retirement. I draw on my experiences to help shed light and deconstruct the "why" behind the events, decisions, thoughts, and feelings that make up an athlete's journey. Our deeper psyche of how we identify as an athlete tells us a lot about why we behave in certain ways or feel certain emotions. For example, why do athletes struggle sometimes to the point of suicide when they retire from their sport? A few other questions we will answer include:

- What does it mean to have an athlete identity?
- Why do we build an athlete identity?
- How do we build an athlete identity?
- How does that affect my life?
- Why am I addicted to winning?
- What are my typical thought patterns?
- How is my identity influenced by my environment?
- What is the underlying psychology that explains the way I feel?

When we look closely at what it means to be an athlete, we uncover many insights, where insights are the building blocks to developing our understanding. With this basis of understanding we can then apply new knowledge and help create positive change. A basis of understanding clears the path for us to truly figure things out. Rather than forcibly struggle through muddy waters trying to survive, we wipe away the mud to view ourselves with crystal clear glasses.

Second Half: Practical Guide

The second half will take the understanding we have constructed of the Athlete Identity and offer a practical guide to navigate difficult athletic terrain. In specific, the second half focuses on the topics of defeat, injury, and retirement.

- Why do I absolutely hate losing?
- How can I soften the harsh blow of defeat?
- How can I be patient when I'm benched due to injury?
- How do I build a new identity in a life post-sport?
- How can I accept my outcomes?
- How have others navigated similar situations?

Viewing the full landscape of our athlete identity with crystal clear glasses allows us to create change when the journey gets tough. The traditional, complacent mindset of "sticking it out" is not only outdated but can be harmful as many athletes have pointed out. In one of the most advanced eras in mental health and psychological wellbeing (and the most physically advanced sports era known to mankind), we owe it to ourselves to pause, dive deep into our athlete minds and utilize available tools and strategies to develop a healthier athlete mindset.

I want athletes to read this book and understand what it means to be an athlete in the first place. I want athletes to develop tools and strategies to thrive through the most difficult competitive moments. I want athletes to better focus their energy on taking care of their mental health just as much as they focus on the health of their bodies. I want athletes to keep this book in their gym bag and pull it out every time they could use support. I want athletes to be open to the inevitable mental and emotional struggle that accompanies elite competition knowing they are equipped to handle it. I want athletes to reach levels of mental strength an entire generation would find incomprehensible. I want athletes to reach levels of mental strength an entire industry would find incomprehensible.

FIRST QUARTER

Mental Health & the Power of the Mind

"I've always been an extremely motivated person
. . . it nearly cost me my life."
—*Alexi Pappas, 2016 Olympian*

Chapter 1

What If...?

You only change what you understand. What you do not understand and are not aware of, you repress. You don't change. But when you understand it, it changes.

—Anthony de Mello, Spiritual Teacher & Psychotherapist

What if athletes took care of their minds just as much as they did their bodies? This is the question American distance runner and 2016 Olympian, Alexi Pappas, posed in a New York Times Op-Ed. Pappas was diagnosed with severe clinical depression following her Olympic performance. She opened up about her struggle with suicidal thoughts and battle with darker emotions and, interestingly enough, she credits the revelation that saved her life to a conversation she had with her doctor. Her doctor suggested a parallel approach to healing her mind the same way she heals her body. Just as you treat a scratch on your knee, you can also treat a scratch on your brain. This thinking was the light switch for Pappas' approach to overcoming her depression.

As athletes, we too can adopt this approach to our minds when we inevitably experience the valleys that "come with chasing a dream."[1] Those inescapable valleys every athlete experiences at one time or another include moments of defeat, injury, and retirement from sport for good. What if athletes had the same level of support to heal those mental struggles as we do to support physical performance? What might an athlete with a well-supported, healthy mind even look like? What might the sports world even look like? What if athletes took care of their minds just as much as they did their bodies?

Let's take a look at the downside of mental health neglect in sports. Consider the following: A 13-year-old volleyball player commits suicide during the pandemic. Suicide is currently the 3rd leading cause of death among NCAA athletes.[2] Swimming Olympic champion, Michael Phelps, contemplated suicide after winning eight gold medals in Beijing, unable to leave his bedroom for weeks. NBA Player, Kevin Love, suffered a panic attack in the middle of a professional game. NFL player, Hayden Hurst, attempted suicide in his apartment. MLB Player, Drew Robinson, lost an eye in a failed suicide attempt in early 2020. Professional soccer coach, Cesare Prandelli, retired to cope with profound distress. Aerial skier, Jeret "Speedy" Peterson, killed himself in 2011 just a year and a half after winning a silver medal. Unfortunately, I could go on, but you get the point. The heartbreaking statistics on athlete's suffering mental health can no longer be ignored.

The intent of this book is not to drown us in sorrow, rather it is written with the opposite intent to illuminate a path that participation in sports doesn't have to look like this. We owe it to ourselves as athletes, fans, coaches, and participants in the world of sports to acknowledge the intense emotional journey of competing. Given how far physical development has come in sports this century, it is about time we developed the same for mental strength and conditioning. It's about time we further develop mental strategies and coping skills so when we inevitably hit the road bumps that make up the daily trials and tribulations of being an elite athlete, we're equipped with the mental strength to handle them. Defeat, injury, and retirement are some of the most difficult moments athletes face on their journey, and this book is intended to support you through them all.

Before we unpack the Athlete Identity, I want to highlight the importance of self-awareness, outline a general concession, and offer a reality check.

Awareness Leads the Way

Would you rather act and not be aware of your actions, talk and not be aware of your words? Would you rather listen to people and not be aware of what you're hearing, or see things and not be aware of what you're looking at?
—Anthony De Mello

Self-awareness, defined as "the ability to see yourself clearly and objectively through reflection and introspection"[3] is the initial torch lighting our path. Without this torch, we simply have no idea where to take the first step. However, this self-awareness torch can be difficult to light as it requires total acknowledgement of who we are, including traits and behaviors that we may not want to admit. We may believe certain characteristics about our personality, but with objective self-awareness those beliefs aren't entirely true. You may think you're a supportive, reliable friend, but if you really reflected on your behavior you may come to find you are not as thoughtful and reliable as you think. Because our lives are lived from within, grounded in a particular experience from which we frame, relate, and understand the world around us, we must take the effort to punch through our rose-colored self-perception.

It can be uncomfortable at times to engage with the human side of us outside of being the perfect athlete, but developing self-awareness is critical to understand who we are (the eternal question). Self-awareness is critical to develop an ability to "make sounder decisions, build stronger relationships, and communicate more effectively."[4] Setting our ego down on the bench, setting our discomfort down on the bench, we are going to take a closer look at ourselves with compassionate curiosity. The deeper and truer we dive, the more headway we make toward better understanding an athlete's life challenges.

You, the reader and athlete, will have opportunities to look inward, really look at who you are, and connect the dots of your athlete journey to draw conclusions and make sense of your world. This is going to be a delightful, confusing, uncomfortable, and priceless experience of self-awareness.

As you're reading and relating back to your own life, be honest. Be honest with yourself. No one is looking at you. No one is recording your progress. Whatever you build here is between you and these pages. You might as well make the most of the process, open up to full honesty with yourself and begin tasting the sweet relief of understanding.

A Minor Concession (and how much we love sports)

Defeat, injury, and retirement are the three most excruciating moments we experience as athletes. At times, it may seem as though I'm writing from a pocket of pessimism, but I am intentionally hyper-magnifying the darker side of sports as those moments require the most care. Losing an important game, tearing your Achilles tendon, or hanging up your cleats for good pose challenges in your life that blissful winning does not. It is the tougher moments that require a bit more time and attention. Before diving deep into these topics, take a moment with me to appreciate the gift of simply having sports in our lives in the first place because despite the more difficult content in this book, I do not want to detract from the overarching goodness that sports provide.

Sports are a fantastic invention. You learn life lessons, have fun exercising, enjoy spectating, and make new friends. You bond with teammates and coaches. You learn how to set goals and dedicate yourself to achieving them. One of the greatest gifts sports gives us is the opportunity to experience tremendous amounts of individual progress. Every new skill learned or game won is a testament to hard work paying off. Tony Robbins, one of the most prominent coaches and motivational speakers of our generation, equates happiness with progress.[5] When we feel improvements, we feel happy. Sport gives us the perfect sandbox to safely observe our progress and reach those feelings of confidence and self-esteem, meeting our emotional and psychological needs.

The potential that an individual can reach in his or her sport is awe-inspiring to witness (or achieve yourself). In 2019, before a global pandemic shut down most of the world's sporting events, I was able to snag a courtside ticket to the U.S. Open Tennis Championships in New York. I remember walking down the stairs to my seat in Arthur Ashe Stadium, watching Roger Federer warm up for his match in the East Coast summer sunshine. Federer was probably 30 feet away from me standing on the baseline, and I couldn't believe how close the seats got you to the players. I also couldn't believe the laws of physics watching him effortlessly hit backhand after backhand at speeds I couldn't fathom while dropping the ball right inside the baseline every single shot. To this day, I still don't fully understand how professional tennis players can hit with such power, speed and topspin to keep the ball inside the court - the same size tennis court I play on. For me, a moment like that watching one of tennis' all-time greats makes me appreciate the mere fact that a sport like tennis exists and I was able to spectate a GOAT (greatest of all time) in his craft. I admire the opportunity to watch an athlete who has dedicated his life to honing every minutia of detail of playing, performing and competing. A moment like that makes me appreciate not just tennis, not just sports, but the incredible athletes that participate.

Sports are also chalk full of drama, and there aren't many things humans love more than drama. Entire industries, such as reality television and tabloid magazines, exist because of drama. There is nothing more exciting than watching a pool of incredibly talented athletes fight for the top spot. When 20 Formula 1 drivers, each thinking he is the best in the pack, rev their engines at the start of a race everyone can feel the unbearable amount of tension and pressure mounting before the start light turns green. We love stories of an underdog, overcoming all odds to defeat the longtime legend. We love speculating who will win in the matchup of old veteran versus young prodigy (think of the 2019 Superbowl game with The Patriot's veteran coach Bill Belichick up against younger prodigy Sean McVay, head coach for the Los Angeles Rams). We love competition. We find gratification in seeing a winner become a winner. We find gratification in seeing losers humbled. Our heartbeat increases when it comes down to the wire. Ancient Rome's gladiator fights set the precedent for the highest of stakes. Countless spectators gravitated to the Coliseum to watch the mano a mano fights and wager on who they thought would walk away a winner. Battles, opponents, and gold medals have been part of human history for as long as any of us can remember. We crave the storylines, the characters, the happily ever-afters and the all-encompassing drama that is sport.

In a more poetic sense, sporting events such as the Olympic Games bring countries from all over the world together in a way that no other activity can. Despite a country's political beliefs or opposing lifestyles, sports create an even playing field for athletes from all backgrounds and cultures to safely compete against one another. The Olympics are a global, cultural icon allowing countries to set aside differences and come together for the sole purpose of sport. How amazing and powerful.

Not to mention we love reminiscing on historical sports moments and legendary athletes. Just like we learn history of empires conquering lands across the globe, we also revel in sports history honoring legends such as Muhammad Ali fighting in The Rumble in the Jungle or Jesse Owens winning four gold medals in 1936. We love to play the games, we love to watch the games, and we love living in the bubble of athletics.

Let's also express gratitude for having sports as a fun way to exercise. If sports did not exist, we would be stuck with treadmills and ellipticals and weightlifting repetitions. At least with sports we can run up and down a field and kick a ball into a goal. We can dive into a pool and swim laps to win first place. We can sprint around a track to beat the runner next to us. We can move our bodies and exercise our physical strength in an activity that also engages our minds. Sports make exercise fun, and I'm glad I don't have to stay fit in a world without games.

Whether playing or spectating, I am grateful I live in this era of modern sport. There are so many jaw-dropping moments of athletic abilities. I love watching the best of the best. I love playing and improving my own skills. I love the gratification of defeating an opponent and proving my efforts to myself. I appreciate the friendships and bonding experiences that no one else will understand. I am grateful for the memories and life lessons accumulated along the way - yes, even the painful ones. I appreciate the entertaining fitness. I crave the drama. I love 'oohing' and 'aahing' at the accomplishments of heroes' past. I truly appreciate an athlete's pursuit of *becoming*.

Take a moment and review your own athlete journey. What have been some of the most inspiring, motivational moments you have experienced? Have you seen a teammate or professional athlete accomplish something incredible? Have you yourself pushed your own limits to achieve a goal you never thought you would reach? Have you bonded with teammates to create lifelong friendships? Have you mentored a young athlete coming up the ranks? Who mentored you as you experienced your own growing pains? There are many positive reasons to express gratitude for sports regardless of your level of competition or longevity in the game. As we appropriately root ourselves with the gratitude sports deserve, we can dig into the tough moments with a healthy perspective that both the ups and downs are part of the journey that make up the very games we love so much.

Reality Check

This book is not going to be your end-all-be-all solution to become an impenetrable force of positivity, happiness, and strength during the toughest moments of sport. That is simply unrealistic for any human being, but we can make strides by educating ourselves on understanding the implications of our athlete identity. We can continue to open more space to have conversations about struggles that have traditionally been publicly avoided. We can proactively make the moments of hurt, hurt less.

Join me on this journey as we take a closer look into the challenges of defeat, injury, and retirement in the life of an athlete. This book will help you adopt new, effective coping skills that leverage renowned psychology principles as well as practical advice to help you thrive when things get tough.

Learn from some of the greatest, world-class athletes in history. Relate to someone who has been through it, as most non-athletes will never understand the unique challenges in sport. Most importantly, find clarity in your own experiences to better thrive for tomorrow. Use this book as your tool to dig deeper, untangle, and make sense of your life as an athlete. And, of course, expect that the work in this book requires practice on your part. Just as we practice our swim flip-turn or basketball jump shots countless times, the same rationale applies to developing our mental skills to cope better during moments of defeat, injury, or retirement. We've taken care of our bodies. Now, we are going to take care of our minds.

Chapter 1 Endnotes

1. Pappas, A. (2020). *I Achieved My Wildest Dreams. Then Depression Hit.* The New York Times. https://www.nytimes.com/2020/12/07/opinion/alexi-pappas-depression.html

2. Capone, Ashley, "Mental Health Issues in College Athletes" (2018). Kinesiology, Sport Studies, and Physical Education Synthesis Projects. 41. https://digitalcommons.brockport.edu/pes_synthesis/41

3. Ackerman, C. E., MA. (2021, April 8). *What Is Self-Awareness and Why Is It Important? [+5 Ways to Increase It].* PositivePsychology.Com. https://positivepsychology.com/self-awareness-matters-how-you-can-be-more-self-aware/#:%7E:text=Self%2Dawareness%20is%20the%20ability,objectively%20through%20reflection%20and%20introspection.&text=Although%20everyone%20has%20a%20fundamental,more%20or%20less%20than%20others.

4. *What Self-Awareness Really Is (and How to Cultivate It).* (2021, April 14). Harvard Business Review. https://hbr.org/2018/01/what-self-awareness-really-is-and-how-to-cultivate-it

5. Tony, T. (2019, April 30). *How to Make Progress in Life by Learning How to Feel Good.* Tonyrobbins.Com. https://www.tonyrobbins.com/leadership-impact/feel-good-now/

Chapter 2

My Athlete Journey

Growing up, I was the epitome of a tomboy and the opposite of a princess. I was sporty, athletic, and hated the color pink. My mom couldn't keep a bow in my hair, and I refused to wear dresses. I would rather roll around in the dirt, play kickball in the street and somehow find ways to outsmart the other kids in the neighborhood. I was scared of adults and incredibly shy. In first grade, while sitting in the dentist's waiting room, I peed in my school uniform because I was too shy to ask the receptionist where the bathroom was. It was less humiliating to pee in my pants than talk to a strange adult. It's funny how we change as we get older. I'm still sporty but I love purple and pink. I also consider myself one of the most friendly, outgoing people I know.

One of my earliest memories of sports is playing wall-ball in elementary school with all the boys. I was the only girl willing to break a sweat and get dirty, so that's exactly what I did during recess. We threw a tennis ball at a large, concrete wall and the goal was to catch the ball first before it bounced. I don't remember if there were more rules, but looking back it must have been funny to the teachers to watch a group of first graders run in a small herd chasing a tennis ball bouncing off a wall. To me, it was the most fun to play with other kids and grow my skills in an activity.

As a kid nothing made me happier than running around outside in the summer heat, and being from Georgia, there was a lot of summer heat. Releasing endorphins and showing off my athletic ability were things I always looked forward to. Especially because I was much better than the boys, of course, so I loved showing off my skills. Part of me indulged the insecurity in the boy's eyes when they had to face the fact that a girl was better than them. I was also a bigger kid, taller (I'm 5'9" now), and I took pride in being able to outshine everyone else. For me, I validated my existence by my ability to move. I was deeply existential at a young age. If I didn't feel my heart beating out of my chest or feel sweat drip off my forehead then I didn't fully buy-in to the whole "living" thing. One of my greatest fears in life, even today, is getting old to the point where I can't move around like I once could. I don't devalue aging, but growing old and weak is something that troubled my mind as a child, even more than actual death. I prided my early identity heavily on physical movement and competition. I feel like I came hardwired this way and was always seeking a space for realizing this desire.

I was also an incredibly hyper and energetic kid. My energy was limitless. When I was in a group of friends, I was always the performer, doing any stupid act to make people laugh. I could never just smile in pictures like a normal girl. I always had to make a funny face or stick my tongue out. At practice, I would make jokes to the swimmers in the lane next to me while we were gasping for air. I loved freaking out the swimmers from other teams when I would throw my waterproof camera into the pool, fake cry that my camera was fried, then laugh as I pulled the camera out of the pool spoiling the prank. Sometimes I think about a career in stand-up comedy if everything else fails me. I like the cathartic nature of leveraging the deepest pain in life toward something funny, light and relatable. When I was 12 years old and qualified for the Southeastern Zone Championships, our age group was heading back to the hotel in a large van after practice. It was nighttime and everyone was exhausted - except me. I was cracking jokes and making fun of the billboards along the side of the road. Everyone was laughing. It was funny.

When we arrived at the hotel our coach kindly pulled me aside and gently told me to dial my energy down a bit. I'm not sure if I said something that offended him or if I was just annoying, but I remember that conversation to this day because of how embarrassed I felt. I never got in trouble, and I didn't know that trying to make people smile could get me in trouble. I was a lot more reserved after that.

My mom signed me up for the summer league swim team when I was five years old. As the story goes, I had a great little summer as a budding 5-year-old champion, so much so that a local swim coach called my mom and left a voicemail message suggesting that I sign up for the year-round club team. That was the big time. I'm not sure how much talent you can see or predict when you are only five years old, but I guess I had something. Tenacity and competitiveness would be my guesses. I was always a fiery spirit. When I was a mere toddler in the crib my mom would stand in the hall and inch my bedroom door open, peering in to make sure I was in a good mood before entering. She could never guess which day I wouldn't throw a Beanie Baby at her. I started on the swim team that fall and loved it - the water, the quiet calm of being submerged, and the feeling of moving and gliding through another element. It was a perfect environment to direct my energy and drain my energy. It was perfect for me.

So, my career in swimming began, but my energy abounded into other sports as well. My dad signed my older brother, Chris, and I up to play kids basketball at the local YMCA. I also wanted to play softball. Being the hard-headed, stubborn young girl that gets what she wants did exactly that. I had the coolest cleats, knee guards, sliders under my Soffe shorts, the jersey and baseball cap. To round it out, my dad bought me a real leather glove and showed me how to care for it with leather oil. He even taught me that leaving a ball inside the glove overnight maintains the glove's shape. I loved learning about taking care of my equipment, the very things that helped me play my best. I played shortstop, the quintessential position. Most right-handers hit the ball to the third base side of the field, so the coaches put me at shortstop because they knew I was quick enough to field the balls and accurate enough to throw the batter out at first. I loved catching fly balls, sliding in the dirt, capturing ground balls at the last second and launching a throw to first base for the successful "out". I batted 4th in the lineup. If things went well with the first 3 girls and they all got on base I would close it out, launching a homerun or deep outfield hit to score a few runs. I remember the first time I hit a grand slam. It was during a night game and those bright, white flood lights lit up the dirty field. There were three girls on base and I came up to the plate, tapped it with my bat, and got into position. The perfect pitch came, I swung with all my power, and launched a ball past the fence. All four of us ran around the bases, scoring four runs with the whole team cheering in the dugout.

Then came soccer. I was a little older in elementary school and had never played the game. My dad took me to tryouts, but I don't think we knew it was for the travel team (which, I guess in the soccer world is much more competitive than your average, local soccer league). A group of coaches stood on the sideline as we played soccer, running back and forth while they took notes on our speed and skills. These other girls were good; I wasn't sure what I was doing here. Maybe I should have stuck with swimming and softball. The girls could maneuver the ball from one foot to the other as if it was nothing. I didn't have those skills. The girls could accurately pass the ball to another teammate, way up the field. I certainly couldn't kick with that precision. But, during the tryouts there was a speed test. We all stood behind a line, shoulder to shoulder, and when the coaches yelled "go", they clicked a stopwatch and we ran as fast as we could to the other line. I won. I didn't have the soccer skills these other girls had, but I had the speed. Apparently, that was something very important to the coaches because I made the travel team having never formally played soccer before.

When I reached middle school, I phased myself out of soccer, softball, and other activities to focus exclusively on swimming. It's a bit nostalgic to look back and think there was a softball game that was my last. But I was improving extremely quickly in the water and decided to focus my effort there. Since swimming is such a time-consuming sport, it didn't leave me much energy to pursue other sports (if you can believe it). I had too many nights of swim practice, running to the locker room, changing into my softball gear sweating pure chlorine, and running to the field to play. So, I swam, and swam, and swam. I broke records for the state of Georgia and by the time I reached 8th grade, I was one of the top female swimmers in the country. I was training eight times a week and the kids at school knew me as the "swimmer girl" with my hair permanently in a chlorine bun. I didn't care. I was sucked into every athlete's kryptonite: winning.

Winning was my first addiction. Tasting the sweet high of standing atop the podium, knowing everyone else knows I'm the best felt so good. It fed my ego. It validated my effort. It would be the start of a winning addiction that would accompany my mentality. I wanted to recreate that winning feeling over and over. In 2007, I won the 50-meter freestyle at 14 years old for the Southeastern Zone Championships. It was my best event, my favorite event, and I was the best in the southeast. I loved that feeling. I loved finishing into the wall and looking up at the scoreboard to see #1 next to Kimberly Carducci. My whole state of Georgia team jumped alongside the pool cheering. I could get used to that.

Another thing that drove me to be #1 was my desire to stand out from the crowd and be different. To me, 2nd through last place were the same. The only one that was different was 1st place. Not only did I want to be the best, but I wanted to be different. I couldn't stand the thought of being the same as another girl. I couldn't stand the thought of being average, forgettable. I liked attention and getting noticed. I was a show-off. I liked being unique. Even in my adult life I like to do things different. I had the opportunity to work for one of the largest software companies of our generation, but I turned down the job offer because I couldn't see myself being another cog in the wheel at a global corporation. I didn't want to get lost in the mix and be just another person. I want to be *somebody*.

Sports gave me the opportunity to excel, differentiate who I was and root myself in an identity I could be proud of. I discovered I had talent for athletics and, coupled with my competitive feisty nature, this passion would become my entire life. Many top athletes fall into this mode of thinking, and I'm sure you can relate to the stories I've told about my sports-centered childhood. As a young athlete my malleable ego fell prey to fully attaching itself to the "Athlete Identity". I wasn't in a band. I didn't participate in extracurricular activities. I wasn't in clubs. I didn't have many friends. I just wanted to swim and win. Swim and win. This is sometimes referred to as 'Identity Foreclosure', and we'll unpack this in Chapter 9. I was nothing and no one without sports. I was nothing and no one without being good at sports. I was nothing and no one without being the best at sports. That was my life.

Summer 2007

The first time I felt depression I was 14 years old.

Almost every swim meet I entered, I won. Winning overtook me, and I wanted to go all the way to the Olympics. My passion bled into every other aspect of my life. My identity was not just being a good swimmer, but the best. I trained 12 months out of the year (with an aerobic sport such as swimming there really is no time off). I was extremely strict on my nutrition. I refrained from eating sugar during training, and I timed my meals according to the book *Paleo for Athletes*[1] so I could optimize my recovery and energy. I napped when I could to expedite muscle recovery and ensure I had enough energy for afternoon practice, which was usually three hours. Over the Fourth of July, my family went to New Jersey to visit relatives in which there was a fireworks celebration at midnight on the beach. I couldn't risk staying up that late, so I slept in the car in the parking lot to make sure I got enough rest for morning practice. I was dedicated, overly dedicated, but that's what it took to be the best. I was 14.

The beginning of the summer, after short course season had ended and long course season started, my teammates and I aligned with our coach to set goals for the championship meet at the end of the summer. We solidified what races we wanted to focus on, what our goal times were, and clarified any vacation time with plans to compensate for missed practices. It was a full-proof plan for success. My coach encouraged me to think about qualifying for Olympic trials, which would be the following summer in 2008. Really? I'm only 14, but I guess I could certainly qualify for the meet even if I don't actually make the Olympic team. I'd been swimming great and dropping time like crazy, so it's probably doable, I thought to myself. That would be amazing at this age. The goal time I need to make the Olympic trials meet for the 50-meter free, my best event, was 26.39 seconds. My current best time was 27.54 seconds. So, I had to drop 1.15 seconds in one race to make the cut to swim at the Olympic trials. One second seems like nothing in ordinary life, but it is substantial, especially for the shortest race where every millisecond counts. Regardless, I had my eyes on the prize and I was going to do whatever it took to swim that time.

Toward the end of that summer, our elite group took a training trip to Flagstaff, Arizona. In Flagstaff, the elevation is almost 7,000 feet, much higher than the 1,000-foot elevation I was used to in Atlanta. This is what we called altitude training, and it was a bitch. Comparatively, swimming at sea-level is fairly easy. You can move through the water with ease and have plenty of oxygen to fuel your system. When you jump to 7,000 feet for the first time, you can barely walk up a flight of stairs without heaving for air. Then, put yourself in a pool of water, attach weights to your waist, and try swimming a few laps. It was painful and a few of us got sick. For altitude training to take effect, you need to stay at high elevation for 10-14 days, but the longer the better. So, we trained for almost two weeks, depriving our muscles of oxygen to condition our bodies. Once we adjusted, we came back down to 1,000 feet and our bodies rebounded with energy and a surplus of oxygen, the intent being to swim faster thanks to an increased O2 supply for our muscles.

When we returned to Atlanta, I was feeling good. We were all feeling good. The championship meet was just a couple weeks away, perfect timing to taper and be at optimal performance level. In swimming, when you taper you gradually lessen the exertion and distance you swim during practice to rest your body in preparation for a meet. It is critical for sprinters and less so for distance swimmers, but it allows us time to recover and rest from months of hard training. Two weeks of taper went by, and it was time to race!

At the meet, I swam my race and did my best. I dropped a full half second, bettering my personal record to 27.04, which is an outstanding time drop for a sprint event. Still, that wasn't 26.39. To drop half a second in the 50 free is awesome – any ordinary person would have pat themselves on the back for that. But my goal was 26.39, Olympic trials. I had 26.39 written on my bathroom mirror. I woke up, lived, and slept 26.39. My coach encouraged me – he let me think I could do it. I let myself think I could do it. I believed it. It consumed me. It became me. I was going to be a hometown hero, the first of my friends to make Olympic trials. When I touched the wall at the end of my race, gasping for air and looking at the scoreboard glaring 27.04, I was crushed.

How did I not swim 26.39? If I gave my everything, literally every second of every day, to be better and meet my goals and still didn't achieve them, how do I bounce back from that? I dedicated myself to a strict nutrition plan. I gave my best. I gave everything I had. There is nothing left in me to give. Nothing. My parents spent the money to send me on the training trip to Flagstaff. Every other time in my life I set a goal, worked my butt off, and won. If my best and everything in me gets me 27.04, why continue? Why is this time different? If I can't control my outcome, what is the point? What is the point of swimming? What is the point of life? This is what troubled my 14-year-old mind. For the first time, my best was not good enough and I had zero energy.

After that meet, it was the end of summer. Our coach graciously gave us two weeks off. It was August in Georgia, and the heat was thicker than molasses. School was still a few weeks away, and I sat next to the window in my bedroom looking out at the backyard. As I sat there, I just felt emptiness. No energy. The sun could not put a smile on my face. I hated swimming. I had no more to give. I decided I was going to quit.

Once a new school year began, I signed up to play junior varsity softball. I was not swimming. I would not go back to a sport that I poured everything into only to get slapped in the face back. Swimming was over for me. It had been years since I played softball, and I was rusty. It was fun, the teammates and coaches were enjoyable, but I didn't have the spark and drive for the sport like I used to have for swimming. Softball, although a breath of fresh air from the torment of swimming, was just exercise and a reminiscent practice from my elementary school days. After the season ended, I was relieved and found myself thinking about swimming.

No. I'm not going back. That sport is the devil. My coach deceived me. I deceived myself. I'm not getting fooled again and wasting my precious youth believing in far-fetched dreams that are apparently not meant for me. Never again am I doing that.

A week later I was back in the pool. I somehow found myself in the locker room putting on my swimsuit. I can't remember if I wanted to be there. It was October and the next championship meet was at the beginning of December – I knew because it always fell on my birthday (December 4th) and was always the last meet I had before I aged up into a new bracket (9-10, 11-12, 13-14, 15 and up). Two months is seriously not enough time to train for a championship meet, but I got in the pool with no real goals and just swam.

Part of me was subconsciously lured back to the chlorine because I didn't know who I was without it. Relatives always kept up with my swimming accomplishments, I missed school days for travel meets, and I took pride in my ribbons and medals hanging in my room. It wasn't just a sport for me, it was a way of life. Swimming was my identity and a distraction from the mundaneness of the world. It might have been painful, but it was familiar. I got sucked back in because it was all I knew.

High School & College

I switched teams in high school, finding a coach that clicked with my personality. Coach Ian was the type of coach that didn't care if you went to practice or not. Let me rephrase that. Coach Ian was the type of coach that didn't reprimand you if you didn't go to practice. Of course he cared, but his philosophy was giving the athlete ownership of their success. He was there anytime and always to help, offer advice and write the most effective sets in practice, but the responsibility to show up and do the work was on the athlete. I loved that. I admired him for that. It made me want to perform even better, for myself and for him. If he was the type of coach that yelled at me, like I experienced in college, I would not have trained my best.

One season, I really wanted to become stronger at kicking because that was my weakness. I have strong shoulders and arms, but my legs lacked the flexibility and stamina to help propel me like other swimmers. So, I told myself during practice, "I don't care how tired you get, you can't stop kicking. Everything else must fail first before you stop kicking." In Ian's practices the lanes were divided based on interval times (fastest to slowest) with lane one typically being the fastest lane. I would often find myself in lane seven or eight because I was trying so hard to constantly kick. Your glutes and quads are the muscles in your body that take up the most oxygen, so you can imagine with my new strategy of constantly kicking I had very little air to breathe. I was swimming slow (because I was dying), but I was always kicking. On another team, a coach may have yelled at me or put me in lane one or two regardless of anything else. Ian never expressed concern of my slow times in practice. He let me train however slow or fast because, ultimately, putting the effort in was up to the athlete. This was his philosophy.

That season was my best high school season and positioned me to be able to swim on a Division I team. I swam lights out at the championship meet, and I remember telling Coach Michael, our assistant coach, that I felt like I had the stamina to easily crush 500 after 500. Which, as a sprinter is not something you hear often. Swimming with Coach Ian I not only swam some of the best times in my entire career but enjoyed the thrill of the sport again.

However, senior year of high school rolled around and I began to feel lingering feelings from when I was 14. I still had not qualified for Olympic trials, and every summer that went by where I didn't qualify while all of my friends did felt like a good reason to quit. It was getting harder for me to stay motivated to train exorbitant amounts every week. I didn't have much of a desire to swim in college like most of my friends. I yearned for a life with no commitments. I was burnt out from hardcore dedication. I wanted to relax. I wanted to eat M&M's late at night. I wanted to just put my legs up on the couch and not do anything for once. I was so tired. I felt bad for my parents. They paid for swimsuits (competition suits are $300+ and only last a couple meets), club team memberships, meet entries, travel, and more. I couldn't not fulfill the last stage of the journey by not swimming in college. All of my friends and their parents were excited to sign with a university and begin a collegiate athlete career. Not me. My times (thanks to Ian) and academics were just good enough to swim on a Division I team, and I didn't want to let my parents, family and coaches down, so here I was at the beginning of my freshman year at The University of North Carolina, training again. But at my core, I was burned out.

Freshman year went by. I swam personal best times and even garnered "College Swimmer of the Week", but I didn't make the ACC team. Which was fine. It would have been nice to reap the rewards of a year of hard work, but at this point I didn't care enough to get worked up over it. I knew I was finally at the point of being done. I went home for the summer, talked to my club coach and parents, and decided to retire from the sport for good.

But don't you want to swim all 4 years? No.

Don't you want to be a NCAA student-athlete? Not really.

Don't you want to train 24 hours a week and miss out on other college experiences? No.

I wasn't going to make the Olympics; I never even made Olympic trials. I might have made the ACC team, but it wasn't worth the training effort. I couldn't bring myself to endure three more years of 5:00am practices and a challenging training schedule on top of classes for marginal improvement. It just wasn't worth it to me, and I was at my limit. So, I retired very unceremoniously. And then came the most excruciating, heartbreaking, lost period of my life. The five-year-old sporty Kim that grew into an elementary school tomboy who then burgeoned into an elite high school swimmer was, for the first time ever, living a life without sport.

I retired. Now what?

To say I had no idea what to do with myself with the absence of swimming in my life is an understatement. What do you mean I have no practice to rush to? What do you mean I can eat whatever I want? What do you mean no one is counting on me? What do I do in December and April when I'm supposed to show off my training at the championship meets? Where am I supposed to go? What am I supposed to do? Who am I supposed to be?

My life came to a screeching halt. For the first time since I was five years old, I had abandoned swimming for good. I don't even remember 99% of my life before age five, so this was really the first time I had known a life without swimming. Because swimming had dictated so many aspects of my life during training (diet, friends, vacations, school, everything) I had an influx of freedom I had no idea how to handle. Not only was it an influx of freedom, but it was a total identity release I had never experienced. I was no longer "the swimmer girl with the wet hair". I was no longer somebody. All the criteria I used to base my identity on (being fast, being a record-breaker, being a teammate, etc.) vanished. I had no clue who I was or how to fill the hours of my day. It felt as if gravity, the commonality that kept all beings rooted on Earth, suddenly stopped and I had no idea what was up, down, or sideways. It sounds like such a first-world problem – so much free time and nothing to do. It was paralyzing. It almost drowned me.

Some people say college is the best time of their lives. For me, college was the worst time in my life. I didn't know basic skills like how to make friends – all my life my friends were given to me because we were teammates that trained 20 hours every week together. In college I partied hard, binge drinking to numb my internal fatigue and confusion. I changed my major, but I really had no idea of what I wanted to be, what I wanted to do. No career path was particularly interesting to me. I pulled up the list of available degrees offered on UNC's student website and read each one aloud. Every single degree was followed by a "no". I eventually settled as a Communications major and minored in Writing for the Screen & Stage. Still, every door I opened led to more doors that needed to be opened and I eventually felt so lost. I was overwhelmed, confused, down and that spiraled into a deep depression. My life was out of control, and I couldn't stop it.

Drinking was an unhealthy coping mechanism for me that escalated my feelings of depression. Every weekend, and even some weekdays, was an opportunity to drink until oblivion. It was the only time I felt like I was having fun. One afternoon, already blackout drunk, I got into my car and sped off down the country backroads of North Carolina. I can't remember having a destination. I was just driving speeds of 90 mph, secretly praying something would happen and I would have an excuse not to be on this planet anymore. I was destructive. I was self-sabotaging. I was apathetic. I was exhausted. I was lost. Every day that went by I was further and further away from anything resembling "good" and "healthy". My life was dark, heavy, and depressed.

My depression got so bad my junior year that I checked myself into the university hospital for suicidal thoughts. It is an odd stress-reliever to think of yourself no longer on this earth, but those thoughts helped me cope. It would be really hard for me to sit here and say I would actually harm myself, but wow it was nice to think about. You mean I don't have to deal with guilt, shame, feelings of inadequateness? Sign me up. Those feelings inside me were so painful, and I didn't know how to handle them. They don't teach you in school how to manage depression or cope with a darkness you've never felt before. But to think there was always a way out provided the relief I needed. After four days in the maternity ward because the psychiatric ward was full (hmm doesn't that tell you something about our modern world), I was released from the hospital. I remember standing outside on the sidewalk with my bag of clothes. The dispatch lady was a yoga instructor, and she stood by me until my friends came to pick me up. I don't remember her exact words, but she said something along the lines of "take care of yourself, it gets better." I hoped she was right, but I didn't believe her.

After the hospital I took all the prescribed measures to get better. I went to counseling and got on medication. I didn't feel it helped much. In my senior year I was sucked back into the enabling party culture and adverse effects of self-loathing. I prayed college would end and I could put this whole chapter behind me. One night, I drank until I blacked out, laid in the shower and let the water run over me for hours in an attempt to get sober. The sounds of running water woke my roommate up. In the middle of the night, she perked up and entered the bathroom. She found me passed out in the tub, blacked out and close to drowning. This, unfortunately, is just one example of how I wasn't taking care of myself. I wasn't resolving my identity. I didn't know what was really wrong. I didn't know how to acknowledge my thoughts and feelings. I didn't know anything at the time. I was just trying to survive.

That December, I graduated one semester early. I crammed all my final credits into that last semester to not prolong my time at school. I moved back home with my parents and was able to slow down. I needed to be out of the environment that triggered memories of swimming and enabled party culture, catalyzing my journey to the bottom. I continued counseling, but my therapist talked a lot at me instead of letting me express myself. I didn't feel any shifts or changes in my perspective of life and who I was. I still struggled with moving on from an identity that had been embedded into my soul for almost 15 years, the most formative years of my life. I was a "swammer", favoring the past tense and holding on to the good of what used to be. I hated my party behaviors. I hated my overly critical mind. I couldn't stand my perfectionist attitude and intensity. Every day was a race, a competition and nothing was meant for simple enjoyment. I was always going, doing, going, doing and I hated how I couldn't even let myself make mistakes or sit still and be okay with doing nothing. My intensity, perfectionism, competitiveness, and hypercritical nature all stemmed back to being an athlete and that approach to my life was ruining my life. How do I undo 15 years of reinforcement?

While I tried to figure that out, I got a job. I picked up a number of self-help books. I went to hot yoga and tried to sweat out years of alcohol. I wanted to do the work, to be happy. I wanted to resolve and grow and enjoy life. Working, reading and yoga surely helped me feel accomplished in my day-to-day life, but it didn't cure me from my chaos. The work I needed to do was deeper, much deeper. But, for what I knew at the time, those coping activities were all I had.

My first job was a leasing agent for apartment communities - nothing interesting or life-changing. I wasn't in medical school. I wasn't becoming a lawyer. I wasn't on the trajectory of landing some high-paying job with a notable firm. But honestly, it was so relieving to have simple responsibilities with zero pressure for the first time in my life. I did simple paperwork and felt unbothered by how my days flowed. The job itself was easy. I could accomplish a full, easy day's work, make my boss happy and go home every night with no stress or pressure or over analytical thoughts about how I did and what could be different next time. I could complete tasks with no repercussions on my self-worth. It was so simple yet so cherished. This new activity log was the very first time I felt the constraints loosen on my brain that I was only swimming. After 15 years of what felt like constant running, I finally sat down.

Over the next five years I held a few corporate jobs, working in software sales and digital marketing. They were good jobs that I was initially excited about, but the newness always wore off and I felt like I was distracting myself from healing my college trauma. While my days were filled with tasks and workouts and social events making me feel like I was accomplished, I wasn't aware of how I was avoiding the deeper work. I knew but didn't really know there were still lingering parts of my athlete journey affecting all aspects of my present-day life from work, relationships, and self-image.

I really struggled with who I was as a person. The qualities that made up who I was. Being an athlete and someone who remained incredibly private about my deeper feelings (it's ironic I'm writing this book), I was jealous of friends that held such empathy, compassion, and kindness not only to themselves but to everyone around them. Others were able to forgive themselves for silly mistakes and build friendships based on mutual empathy. Others were able to openly express vulnerabilities, worries and shortcomings while I avoided mentioning weaknesses at all costs. Here I was, a critical perfectionist with no tolerance for mistakes. Not for me. Not for other people. You can imagine I was a great, easygoing friend (not). You can imagine it's fun to date me (not). I didn't expect errors. I didn't welcome apologies. My mindset was "get the job done or you're not worth my time." I held that same mindset for myself. I was so incredibly intense about every single thing. Just as you can "break" a horse when it's trained to be ridden from its free nature, I wished to somehow "break" my personality. I hated who I was that much that I wish I could've woken up an entirely different person. My intensity wore me out. My lack of empathy made me feel like a terrible friend. My competitiveness drove wedges between me and everyone else, including myself. I was so tired of me.

One thing I learned during this time is that my behaviors tell a lot more about me than any thought could. If you really want to know the truth about people, watch what they do and not what they say. When I looked at what I acted upon and the decisions I chose, it shed more light on who I was than my thoughts ever could. I thrived in relationships that gave me the love my own self could not give me. I needed someone else to tell me I was worthy enough, good enough, and validated to really think I was. I worked sales jobs for that competitive adrenaline and praise that I needed to fill a void of external validation. Even when I felt burnt out and ended up resenting sales pressure, I continued to validate my intelligence and worth by staying in a career that wasn't aligned with my true self. I behaved in patterns that were familiar even if they were not healthy. I didn't realize it at the time, but my self-love and self-esteem were at their lowest points.

The Straw that Broke the Athlete's Back

In the summer of 2020, I played a tennis match that would become the impetus to write this book and do the work I'm doing today. Partnering with my boyfriend at the time, we played a mixed doubles tennis match to qualify for the next round of playoffs in the championship bracket. We played awful. We didn't communicate. We hit bad shots and we lost. I was so upset over losing because I envisioned my boyfriend and I making it all the way to the championships and winning together. That was special to me, so I took the loss incredibly hard. I walked to my car fuming after the match, sitting in silence for 10 minutes to cool down. That night, I wrote a lengthy email to my boyfriend about how the loss was his fault, pointed out how he was the weaker player on our team, and told him that I was never going to play tennis with him again. Yes, I sent the email. Yes, I cringe when I think of how mean I was. Again, this is a great example of my intolerance of simply being a human being; my competitive intensity reared its ugly head after this match. The following day after I hit "send", I woke up with a pit in my stomach. Why did I have to attack him for a loss that was both our faults? Why did I feel the need to be so mean? Why was I so attached to winning? Can I not lose a tennis match? Why can't I move on like everyone else does when they lose? What is wrong with me? These were all the questions I asked myself and could not answer. The only thing that came to mind was my unmanaged and unresolved identity attachment of being a relentless competitor. Being an elite athlete. I simply could not play a game for fun.

This tennis match was the last straw because I so deeply hurt someone I loved. The intense, competitive person I was lashed out and created a fissure in a relationship I cherished. The friction I already felt about myself plus the now destructive behaviors stemming from my intensity was the wakeup call for me. Creating suffering for myself is one thing. Hurting those around me is another. Enough was enough.

Life Lessons

The period of my life in writing this book I call my "awakening". I quit my 9-5 job. I signed up for therapy twice a month and began listening to incredible podcasts on thought models. I read a number of self-help books and journaled every day. I meditated. I sat in my thoughts and in my pain. I created mood playlists, read articles online, and began recording hours of voice memos on my phone. I started to walk myself through what I was thinking, feeling, and observing to help me reach conclusions. I practiced self-love. I talked with others about their own athlete journeys. I interviewed Olympians and professional players. I watched athletes compete and behave on the biggest stages. There was work I needed to do, so here I was taking a big bite.

One thing I really do love about myself is my commitment to growth. I may fall down hard, but I will never give up on myself. I know I have the desire to progress, to improve and to grow. I love that I am constantly leveling-up who I am as a person. I really dove deep into the inner work I so desperately needed to uncover the roots of who I am. I needed to expand my self-awareness so I could expand my self-love, which was so obviously missing from my life. My growing self-awareness allowed me to better notice times I was being incredibly harsh and when I was, I was able to practice forms of self-love, such as affirmations and forgiveness, that changed how I felt about myself.

Today, I'm still competitive when I play tennis, but I don't let it ruin relationships or eat me alive. When I lose, which is something I certainly do not enjoy, I let myself feel frustration and anger, but I don't indulge the endless "what ifs" about my performance. I can look at certain errors for improvement or additional practice, but I don't torture myself by arguing with what is reality. I dive deep into defeat in Chapter 12.

I feel peace about my swimming career. I've updated my thoughts about how things turned out and leveraged practices I mention in this book to reach closure and practice acceptance. I root myself in reality over and over. I'm deliberate in managing my mind as opposed to letting certain characteristics take over: competitiveness, intensity, lack of compassion. I'm not scared to feel uncomfortable feelings or pain because I know the discomfort is temporary and I have the tools to navigate through those emotions in the healthiest way. I dive deep into retirement in Chapter 17.

I practice my lifelong journey of self-love. For me, it was always hard to show myself kindness because if whatever I did wasn't the best or the fastest or the greatest, I didn't like it. It wasn't enough. I am my own worst critic and am the meanest to myself - thank God my thought track doesn't play out loud or some people would be frightened. To counter what feels natural to me as an athlete, the mean thoughts in my head about what I'm doing, I practice loving all things about me as a person. If I make a mistake, I show myself compassion that I'm human and not some robot-perfect-athlete. **I don't expect perfection, I expect a human.** I shower myself with kind words when I need it most, when I do mess up or say something stupid or feel insecure. I'm my own biggest fan and supporter. I'll talk about how to break the perfectionist curse in chapter 17.

I don't shy away from life. I also don't live in fear of what other people think of me or what might happen. When unexpected or unwanted situations arise, I find comfort in the fact that I know I can manage it. I know I can process it, work through it and that, ultimately, it will pass. I'm not perfect at this. On occasion, I'll find myself in old thought patterns of being affected by the thoughts and actions of others. In those moments, I double-down on my own thoughtwork. Something must be off in my thoughts, so I re-root myself in the reality of the situation. "Every time you are unhappy, you have added something to reality. It is that addition that makes you unhappy."[2] Doing this work is like eating soft, cooked noodles versus crunchy, uncooked noodles. I could avoid the work and continue to eat uncooked, crunchy pasta or I could sit with what's uncomfortable, root myself and update my thoughts and actions about the situation to eat soft, cooked pasta. I'm Italian (and Irish), so it only makes sense I throw in a pasta analogy.

The most substantial aspect of my life I've noticed changing in a positive way is how I approach and participate in social situations. Social gatherings always felt like big commitments for me. My social anxiety about saying the right things or not offending someone or showing too much of myself that could harm me down the road caused a lot of headaches for me when it came to making friends, hanging out on a regular basis, or going to large events. Mix that in with my fear of being disliked (people-pleasing tendencies) and I drained all my energy thinking about the event before I even got there. Now, because I have much more compassion for myself and others as human beings, I look forward to simply connecting with people. Social events no longer feel like some major, planned circumstance that I need to prepare for. They are low-barrier moments in time to connect, learn, grow, help and practice simply being a human being. After all, connecting with others is largely what we seek to draw meaning from our lives. In Brene Brown's book, Daring Greatly, she explains our desire to connect with others:

> Connection is why we're here; it is what gives purpose and meaning to our lives. The power that connection holds in our lives was confirmed when the main concern about connection emerged as the fear of disconnection; the fear that something we have done or failed to do, something about who we are or where we come from, has made us unlovable and unworthy of connection.[3]

I choose to live with this mindset because, for me, it is my most effortless way of living. Imagine you were squatting 200 pounds. For me, 200 pounds would be incredibly challenging. Then, your spotter removed 180 pounds from the bar, and you were left to squat only 20 pounds. Wow! It feels so light and easy. You still have to squat, but it feels so much better. That is how the change in my life feels. I still have to squat, but I have a much easier, healthier, and wiser way of handling life when it doesn't go according to my perfectionist standards. I don't ruminate on the negative, I've drastically reduced anxiety about social situations, I don't take preemptive action out of fear and I can sit with discomfort and simply "be" without it hurting so bad. Everything feels perfectly imperfect.

Why Me to Write This Book?

Of all the athletes in the world, many of whom were much better than I at their sport, why me to write this book? I'm not a psychology major (although I did score an A in all my psychology classes). I'm not a licensed psychologist or psychiatrist. I never made it to the Olympics. You would think on paper, there are a million other athletes or psychotherapists more qualified than I to write this book. Maybe there are. Maybe there aren't. My existential mind combined with my own personal sports journey puts me in a perfect position to dissect information, experiences, stories and data about athletes and analyze the sports experience.

I'm someone who simply gets it. When it comes to the trials and tribulations of being an athlete, I get it. I understand the struggle. I understand the pressure of being in the championship with everything on the line, and its related drama. I understand the desire to rip your opponent's head off, and the crushing, agonizing feeling of losing a match. I understand a bruised ego and, consequently, the bonfire it ignites to restart. I understand the sacrifice of skipping sleepovers or friend dates and altering your entire life to be dedicated to your sport. The goals and accomplishments in my career truly mattered to me. I cared about the effort I was putting forth and the records I was breaking. I was totally invested in being an athlete, a swimmer. I got lost in my own athlete identity and dug my way out, analyzing each component and the "why" behind it every step of the way. I understand the complexity and drama of modern sports, having grown up in the 90s and 2000s. I understand, and will forever continue to grow my understanding, of what it means to be an athlete.

However, I don't stop at the simple understanding of why athletes are the way they are and what comprises the rollercoaster of an athlete's journey. My work is taking that understanding of the athlete identity and applying real frameworks to navigate through the intensity. I've learned mental tools and strategies that have saved me years of heartache - even retrospectively - and I wouldn't be sharing my thoughts with you if they didn't work. I wrote this book to help myself first.

I understand there will always be the inevitable ebbs and flows of gains and losses, good and bad, joy and suffering in life. Reading a book, getting a job, talking with a counselor, or traveling the world are not end-all-be-all's to life's problems. Don't let *Eat Pray Love* fool you. But adopting modern tools and mental strategies to enrich your own life's learning will set you up for fulfillment, gratitude and compassion, a combination of qualities I envision in the ideal person I strive to be every day. We are constantly evolving specimens in a constantly evolving environment. Don't let that daunt you; this gives us so many opportunities to grow deeper with ourselves, learn about others and enjoy the silver linings in life. As my dad always told me, life is a journey to be experienced and not a puzzle to solve. If only my five-year-old self actually listened.

Today, I help other athletes retrain their minds to operate in ways that best serve them, not work against them. With my organization, Everything Athletes, I offer online courses, podcast episodes, blog posts, book reviews, and now my own book related to the topic of athletes and mental health. I've interviewed Olympians, Professional Athletes, and amateurs about the tough moments on their own respective journeys. I've researched scientific journals to identify psychological trends among athletes. They say the best learners are those most passionate about the topic, and if you haven't picked up by now that I love sports – I love sports. I value my sports journey, and I enjoy watching other athletes achieve their goals. I do this work because I want every athlete to compete and train and perform at levels that are the healthiest for them. In a world where physical attributes dominate, I'm standing up to say the mind can't be ignored any longer.

So why me to write this book? Read on.

Chapter 2 Endnotes

1. Cordain, L. P. A. J. F. (2021b). *Paleo Diet for Athletes A Nutritional Formula for Peak Athletic Performance*. Rodale Books.
2. DeMello, A. (2021). *Awareness: The Perils and Opportunities of Reality by Anthony De Mello (1990) Paperback*. Image Books.
3. Brown, B., PhD. (2021). *BY Brown, Brene, Ph.D. (Author) [Daring Greatly] 04–2015 Paperback*. Avery Publishing Group 2015-04-07.

Chapter 3

Why is Mental Health so Important?

Emotions are as much a part of the competitive sports experience as physical conditioning, equipment, technique, strategy, and teamwork. It could be argued that emotions are the 'raison d'être' of sports competition.

—Dr. Jim Taylor, former world-ranked athlete and author of Train Your Mind for Athletic Success: Mental Preparation to Achieve Your Sports Goals

---

Mental health is defined as a person's condition with regard to their psychological and emotional well-being.[1] The sport world's ability to avoid mental health concerns has become more difficult over the last decade. The countless athletes that have come forward sharing their experience with inner turmoil and darker emotions has certainly helped raise social awareness on mental health in sport. However, if you ask any one of them, they would probably all agree that there is still a long way to go considering the "dynamics of modern sports provide an especially dangerous landscape that fails to prepare athletes for long-term physical and psychological health."[2]

Growing awareness around mental health in sport is so incredibly important for three main reasons: to accommodate the intense emotional journey that comprises modern elite competition, to remove the stigma that suppresses human vulnerability in sport (and we all know what happens when you attempt to suppress) and finally, to prevent further widespread trauma to athletes. As sport has advanced on every pressure-filled physical level to catapult athletes to unprecedented performances, we haven't caught up on a mental health level to protect our headspace. The consequences of not catching up our mental standards to the standards of our physical priorities are cringeworthy and a disservice to the very participants that make up the sport in the first place. As a collective sports community, maybe we could reduce the percentages of struggling athletes as shown below:

- According to the NCAA 2020 Gallup Survey, **46%** of former student-athletes struggle with purpose wellbeing (Purpose Wellbeing: Liking what you do each day and being motivated to achieve your goals.)[3]
- **35%** of elite athletes deal with a mental health crisis.[4]
- The **3rd** leading cause of death among NCAA athletes is suicide. [5]
- **45%** of male team-sport athletes report having anxiety and depression.[2]
- A 2016 study by researchers at Drexel and Kean universities found that nearly **25%** of collegiate athletes have reported symptoms of depression.[6]
- Only **10%** of college athletes with mental health conditions seek help.[7]

Modern Sports Brings Emotional Intensity Like Never Before

An athlete's world of high pressure, high stakes competition presses the pedal to the medal shooting our emotions in one direction or the other. You either find yourself winning, on top of the world with overwhelming feelings of elation and pride. Or you find yourself defeated, at the bottom of the earth looking into space and questioning everything you've ever known. Intense competition does this to you. Enormous prize money and contracts worth millions of dollars does this to you. Total commitment to being an athlete does this to you. Particularly for athletes, "the range of events and emotions that are experienced through athletic involvement seem to be both numerous and extreme compared to the normal population."[8]

Essentially then, taking care of your athlete mind is like getting your car's oil changed. The rule of thumb is to change your car's oil once a year or every 5,000 miles. If you hit the 5,000-mile mark in the first month, would you wait 11 months more to get your oil changed? No. You would make an appointment at the service center to change your oil and keep the car running smoothly. Athletes live in that world where so much mental and emotional ground is covered in short periods of time, compared to your average non-athlete. Thus, it requires more time, attention, and visits to the service center to keep your mind and emotions healthy.

Competition in our modern world has also become so cutthroat thanks to advancements in training, adding to the emotionally intense journey. Athletic gear has become incredibly custom, training is smarter, and nutrition is honed for optimal recovery and muscle growth. If we time travelled to 2005 - we wouldn't have players like Serena Williams still competing in Grand Slam finals at the age of 39. We wouldn't have Olympic swimmers like Dara Torres still winning medals at the age of 41. We wouldn't have Professional Golfers like Phil Mickelson winning a PGA Championship at the age of 50. The incredible, shared knowledge around how to rest, train and compete and optimize that cycle has prolonged careers and contributed to the most competitive sports environment we've ever seen.

This intense level of competition leads to an almost nonexistent margin of error between winning and losing and thus the pressure on athletes has exponentially increased. Think about sports like golf or timed races at the Olympic games. A single golf putt could be the difference in winning $700,000 of prize money. A fraction of a second separates 1st place and 2nd place in sports like track & field and swimming. At the 1966 Olympic Games, the time that separated first from second in the women's 100m freestyle was .40 seconds. The time that separated second place from third place was .90 seconds. Fast forward 50 years to the 2016 Rio Games. In the same event, first and second place tied to the exact millisecond (.01) to each earn a gold medal. The difference between the two first-place finishers and third place was .20 seconds.

This trend for decreased margin of error in sports has become increasingly prominent with time, technology, and knowledge. Losing by a barely noticeable fraction of a second is a more common occurrence in sport than ever before and contributes to the intensity of competing.

I recently sat down with a family friend, a mother of three, and chatted about athletes and kid's sports. She said to me "I would never have my child play professionally because of the enormous pressure." This is how people view sports now. This is what sports have become. They're not grandiose, old-school games of glory, passion and winning. They have become data-driven (Moneyball, analytics changing the NBA), gear-reliant (the now outlawed 2008 Speedo Fastskin LZR Racer suit that helped 23 out of 25 WR's get broken in a single meet) hyper-competitive cesspools for mental health troubles because, just as Americans do with almost everything else, we've maxed it out. We have physically maxed out sports and left our minds behind.

I'm fine, I'm fine, I'm fine (the stigma)

As competitive athletes, we voluntarily throw ourselves into the gauntlet of sport over and over again for the chance of winning, blind to the actual heat of the flames. By "blind" I mean ill-equipped to manage our minds during moments of intense emotion, and intense emotion is something athletes know all too well. There is no real handbook or best practices to navigate these emotionally exhausting periods in a healthy way. There aren't tried and true methods widely shared among athletes to help during the tough stuff. Not having readily accessible knowledge on how to navigate defeat, injury and retirement is hard enough, but what makes matters worse is the stigma in sports culture of avoiding vulnerabilities, ignoring weaknesses, and pretending you're strong all of the time.

If we continue the "tough it out" attitude and encourage stigma-reinforcing behaviors, we will never get to a place where sports are healthy and fun. We will continue to harm athlete's emotional well-being both during and post-sport. Why aren't athletes given the permission to feel? Marc Brackett, Ph. D. and Director of the Yale Center for Emotional Intelligence, wrote an entire book titled *Permission to Feel*. On the very first page of the prologue he states, "To stop feeling would be like to stop thinking. Or breathing. Impossible. Our emotions are a big part – maybe the biggest part – of what makes us human."[9] When athletes aren't encouraged to express emotions and are banned from being human, they are being harmed. This is why mental health has become such an issue in sports today, and there is no longer the option to continue to take a back seat. If we don't take measures or share knowledge or encourage mental rest for athletes thrown into the fire, there will unfortunately be many more dismal statistics to share.

A large part of the mental health taboo is the general perception that athletes are perfect. Emma Vickers, a Sport Psychologist, explains that "top elite athletes are idealized within the media, often subjected to a large fan base, potentially giving the perception that they are immune to such problems."[10] As athletes we also attempt to satisfy the self-fulfilling prophecy of being "perfect" while holding "fear that their mental health concerns could negatively impact their reputation and future contract negotiations."[11] In a 120-page report from the NCAA, the thoughts about why athletes fear expressing mental health concerns are explained below:

Athletes often consider seeking help as a sign of weakness, feeling that they should be able to 'push through' psychological obstacles as they do with physical ones. Athletes may not have developed healthy coping behaviors. Athletes may also be at greater risk for mental health issues in that they are less likely to seek treatment, may be afraid to reveal symptoms, may see seeking counseling as a sign of weakness, are accustomed to working through pain, may have a sense of entitlement and never had to struggle, and/or may not have developed healthy coping mechanisms to deal with failure.[12]

To compete at the highest levels, we brush aside anything that threatens our ability - such as mental or emotional instability - and maintain a stoic persona of perfection. Regardless of everything else going on in our lives we reinforce this facade of toughness. An athletic prowess that can't be dimmed. Don't show weakness, especially to an opponent. Don't show weakness for fear you may start to doubt yourself. Don't show weakness. Period. Kerrie Thompson Mohr, psychotherapist and founder of A Good Place Therapy & Consulting, explains that "perfectionists work harder to hide perceived flaws because they are constantly comparing themselves to people around them. They place a high value on an all or nothing 'perfect' standard, but the result of this obsession can be very isolating."[13] The fear of stepping forward as an athlete and suggesting a mental struggle (even confidentially confiding in a coach does not always feel welcome), the external expectations placed on athletes to be perfect at all times, and the lack of awareness on how to actually engage with our mind during periods of struggle contribute to sports' avoidance of mental health.

This stigma and avoidance of mental health couldn't be more opposite to the response athletes receive when it comes to physical struggle. When there is a potential threat to an athlete's body, there are limitless resources available for aid: physical trainers, hyperbaric chambers, cryotherapy, protein shakes, pre-workout supplements, weightlifting sessions, graston, sports massages - the list truly goes on. Anything we can do to improve muscle strength, flexibility, core, or stamina is served up almost immediately.

In Brett Rapkin's HBO documentary, *Weight of Gold,* American figure skater Gracie Gold highlights the immediate response she receives to her request for a physical trainer when she has a physical injury.[14] Any physical ailment, even the mention of it, warrants a barrage of trainers and medical specialists to expedite healing and recovery. However, there is no protocol in place if an athlete mentions a struggle with depression, stress, or anxiety - common mental states in high-profile, high-pressure arenas. Gold never even received a response from the committee when she requested help during her time of disordered eating and depression, a sad but clear example of how sports culture views mental struggle. It seems silly that our most complex organ is widely ignored when our mind has more power than our bodies could ever fathom.

In time and with more awareness, we can end the stigma and open opportunities for athletes to take care of their minds. The trend has already started with some of the world's most remarkable players sharing stories or withdrawing from competition, sending the message that winning gold is not worth a damaged psyche. In his remarks on changes from the time he played over a decade ago to now, former NFL Player Michael Robinson comments that "When I first got to the NFL [in 2006] you would have never seen any pieces like this [NFL Mental Health Video Series] where guys are sharing some of this information. Now, you're seeing guys raise their hand and say 'hey, I'm willing to share my story because if my story can help somebody else out there, that's all that matters.'"[15]

Power of Acknowledgement

Because athletes are traditionally conditioned to avoid emotions, here's a simple reminder to acknowledge how you feel. When you're in a down moment, one of the best practices to help open a pathway for emotion to move through you is the practice of acknowledgement. Acknowledgement is recognizing and allowing any and all emotions within you. Take it from Marc Brackett, author of *Permission to Feel*. Giving yourself the simple permission to have emotions – good, bad, and ugly – is the first step to grow skills for your own emotional well-being.

Acknowledging your emotions is the opposite of suppression, which only makes those emotions grow stronger. This seemingly simple yet often ignored technique removes the power your negative emotions have on your mind. Simply saying "this sucks" or "I'm not happy" or "I'm incredibly frustrated" aren't common phrases we say out loud to acknowledge the state we are in. We talked about the mental health stigma in sports and the fear athletes have in admitting darker emotions. For us, it may feel unnatural to say to ourselves, "I'm having a hard time". It is the opposite of what athletes are portrayed to be - indestructible, undefeatable, strong. When you do acknowledge the true sentiment of what you're feeling, you release the power those emotions have over you and clear a path in your mind to begin the work.

Try it for yourself right now. What are you feeling in your life? Say it out loud. "I'm calm" or "I'm frustrated" or "I'm not looking forward to next week." It's like taking a broom to the floor of your brain and every time you acknowledge exactly how you feel, you're clearing the way to move through that feeling. We will continue to reference the power of acknowledgement throughout this book.

Emote Baby, Emote

No human can think their way through periods of struggle without feeling the struggle itself. As humans, creatures with feelings and emotions and conscience's, we must face the undeniable truth that no matter what thoughts are in our head we will sometimes feel sadness, joy, anger, excitement, frustration, happiness, confusion, and all the unlimited emotions we feel that even our modern vocabulary sometimes can't cover. We're human. We feel. We think. And we can't avoid either of those.

One of the best ways to tap into your emotions and feel is through music. Music can help athletes learn how to allow emotions pass through them, a practice athletes may not know how to do. Rosie Mead, a Soulful High-Performance Coach, teaches individuals how to tap into emotions and, quite literally, change the way you feel.[16] She uses a method called desire mapping, coaching high performers to regulate emotional responses, tap into our hardwired response to rhythm (we all have a heartbeat) and easily access our desired feelings. Why do athletes listen to music before competing? To hype them up and get them "in the zone". It is the same for other desired emotions as well.

The power of music is incredible and has the power to bypass any thought in your head and hit you straight in the heart. Go wherever you stream music (YouTube, Spotify, Pandora), search for cinema scores and just listen. Some of my favorite movie theme songs are Finding Nemo, Pirates of the Caribbean and Jurassic Park. When you listen to the beauty of an entire orchestra playing harmonious notes that tell a story and take you on a journey in your mind there is so much energy and life to the songs. There is so much sentiment in the notes. You yourself probably feel some type of way when you hear the theme song to Harry Potter or Star Wars. We can't even quite describe the experience of listening to cinema scores through written word. Go listen to John Williams, the composer behind some of the most iconic movies of our time, and then continue reading. Visit Rosie Mead's Instagram page (@iamrosiemead) to learn from an expert on how to leverage music as an athlete.

It is normal and healthy to feel sad. It is normal and healthy to feel frustrated. It is normal and healthy to feel dismal. There aren't any magical words or advice I could offer about the range of human emotion other than feeling the negative is simply part of the human experience, just like feeling the positive. All emotions you've felt in your life or have yet to feel simply come with the territory of being a human being. Do you expect yourself to live 100 years on this earth without a single moment of sadness? I think we'd all like to minimize sorrow and pain and enjoy as much of our existence as possible, but there is no magic pill or practice or advice that would allow you to circumvent feeling the feelings despite how much we want to. And I know we want to. The self-help industry is predicted to be worth $13 billion by the year 2022.[17] It is clear our population wants to feel better, grow stronger, learn strategies and tactics on how best to cope and thrive, which are all great goals. But nowhere in those $13 billion will you find a remedy that allows you to avoid feeling feelings. Sometimes, you're just going to feel down and holding space in your mind for that expectation is half the battle.

Imagine if...

Imagine, for a moment, you applied the same effort toward your mental health as you do your physical health. The hours you spend in the gym, the reps you push yourself to complete and the extra cross training included in your schedule all to enter every competition with peak physical ability. While our bodies are the very tools that accomplish some of the amazing athletic feats we can point to in our careers, we forget that our bodies are controlled by and highly connected to our brain. If, in a Frankenstein world, I swapped out my body with Michael Jordan's but had a bad attitude and no desire to put my shoes on, the elite specimen that is Jordan's body would go to waste. I would stay put on the couch, defiant and unwilling to compete. While this is a silly example, it demonstrates how crucial a healthy mind is to complete a strong athlete.

What would your life look or feel like if you improved your mental health focus by 10%? 30%? How would you feel different waking up every morning? Instead of thoughts rushing to negativity or insecurities, your thoughts exude confidence, ease, and calm. Imagine how practicing strong mental health strategies could expand your capacity for patience and perspective. Not only will you find that your calming, non-judgmental thoughts provide instant relief in your present moment, but you find that by eliminating negative hurdles that create an overall sense of constantly running uphill you are able to slow down and create mental space to see life clearer.

When you're really feeling down, hope is often the missing piece needed to begin creating momentum in your life toward a better outcome. When you don't think things could ever get better the apathetic feelings hopelessness inspires are dangerous. This "hope" I'm talking about is the same feeling of excitement someone gets when they start a weight loss journey, buy a lottery ticket, apply for a job at their favorite company or begin falling in love. It is the thought about how that future might look that generates excitement. Think of two prison inmates, both serving a one-year sentence. Inmate A is told that his sentence is exactly 365 days while Inmate B is told he will serve life. Even though both inmates will only serve one year, Inmate B will likely have a worse experience in prison over the course of his year than Inmate A. Inmate A might take advantage of the library and learn a new skill for possible future employment. Inmate B, perceiving his future as 365 days x 60 years in prison, might become apathetic and spend his days in bed because - what's the point? Knowing there is a possibility that the future could be brighter changes everything. Conversely, lack of hope that the future is brighter evaporates energy, a defining characteristic of many mental health disorders.

Visualize what your own life would feel like if you consistently woke up with a clear mind and practiced healthy mental habits. What would be the first thought in your head when you woke up? Would you smile more? Talk to friends more? Have more time? Ruminate less? What does it look and feel like for you? When you think of living your life this way, with a formidable mind strong enough to handle whatever life throws in front of you, it sounds pretty nice, right? With a bit of work, a bit of insights, a bit of understanding you can reach a life filled with ease, clarity and light. Right now, reading this book, you are on your way. I'm not sure about you, but I would rather live my life as Inmate A.

One More Thought. . .

While this is just one small book in the world, growing our understanding of the intense nature of competition today and the importance of protecting our mental health begins our journey to grow stronger as athletes and human beings. As athletes, we place ourselves in some of the most stressful situations we might find ourselves in in our entire lives. Learning how to handle those situations and the emotional byproducts that accompany them can save us a lot of heartache and mental anguish. We can't prevent heartache and pain, but we can certainly take a proactive approach in growing our awareness around the most complex organ in our body, our brain.

Your mind is so incredibly powerful. The thoughts inside that brain are incredibly powerful. Those thoughts can materialize into the very life you lead. The daily choices you make, who you spend your time with, where you live, what you do for a living - everything is generated from thoughts. Manifestation, or bringing something tangible into your life through attraction and belief[18], and universal laws such as the Law of Attraction, the belief that positive or negative thoughts bring positive or negative experiences into a person's life[19] are living proof that thoughts truly come to life. The placebo effect, the idea that your brain can convince your body a fake treatment is the real thing[20], has actual, proven results to reduce symptoms of severe illnesses such as cancer. It is remarkable yet simple that to think a thought and believe in the integrity of that thought creates real effects, both positive and negative depending on the thought. With this incredible amount of power, wouldn't you like to better manage and work with your mind to serve you in the healthiest way possible? Why would you not want to learn and dive into your mind's operation to understand and optimize the very thoughts that become your life?

The more we grow our awareness, the better we understand. The better we understand, the more educated decisions we can make. The more educated decisions we can make, the happier and healthier we become. Are you seeing a trend here? (awareness → understanding →insights → positive change)

Chapter 3 Endnotes

1. Oxford University Press (OUP). (2021). *mental health*. Lexico.Com. https://www.lexico.com/en/definition/mental_health

2. LIZ HENDERSON liz.henderson@gazette.com. (2021, February 8). *Athletes struggle to find purpose, identity after sports | Special Report*. Colorado Springs Gazette. https://gazette.com/news/athletes-struggle-to-find-purpose-identity-after-sports-special-report/article_ea000d90-220f-11ea-b1ac-9f79e1310dd8.html#:%7E:text=Experts%20say%20the%20dynamics%20of,term%20physical%20and%20psychological%20health.&text=The%20pressure%20to%20recover%20leads,them%20especially%20susceptible%20to%20depression.

3. Gallup-Perdue. (2016). *Understanding Life Outcomes of Former NCAA Student-Athletes*. NCAA. https://ncaaorg.s3.amazonaws.com/research/other/2020/2016RES_GallupNCAAStudentAthleteReport.pdf

4. McMillan, B. (2019, May 16). *Mental Health and Athletes*. Athletes for Hope. https://www.athletesforhope.org/2019/05/mental-health-and-athletes/#:%7E:text=But%20of%20college%20athletes%20with,burnout%2C%20or%20depression%20and%20anxiety.

5. Capone, Ashley, "Mental Health Issues in College Athletes" (2018). Kinesiology, Sport Studies, and Physical Education Synthesis Projects. 41. https://digitalcommons.brockport.edu/pes_synthesis/41

6. *Depressive Symptoms Prevalent Among Division I College Athletes*. (2016). DrexelNow. https://drexel.edu/now/archive/2016/January/Depression-College-Athletes/

7. Velasco, H. U. T. (2017, July 21). *Few student-athletes with mental illness seek help*. College.Usatoday.Com. https://eu.usatoday.com/story/college/2017/07/21/few-student-athletes-with-mental-illness-seek-help/37433787/

8. Taylor, J. (2017, June 28). *Articles/Chapters*. Dr. Jim Taylor. https://www.drjimtaylor.com/4.0/writing/articleschapters/

9. Brackett, M. (2020). *Permission to Feel*. Celadon Books.

10. Vickers, E. (2013, December 19). *The stigma of mental health: is it increased for athletes? - BelievePerform - The UK's leading Sports Psychology Website*. BelievePerform - The UK's Leading Sports Psychology Website. https://believeperform.com/the-stigma-of-mental-health-is-it-increased-for-athletes/

11. Miller, K., & Bissoy, J. (2018, October 1). *Destigmatizing mental health in sports*. MPR News. https://www.mprnews.org/story/2018/10/01/kerri-miller-destigmatizing-mental-health-in-sports

12. NCAA. (2014). *Mind, Body and Sport: Understanding and Supporting Student-Athlete Mental Wellness*. NASPA. https://www.naspa.org/images/uploads/events/Mind_Body_and_Sport.pdf

13. Mohr, K. T. (2017, May 7). *Perfectionism's Dark Side: Lessons from Japan*. Psyched in San Francisco. http://www.psychedinsanfrancisco.com/perfectionisms-dark-side-lessons-japan/

14. Rapkin, B. (Director). (2020). *Weight of Gold* [Documentary]. Podium Pictures.

15. *NFL Mental Health & Wellness Series | Michael Robinson*. (2021, May 6). NFL.Com. https://www.nfl.com/videos/nfl-mental-health-wellness-series-michael-robinson

16. M. (2020b). *Rosie Mead*. Musica. https://musica-music.co.uk/rosie-mead/

17. Sinclair, M. (2019, August 6). *Why the Self-Help Industry Is Dominating the U.S. - Featured Stories*. Medium. https://medium.com/s/story/no-please-help-yourself-

981058f3b7cf#:%7E:text=Now%2C%20business%20is%20booming%3A%20 In,next%20four%20years%2C%20by%202022.

18. Zapata, K. (2020, December 23). *How to Manifest Anything You Want or Desire.* Oprah Daily. https://www.oprahdaily.com/life/a30244004/how-to-manifest-anything/#:%7E:text=Essentially%2C%20manifestation%20is%20bringing%20 something,it%2C%20and%20it%20will%20come.&text=via%20your%20-thoughts%2C%20actions%2C%20beliefs%2C%20and%20emotions.%22

19. *Let the Law of Attraction Help You With Positive Change.* (2020). Verywell Mind. https://www.verywellmind.com/understanding-and-using-the-law-of-attraction-3144808#:%7E:text=The%20law%20of%20attraction%20is,negative%20 thoughts%20bring%20negative%20outcomes.

20. Harvard Health. (2019, August 9). *The power of the placebo effect.* https://www.health. harvard.edu/mental-health/the-power-of-the-placebo-effect#:%7E:text=The%20 idea%20that%20your%20brain,as%20effective%20as%20traditional%20treatments.

SECOND QUARTER

The Athlete Identity

"There is about world-class athletes
carving out exemption from physical laws
a transcendent beauty
that makes manifest God in man."
- *David Foster Wallace, String Theory*

Chapter 4

Studying Identity

Identity is such a complex notion, and we will spend our entire life uncovering our evolving selves. Like a snake shedding its skin, we grow and shed past beliefs, habits, and thoughts as we become a wiser, older version of us. As we grow, we adopt different opinions, meet new people, form new beliefs, and connect the moments that create our internal story of "me". Studying identity and learning about how identities are formed is so important as they provide us our basis of perception, or the "process of actively selecting, organizing, interpreting, and evaluating information, activities, situations, people, and essentially all things that make up your world."[1] This perception is what we rely on to interact with our world every day. Imagine this morning you woke up and were of the opposite gender. Each moment you experience would be perceived from a totally distinct lens, foreign to everything you know. Every interaction holds a different meaning and the story your inner dialogue builds about who you are is from a totally unfamiliar perspective. Beyond gender, our identity labels extend to the interests, activities, families, and other components of life we involve ourselves in. The label of "jock" connotes much different images and emotions than the labels of "preppy students" or "goth kids". Even as you're reading these labels certain stereotypes come to mind. These identities – such as male, female or athlete – help us contextualize and categorize the world around us, providing a basis of where we fit in, where others fit in and what it all means. When so much of what we think, say, do and perceive is based upon the identity framework we've built about ourselves and others, growing our knowledge of those identities and its implications is the necessary starting point required to decipher meaning from the events in our lives.

Hovering our magnifying glass over the athlete identity, we cannot appropriately dissect and understand an athlete's life journey if we don't first know what it means to identify as an athlete. Some experts such as John Murray, a clinical sports psychologist, claim that "the more elite the athlete is, the more identity is …wrapped up in the athlete role."[2] While a correlation does exist based on what Murray suggests, I also believe that regardless of an athlete's competition level, the meaningfulness of being an athlete to the individual is a greater cause for identity formation. For example, an Olympic gymnast having spent her entire childhood training and building her life around gymnastics could enter retirement seamlessly with little to no mental friction. Maybe she had a great social life and dove into a career she loved without looking back. To her, cataloguing gymnastics as a chapter of the past was easy and natural. On the other hand, a collegiate rower who depended on their identity as an athlete to validate or overcompensate parts of their life might have a more difficult time reconciling who they are in a post-sport world. Maybe they grew up with limited means and being a rower granted them opportunities they never would have accessed if it weren't for sport - like college. Shedding the athlete identity has greater mental implications for the collegiate rower than the Olympic gymnast, although competing at the Olympic level is significantly more "elite" than performing in college. I prefer the simple, explanatory definition from Myanna Webster, a former athlete and counselor, who instead suggests that an athlete identity is "the extent to which a person aligns with the role of athlete within their life."[3]

Being an athlete, particularly in our modern, sophisticated world, is an identity that runs much deeper than the surface-level traits of dedication, competitiveness, and athleticism. There is much more to an athlete than a packed training schedule and a desire to win. How do others perceive athletes? How do athletes perceive themselves? What are the typical thought patterns of an athlete? How do the defining characteristics of athletes come to be? Why do athletes think what they think and do what they do? Why are athletes so selfish? What is an athlete's greatest fear? Like an archaeologist dusting off fragmented fossils, the deeper we dig the more fossil we find, each of which builds a bigger picture of who we are.

Imagine for a moment you never heard of the flu. Influenza. That combination of syllables never rung your eardrum before. One day, you start feeling sick. You have the chills. Your body aches. You run a fever. You start thinking to yourself, "oh my God. Are my organs failing me? Why do I feel this awful? Am I dying?" It sounds silly, but if you don't have previous knowledge of these symptoms, it seems probable that you're on the fast track to death. You write your will and bid adieu to your friends as you visit your doctor and hope you're not terminal. Your doctor checks your vitals, runs a few tests, and diagnoses you with a mild case of something called "influenza". She then explains it is a rather common illness and can be treated with an antiviral medication and your choice of over-the-counter home remedies. Phew! You're not dying. What you have is something treatable that many people come down with. Although your body aches, you feel relief because you understand why your body feels the way it does. Our minds crave the true explanation of why things are the way they are, providing relief to the fear-based stories our ego gravitates toward to prepare us for the worst.

Just like understanding your aches are due to a mild flu, recognizing how the decisions you make, the thoughts you think, and the feelings you feel stem from your athlete identity also provides relief and clarity to your mind. We don't have to subject ourselves to worrisome, unrealistic conclusions that cause stress. We don't have to beat our heads against a wall repeating the same life lessons. We don't have to guess about how we should navigate our life because we don't have a basic understanding of who we are. When we reach newfound explanations about our athlete identity, we position ourselves in the best spot possible to begin mindset strategies. We uncover the fossil bones, that is, we piece together the full dinosaur and with that whole picture view we are able to draw conclusions.

Crushing defeat, frustrating injury, and confusing retirement are all moments that feel less heavy when we can better understand the underlying mechanics at work in our athlete mind. Growing our understanding of how we've built our own athlete identity allows us the chance to deconstruct attachments that no longer serve us once we enter a post-sport life. Growing our understanding allows us the chance to choose healthy behaviors in periods of turmoil, such as defeat and injury. The exploration behind our thoughts and actions in these crushing moments provides insight on how best to make healthy decisions to move forward. When you understand who you are and why, making intelligible decisions that guide you through those circumstances in the healthiest way possible becomes a much easier practice to practice.

Chapter 4 Endnotes

1. Duck, S., & McMahan, D. T. (2020). *Communication in Everyday Life*. SAGE Publications.
2. Webster, H. (2014, July 21). *How to Overcome Depression After a Sports Injury*. U.S. News. https://health.usnews.com/health-news/health-wellness/articles/2014/07/21/how-to-overcome-depression-after-a-sports-injury
3. Academy, S. U. S. (2020, February 11). *Why Athlete Identity is an Issue*. The Sport Digest. http://thesportdigest.com/2020/02/why-athlete-identity-is-an-issue/

Chapter 5

The Reasons We Play

There's an American doctor who wrote about the effect of competition on his life. He went to medical school in Switzerland and there was a fairly large contingent of Americans at that school. He said some of the students went into shock when they realized that there were no grades, there were no awards, there was no dean's list, no first or second in the class at the school. You either passed or you didn't. He said, 'Some of us just couldn't take it. We became almost paranoid. We thought there must be some kind of trick here.' So, some of them went to another school. Those who survived suddenly discovered a strange thing they had never noticed at American universities: students, brilliant ones, helping others to pass, sharing notes. His son goes to medical school in the United States and he tells him that, in the lab, people often tamper with the microscope so that'll take the next student three or four minutes to readjust it. Competition. They have to succeed, they have to be perfect.

—Anthony de Mello, *Awareness*

Desire to Compete

Athletes are born out of the people who respond to competition. This is the hallmark trait of an athlete above all else. When an athlete comes across someone doing the same activity as them, they want to do it better. There's an immediate internal response, a "competitive drive to win and demonstrate superiority over opponents."[1] If you're an athlete reading this, it may feel foreign that there could be another way to live. Can you really meet someone who is also a [insert height], [insert weight], [insert age] and [insert sport] and not desire to prove that you are more elite? More skilled? How can I just sit back and watch? Some people, however, do have a more calm, cool and unaffected disposition as opposed to fearless fighter. Some people's veins do not circulate lethal doses of competitiveness. But, when you have an athlete, they want to fight. Athletes want to be in the thick of the excitement for the chance of tasting glory. Athletes. Want. To. Compete. The impulse to compete and prove dominance is *the* natural, hallmark trait among elite athletes.

A classic tale of an athlete's desire to compete, to be right there in the drama, in the fight for the title is Rocky Balboa. Rocky took on the challenge of fighting Apollo Creed to see how far he could go. Regardless of win or lose, being part of the fight, part of the game and part of the pursuit drives purpose. Training. Becoming. Eating raw eggs. Using meat in a meat locker as his punching bag. Of course, the goal is to win and we'll talk about that soon. Rocky Balboa lost the match in a split decision, but the movie remains an epic tale of an athlete stepping up to the challenge. The very definition of "compete" begins with the word "strive": strive to gain or win something by defeating or establishing superiority over others who are trying to do the same.[2] In this definition, there is no guarantee of win or lose. There is only the mention of striving for, seeking out and pursuing. Competing is the journey of becoming, and there is something so admirable about throwing yourself in the midst of competition and testing your own skills.

Where does this desire come from? There is the long-standing question among most personality traits, athlete or not, of nature vs. nurture. Was I born motivated or was I conditioned to be motivated? Was I born with a musical ear or was I trained to listen to notes? It is a question that neither experts nor myself will ever fully be able to answer. I believe the desire to compete is largely determined by nature (competitive personality & physical attributes) and strengthened over time with nurture (opportunities to play, coaching, tasting success). You can note how children, 3 and 4 years old, have drastically different approaches to games, playgrounds, and contests. Some children are timid and fear-based with no desire to conquer the rock-climbing wall on the playground. There are other children, the pre-athletes, who run to the front of the line, are motivated by the blue ribbon and fearless of trying something new. It is so fascinating to see that from such an early age not everyone is wired to compete. Some people simply don't respond to competition.

Then let's talk about the physical, especially because sports are physical activities requiring favorable physical attributes to succeed (but, of course, there are exceptions). Nature determines your height, wingspan, right or left-hand, and other physical qualities that make up how you look and feel. Not that it would be impossible, but it is much harder for a 5'2" player to compete successfully in the NBA than a 7'2" player. The shortest man to ever compete in the NBA was Muggsy Bogues at 5'3" and only 25 players in NBA history have been at or below 5'9".[2] Potentially, you could have the most competitive, driven 5'2" man that ever existed but even at his ultimate best he may be considered an average player in the league. In this hypothetical situation, maybe his desire to compete declines because he can never dunk or hang with the 7-footers. While nature determined his competitiveness and physical attributes, nurture negatively impacted his competitive drive. In the opposite scenario - the recipe of most elite athletes of our time - someone could be born with the competitive drive and combined with favorable physical attributes was able to find success early and often. This combination of nature and nurture further strengthened the desire for this athlete to compete. Ultimately, I believe the competitive trait is something people are born with and combined with favorable physical qualities creates an even stronger bond to competing.

Moments of Competition

When we compete, we momentarily drop out of standard reality and enter an alternate universe of pure adrenaline. We cross through a portal. It's a non-place, somewhere solely based on feeling. Adrenaline takes over, biologically preparing your body to do whatever necessary to win. Blood circulation increases. Breathing increases. Normal patterns of thought vanish. Pierre Gasly, French Formula 1 Driver, describes his competition mindset:

> In Monaco it gives you so much adrenaline. As fast as you can but without losing the concentration otherwise you are in the wall. Your level of focus is just so high. You switch to a different mode. Unconscious. You do what you do based on your feeling. You just switch to a different person.[4]

I like to imagine the contrast of non-athlete life to the alternate universe of athletic competition as analogous to an ocean. On the surface, everyone exists. You have non-athletes and athletes alike enjoying surface water activities. Some drive around on their boats. Some decide to kayak. Some stay on the beach. Some are more courageous and decide to swim. But everyone stays at the surface and thus experiences that limited exposure of the world. Athletes, when called to compete, are the ones who plunge deep. Athletes take a breath and dive down, experiencing a totally unique environment. Fish, seaweed, coral, currents, rocks, shells, shipwrecks, and everything else are unknown to surface-people in this way. Below the surface, athletes watch as fish are swallowed whole, witnessing an entire ecosystem different than what's on the beach. When we resurface, catching our breath and calming the adrenaline rush, we could describe the things we witnessed but no vocabulary or descriptive adjectives match the experience of diving down deep.

No description could accurately describe how it feels to race. To compete. Surface-people may try to understand, but they'll never really know.

This deep ocean of the moments of competition is something that uniquely bonds all athletes together. Only other athletes truly know what it's like. Think of your own moments of competition, when you're in the heat of the race - sweaty, alert and incredibly alive. Your moments in the game are probably some of the most vivid memories you have. The elusive, adrenaline-filled competitions separate athletes further from the ordinary person which then further creates an athlete identity.

Elements of Competition

The fun in competing is figuring out how to win. What training program will give your body the best preparation? What visualization and mindset techniques will get you in the right headspace to focus? Which coach and team are the healthiest environment for your success? How can you maximize your strengths against your opponent's weaknesses? What is the best nutrition plan for optimal muscle recovery? There are endless tactical questions to ask that help design your perfect formula for success. If Rafael Nadal, one of the top men's professional tennis players, likes to line up his water bottles in the perfect spot on his bench before matches to help him win, that is a component of his competition strategy to perform his best. It's like developing your own homegrown recipe as you determine what amounts of which ingredients are included or excluded at just the right times. Hopefully, when the cake comes out of the oven it's perfect.

Strategizing and outsmarting your opponent is one of the most fun elements of competition. I'm in my late-twenties and grew up with internet and video replays, so it's interesting that sports existed in a time where you couldn't watch old matches and games to dissect an opponent's style. You couldn't YouTube tennis player Bjorn Borg and figure out where he would serve based on behavioral patterns. Today, there is such a huge competitive advantage to be able to watch so many of other athlete's competitive moments to learn from them and leverage yourself against their weaknesses. Chris Bosh, former professional basketball player, highlights some of the best strategist-athletes of our time: Aaron Rodgers, Quarterback for the Green Bay Packers, can famously recall plays from years ago. Lebron James' photographic memory of every play shocks reporters when he recalls them in post-game interviews. Greg Maddox, former MLB player, ended his career in the top 10 of all-time for strikeouts and wins due to his study of every single hitter's weakness and tendencies.[5]

There is deeper psychology you can tap into when it comes to strategy. Nico Rosberg, former Formula 1 Driver explains "psychology plays a big, big role in sports. It's huge. Everybody has self-doubt... so you need to try and amplify that... you can really force him (Hamilton) into mistakes."[3] Sometimes, competing feels like a real-life Super Smash Bros. video game. How can you see what your opponent is doing and attack their weaknesses? How can you deteriorate their strengths? What can you practice to get even better, stronger, faster than them? What potential leverage can you gain to win? It is an athlete's simple, competitive nature to figure out tactics and strategies that offer the highest probability of winning. It is a healthy mix of offense and defense. In the video game, you're pressing all the different button combinations on your controller to outsmart your opponent and emerge victorious. Strategizing is one of the most fun yet pressure-filled pieces of participating in sport.

Even more gratifying is mastering your own skills. Maybe 10 weeks ago you couldn't successfully perform your gymnastics routine without making an error, but you needed this skill to have a chance at the podium. So, you trained and learned and practiced. Over and over. Over and over. Then one day at practice, your routine was perfect. Every movement was precise. For lack of more sophisticated language: you got better. Adding a new skill to your repertoire of competition strategies feels so good, building your confidence and strengthening your ability to compete.

When done successfully resulting in a win, an athlete experiences a surging sense of mastery. They were able to outsmart everyone else, ultimately and objectively being considered "better" than the opponents. All your effort, strategy and fight worked. Guess who eats this up and licks every drop? The ego. Eckhart Tolle, best-selling author and spirituality teacher, explains that the "Ego is our false self, the person we become so other people will like us, admire us, and accept us…[our ego has] The need to stand out, be special, be in control; the need for power, for attention, for more."[6] You can imagine the smile on our ego's face when we successfully compete, or win. It's like dropping blood in front of a shark. The addiction begins.

Winning

Ah, yes. The sweet, sweet thrill of winning. Holding the trophy in the air. Wearing the gold medal around your neck. Looking up to the scoreboard and seeing your name, your country represented. What could be better than winning? Pat Riley, former Head Coach of the Miami Heat, says "There's winning, and then there's misery."[5]

Winning is the most addicting part of our sport. It is the part that keeps us coming back for more despite every challenge we face. We sacrifice so much of our lives for the opportunity to taste a win. It is why we compete. It is what drives us to push. Winning is the ultimate high, the ultimate satisfaction. Sugar Ray Leonard famously exclaims "Nothing could satisfy me outside the ring… there is nothing in life that can compare to becoming a world champion, having your hand raised in that moment of glory, with thousands, millions of people cheering you on."[7] Andre Agassi, one of the top men's tennis players of the 90's, appropriately describes his first grand slam win in 1992 at Wimbledon as a "hysterical serenity."[8]

> I raise my arms and my racket falls on the clay. I'm sobbing. I'm rubbing my head. I'm terrified by how good this feels. Winning isn't supposed to feel this good. Winning is never supposed to matter this much. But it does, it does, I can't help it. (Agassi, 2009).

Winning proves that you are the best. It proves that you're the fastest, smartest, strongest, best athlete of anyone else in the field. You are the one. Winning validates every drop of sweat, blood, and tears is worth it. Winning provides overwhelming relief because everything make sense. When you win, it feels as if you placed the last toy on the shelf in the right spot and everything lines up perfectly. Winning beautifully closes the loop on all the work you've done to achieve that win. Winning evolves us into Rainbow Mario - an indestructible version of ourselves able to break through anything. And it feels so good.

When you're proven to be the very best of the competition, you feel furthest away from your biggest life fear: mediocrity. The coveted number one spot squashes any insecurity about not being good enough. Winning proves to yourself and to the world that you are talented and skilled and, most importantly, above average. Because winning keeps us at a preferably far distance away from any acknowledgement of shortcomings or mediocrity, we feel an inner sense of peace and safety knowing that, at least for the foreseeable future, there is nothing mediocre about us. We are the best.

Winning is so addictive because it absolves past hardships and shortcomings. Winning is the key component in how we leverage our greatest performances to rationalize inferior parts of our lives. We may have 10 bad meets in a row, but if the 11th meet is where we win and break records, we forget about the 10 bad meets. Actually, we add those 10 bad meets into our story of how we were able to secure that 11th win. The bad times, the tough times, the stressful times feel genuinely worth it and absolved when we reach the win. Agassi positions his win - "Without Nick I wouldn't be here. Without all the ups and downs with Brooke, even the misery of our final days, this wouldn't be possible. I even reserve some gratitude for myself, for all the good and bad choices that led here."[8] Outside of the surface level knowing you're the best, winning is the drug that quashes the insecure question of "is this all worth it?"

Athletes also become addicted to winning based on our inner desire to repeat dopamine-releasing behaviors. Quite literally, winning is a chemical addiction similar to alcohol or other drugs. When you win and your body and mind are overcome with a wave of dopamine and pleasure, you want to experience that good feeling again and again. Think about your own wins. Have you ever won a race or a game and felt satisfied enough that if you never won again you would be okay? Probably not. You want to win again. And again.

Part of why winning feels so good is because it is genuinely deserved, unless you're a cheat. You train like nobody's business with the utmost dedication to elite competition. Observing your hard work pay off with the ideal result is incredibly gratifying, perfectly closing the loop on your intention. An easy win or easy shortcut might feel good at the time, but the depth of gratification is not there. Racing a 400-meter dash against a bunch of kindergarteners will certainly garner you a gold medal, but how is that gratifying? Winning the lottery would sure feel nice, but what if you built a company from the ground up, worked your butt off and then sold the company for an amount that dropped your jaw to the floor? It feels more gratifying to work hard for something and genuinely earn it rather than be handed a prize with little merit backing it up. This genuine, deserving feeling that athletes feel when they win is an untouchable asset that can't be bought or traded. This rare commodity can only be felt by reaping the rewards of plain and simple hard work. This deepens the satisfaction of winning.

After a certain threshold of winning, you become a bona fide champion. To win The Masters once is amazing but to win it five times: Tiger Woods. To win a tennis Grand Slam once is amazing but to win over 20 times: Serena Williams and Roger Federer. To win Olympic Gold once is amazing but to win 8 golds in a single Olympics: Michael Phelps. To win a Superbowl once is amazing but to win more Superbowl championships as a player than any franchise ever: Tom Brady. The list goes on but not for very long. There aren't limitless superstars among us, just the ones who want the gold bad enough. That is what I truly believe makes the difference between being top 100, being a great player and being a champion - how badly you want to win. When you want it bad enough, you will do anything to achieve it. Will Smith describes his own attitude about wanting something so bad and his desire to literally die for it – "But if we get on the treadmill together, there's two things: You're getting off first, or I'm going to die."[9] In Chris Bosh's book *Letters to a Young Athlete*, he has an entire chapter titled "The Gift of Hunger" where he explains that "hunger will be the difference maker...hunger is the swing vote."[5]

Have you ever heard how an athlete really "dug down" or "switched into a 5th gear" while competing? Maybe you yourself experienced this. Something inside you desired the trophy so much and so bad that your fight turned relentless. Subconsciously or consciously, your mind decided that there was no alternative to winning and thus your behavior changed to match that thought. Losing, as a concept, vanished from your knowledge entirely. Your focus intensified like never before, your pupils were likely dilated, your heart rate increased, and your performance reflected that heightened state. You played better than you ever had because you were desperate to win. In that desperation is where the fifth gear is formed. After all, "desperation [is] a more powerful drug than cortisone."[8] To access a fifth gear, you have to desire gold as if your life depended on it. You have to want it so bad that there is no other option. The fifth gear is where champions are made. Once you access the fifth gear and feel what it's like to fight for survival, there's no turning back. Once you've had desire burn inside you like that, it's like being knighted by the invisible royalty of athlete-hood.

I'm doing my best to describe winning, but sometimes it feels as there is no explanation or vocabulary I could use to appropriately represent the addicting, sweet, high, euphoric feelings of taking home the first-place trophy. If you know, you know.

Chapter 5 Endnotes

1. Menesini, Ersilia & Tassi, Fulvio & Nocentini, Annalaura. (2018). The competitive attitude scale (CAS): a multidimensional measure of competitiveness in adolescence. Journal of Psychology & Clinical Psychiatry. 9. 10.15406/jpcpy.2018.09.00528.

2. Oxford University Press (OUP). (2021a). *compete*. Lexico.Com. https://www.lexico.com/en/definition/compete

3. Wikipedia contributors. (2021a, July 16). *List of shortest players in National Basketball Association history*. Wikipedia. https://en.wikipedia.org/wiki/List_of_shortest_players_in_National_Basketball_Association_history#:%7E:text=Only%2025%20players%20in%20NBA,the%20position%20of%20point%20guard.

4. Gay-Rees, J., Martin, P., Todd, S. [Producers] 2019-2021. *Drive to Survive*. [Series] Netflix.

5. Bosh, C., & Riley, P. (2021). *Letters to a Young Athlete*. Penguin Press.

6. Eckhart. (2021). *A New Earth (Large Print) [LP Edition] (PAPERBACK)* (4570th ed.). Large Print.

7. Bent, Q. (2020, April 28). *A Challenge for all Athletes - Quinton Bent*. Medium. https://medium.com/@quintonbent19/a-challenge-for-all-athletes-ebbc12c9bb27

8. Agassi, A. (2010). *Open: An Autobiography* (Reprint ed.). Vintage.

9. B. (2014, August 11). *THE BLACK BEAT: Oldie But Goodie: Will Smith Doesn't Want To Be An Icon [WATCH]*. Black America Web. https://blackamericaweb.com/2014/08/11/the-black-beat-oldie-but-goodie-will-smith-doesnt-want-to-be-an-icon-watch/

Chapter 6

The Journey Up

At the beginning of your career, your sport is an endless source of excitement. Everything is so new. New teammates, new gear, new practice schedule and new rules. If you imagine your mental and emotional stimulation as a line on a line graph, the first few years of participating in sport would look like a drastic spike to the top.

What do you want to be when you grow up?

Before we ever step foot on the field or tumble across a mat or dive into a pool, we learn that athletes hold a special swag that no other career path can match. President of the United States, Investment Banker, Doctor or Astronaut were the "cool" career paths we talked about in our elementary school days, but nothing felt quite as vibrant as hoping you would one day be able to call yourself a "Professional Athlete". When you're a kid and you realize a career could be made from playing the very sports you practice on the playground, that is what you want to do. Forget money. Forget curing people's illnesses. Forget becoming POTUS. You want to be like Mike (Jordan). As sporty, athletic kids with big aspirations, we dream of the days when we can one day walk out onto the field and call ourselves a Professional Athlete.

This dream is supported by the very consumer products that keep us all living the American Dream (Gillette, Wheaties, Sprite, Kia, etc.). Consumer brands choose athletes to represent them. Only a few select professions have the sort of aura that athletes have, such as musicians and actors. However, unlike musicians and actors, athletes are celebrated for their competitive edge and winning outcomes and tend to have a positive reputation attached to their image. Not doctors. Not bankers. Not astronauts. Athletes. This deliberate decision tells the population that among most career options to be chosen for the commercial spot, an athlete is one of the few that holds the power to represent the brand.

Only an athlete is worthy enough. As mere kids we then view the athlete life as sexy, cool, powerful, coveted, prideful and exactly what we want. We trade signed baseball cards, tell our parents to buy the Wheaties box, and jump up and down incessantly hoping Serena Williams will hit her signed tennis ball to our section of the bleachers. So, when someone asks us "what do you want to be when you grow up?", we want to say, "a Professional Athlete".

Learning the Rules of the Game

First you learn how to play the game. If I pitch the ball fast enough, I can strike the batter out? Cool! If I jump over each hurdle and cross the finish line first I win? Cool! If I dribble past an opponent and score a goal our team wins? Cool! In large, rapid bites we piece together the rules, the tricks, the loopholes and understand what the map looks like. Learning these new rules in a fun new sport is psychologically rewarding. When a new skill is learned our brains generate neural connections that increase our dopamine, the happy hormone, leaving us wanting to repeat the experience. This is the same process our brain goes through when we build addictions. "Our brains reward us when we do something that brings us pleasure"[1] and scoring goals brings us pleasure. The dopamine rush we feel leaves us wanting to score again. And again.

You have likely experienced the desire to repeat actions that provide stimulating feelings of happiness. Have you ever hit a dropshot that surprised even yourself? Have you ever scored a three-pointer you thought you had no chance in making? The repeated dopamine rush ignited by executing new skills creates a burning desire to play more and play often, building our first psychological level of commitment to the athlete identity.

Teammates & Friends

Teammates become our friends as we build our support system. Our coach yells at us collectively, we high-five after a grueling practice and we hang out together off the field. Our teammates are the first people to tell us "good job" and the only people who understand what our life is really like. We rely on our teammates for moral support, reassurance and feeling related to. We see our teammates fail. We see our teammates succeed. We are together every step of the journey. Similar to men who fight in the trenches of war side-by-side, there is an unspoken bond between teammates who fight together to reach their goals.

It is an important question to ask, however, if we would be friends with our teammates if we met them outside of sport. Not to say we wouldn't like our teammates if we met as strangers one day, but it is important to distinguish the fact that we didn't choose our teammates as friends. At the onset, teammates are simply people in a shared environment working toward a common goal. That goal alone is the initial bond between teammates and allows us to circumvent the social niceties that make up normal friendship building. Well-practiced social cues that kids at school depend on to make friendships are glossed-over skills that athletes place on the backburner. It is more important for us to get the job done at practice than learn about our teammate's favorite food. Only as time passes and we grow closer with our teammates do genuine friendships start to form and we uncover traits, similarities, and preferences through time spent together.

Albeit the bond between teammates is incredibly strong, the lack of basic friendship-forming skills is prevalent among athletes. I can remember sitting in a 200-student lecture hall my sophomore year of college, fresh into retirement, and I didn't know how to turn to the person next to me and strike up a conversation. I felt silly. There are 200 people sitting in the same room as me, and I don't have the basic 4th grade skills to make friends with a single one of them. My best friends and my boyfriends had all been swimmers. They had always been given to me by my environment, and I never really had to go out of my way to make a new friend. As athletes, we may not fully realize this until we retire, but bypassing basic friend skills due to the fact that teammates/friends are handed to us is another component of our athlete identity.

With our teammates there is also an awkwardly avoided topic that you want to beat each other or play better than them. In an individual sport you want to beat everyone else including your teammate-friends. In team sports you may want to outshine your teammates to secure your position. While you may consider your teammates good friends, there is always an underlying desire to compete with them and be the better athlete, which can externalize into sabotage. Lewis Hamilton, Formula 1 Driver, describes the tumultuous time where he and Nico Rosberg competed for Mercedes Benz AMG team. They struggled to amicably co-exist and Hamilton shares his thoughts: "It's so important to have the support of your teammate. There was a period of time the guy that has been my teammate has been my best friend. But when you work your life to win and only one of you can win it brings a lot of friction."[2] Because of this, we may not fully divulge our vulnerabilities and true selves with our teammates out of protection. The result is what feels like fake or shallow friendships because you both want to outshine the other and win, and only one of you can win.

When this is the case for an athlete, it leads to feelings of isolation and a "lone wolf" self-view. This has the potential to become problematic when times get tough as the support system for the athlete feels sparse; a strong support system is a critical factor to navigate challenging moments. So, without significant time or energy available to cultivate friendships with non-athletes due to extensive training schedules, athletes rely on themselves for support and tend to keep their troubles private. After a while, athletes might begin to identify themselves as individualist or self-reliant and those identity traits become part of their core human, bleeding into other pursuits and activities outside of sport.

The Uniform

You start to love who you become when you put on your uniform. When I was fresh out of college and looking for employment, I signed up as a background actor for some of the feature films being produced in Atlanta. I figured I could make minimum wage doing something fun on a movie set while searching for full-time employment. Even though I was just one of hundreds of background actors on the edges of the cinema screen, we all had to go through makeup, hair, and wardrobe to make sure we fit the environment of the sci-fi world. Even if just one background actor had a Nike logo or common day outfit it would throw off the look of the scene. My hair was braided like a warrior, dark makeup was painted around my eyes, and I wore cargo pants with black combat boots for the "working world" scene. Even those simple modifications to my appearance made me feel like I wasn't my usual coffee-drinking, smartphone-obsessed self. I was a blue-collar warrior part of the uprising to take down the dictator faction of society. These tiny changes in hair, makeup and wardrobe altered how I behaved and viewed myself, albeit for the purpose for a fake movie environment.

Similar to cinema wardrobes or even Halloween costumes, an athlete's uniform elicits similar identity responses. The uniform symbolizes our change from average Joe to a ready-for-war athlete. We become a Version 2.0 of ourselves braced to fight an opponent. Think of the different uniforms an athlete puts on to compete. A baseball player puts on socks, cleats, pants, a belt, a jersey, a cap, sometimes additional under armor, batting gloves, helmet, and the baseball glove itself. A tennis player gears up with their tennis shoes, shorts/skirt, top, sweatbands, visor and their best friend, the racket. A football player gears up with cleats, socks, pads, a jersey, and a helmet. To top it all off, smear some black war paint beneath your eyes and you're truly ready for war, embracing the fighter inside you.

An extreme example of the psychological effect a uniform has on your behavior is the 1971 Stanford Prison Experiment.[3] In this experiment, which could never be performed today due to ethical standards put in place since, students at Stanford voluntarily signed up for an experiment in which some participants were directed to wear a prisoner uniform and others were directed to wear a guard uniform. In the basement of Jordan Hall on campus, the students lived in a mock prison and played out their assigned roles of prisoner or guard. The experiment was designed to examine the psychological effects of authority and power. After six days, the experiment ended due to the guards taking their powerful role too far, harassing and psychologically abusing the prisoner participants. While this is an extreme example, it is worthy to note how wearing a uniform, a costume, changes your perception of yourself and role in the world, ultimately affecting the very behaviors you carry out.

On the surface, athlete gear are just articles of clothing or tools to use, but when combined for the purpose of accomplishing a goal they have the power to transform the body underneath. You become an evolved combat warrior. Sports are a performance of athletic ability, after all, and when we become that performer with our fighting uniform, it feeds our ego that craves pride and purpose. Our identity latches on to the uniform transformation because it gives us the purposeful, strong version of who we are. Wearing our uniform reassures our existential insecurities that there is something worth fighting for and we are capable of fighting for it.

Goals

We start setting goals for ourselves. Our goals can range from simply beating a friend in a race to winning gold for our country at the Olympic Games. Whatever goal we choose, it serves as our North Star, a far-off guiding light directing our choices and providing purpose to our effort. Going to the Olympics, playing professionally, breaking a particular record, or hitting a certain time standard are all great examples of North Stars. The thought of one day reaching our desired destination offers the much sought-after raw motivation that keeps athletes going even when things get tough.

Athletes often fall down the slippery slope of head-over-heels attachment to achieving their goals at all costs. You can probably remember a time in your own career where you wanted to win so bad you would do almost anything for the blue ribbon. Think of Lance Armstrong and his notorious doping investigation that found him guilty of using performance enhancing drugs for over 10 years. Travis Tygart, the USADA Chief Executive on the case, called it "the most sophisticated, professionalized and successful doping program that sport has ever seen."[4] You don't casually or accidentally do what Armstrong did. In his case, his desire to meet his goals was so great he was willing to risk his integrity and reputation (and commit a crime) by illegally doping so he could have a competitive advantage and win. Competing at elite levels and pushing ourselves to achieve extreme levels of success challenges our ability to walk the fine line between blind ambition and caring for the health of our mind. Building entrenched identity attachments to achieving goals so much so that our self-worth is indisputably tied to whether we make the goal or not is where goals become harmful. Philip Moffit, spirituality teacher and former media mogul, says –

When you cling to desire, you become defined by that desire; you see the world through the eyes of someone who wants that particular goal or outcome. It is a distorted vision; therefore, you measure your life incorrectly. You experience stress, anxiety, dissatisfaction, tension, and frustrated longing. The mind is so contracted around what it is craving that it acts as though getting this one thing would make you happy… oftentimes the goal provides only fleeting satisfaction.[5]

When we dedicate so much of ourselves to attain our goals or become 'someone who wins', 'someone who runs fast', 'someone who lands every combination' we latch on to becoming, becoming, becoming so much so that life feels perpetually unacceptable until we hit the mark - a defining frustration among athletes.

When your performance doesn't meet your standards, calibrating the friction felt between expectations and actual results requires uncomfortable effort. This calibration exercise becomes much harder the better you become in your sport. For anybody else, seven gold medals in one Olympics would be earth-shatteringly incredible. But not Michael Phelps. He wanted to win eight gold medals. For anybody else, 22 grand slam titles would be earth-shatteringly incredible. But not Serena Williams. She wants 24 grand slam titles. As the best-of-the-best push beyond familiar barriers to set unprecedented records and achieve unheard of accomplishments, falling short feels even that much more crushing.

The flip side of the coin is the more positive side, namely, when we do hit our goals or exceed our own expectations. Setting out to run a certain time, score a certain number of points, win a certain medal or any other goal you set for yourself and actually achieving the goal skyrockets your brain to newfound levels of confidence. You can cross that task off your list, pat yourself on the back for a job well done and add another gold star to your mind's dashboard of your athletic accomplishments. A sense of mastery overcomes you, knowing that you successfully completed a mission you set out to fulfill. Having this abnormally high level of confidence contributes to your athlete identity because confidence "roots you in who you really are…giving you a greater sense of purpose."[6] When goals, the most concrete, definitive benchmarks you can lay out, are achieved and your confidence bucket overflows, there is no other alternative for your mind than to sink even deeper into the athlete identity.

While goals push us forward and serve as our journey's North Star, balancing our motivated ambition with a healthy practice of self-worth no matter the outcome is necessary to maintain a healthy mind. Reminding ourselves that although a large component of being an athlete is due to the incredible capabilities of our body, our athleticism is simply one aspect of who we are as a human individual. This is why it is critically important to be mindful that our worthiness as individuals is not solely dependent on whether we attain our goals or not, a challenging practice for most athletes who are head-over-heels dedicated to their own goals.

Time, Effort, Resources

The sheer amount of time required to truly hone your skills as an elite competitor also contributes to becoming "the athlete". You don't practice twice a week; you practice 10 times a week. Your season isn't one month long, your season runs for months at a time if not year-round. You don't peak after 365 days; it usually takes years if not decades to realize your full potential.

A great example of the time commitment required to reach desired levels of success in sport is with professional golfer Phil Mickelson. As a professional golfer, Mickelson competed 13 years before he won a major championship - The Masters in 2004. This is 13 years after he played in college, winning three NCAA Championships. Considering he started playing golf as a child before he started school, his career runs about 30 years before he won his first Major. 30 years! During this ticking time, other aspects of life move forward. Family grows older, school years begin and end, and people weave in and out of your life just as you weave in and out of theirs. As things change around you, your sport remains the same and you continually dedicate an enormous amount of time to improve. Simply put, the huge chunk of our existence spent on our sport quietly deepens our attachment over time to being an athlete.

If you're reading this book, you're likely one of the individuals who wanted to make the Olympic team or play professionally. You never looked in the mirror and said to yourself "This is fun, but I'll probably play for just a couple years, win a handful of medals, and then move on to something else." You went to practice and worked. You put in the effort. You stayed late to perfect the double-play. You didn't just go through the motions for 10th place. You poured concentrated effort into practice and competitions to truly compete to the best of your ability. Hard work. Dedication. Effort. Identifying as an elite athlete, you went above and beyond to not only show up but to *show up*.

This requires enormous levels of effort and energy. It is easy to attend a 2-hour practice and just slide by. It is easy to finish all the reps your coaches lay out for practice without really pushing your own limits. It is easy to do the work without excelling at the work. What is hard is putting in the focused effort. Effort is hard. Effort is draining. Effort requires sacrifice. Effort to be the best you can possibly be requires a level of dedication only the top percent of athletes are familiar with. Every single day an athlete must put forth obscene amounts of effort to continually improve. Focused effort combined with the large time commitment required to compete at elite levels also contributes to your growing attachment to the athlete's life.

Outside of the time and effort commitment, there is a necessary level of resources required to compete with the best of the pack. Modern sports can be expensive. Right now, the going rate for a competition female swimsuit ranges between $400-500, and an elite suit like that only lasts a few meets. Baseball bats, gloves, cleats, tennis rackets, tennis shoes, goggles, leotards, sweatpants, protective pads, jerseys, helmets, the balls themselves. The list goes on, and those items cost money. This cost doesn't even mention additional expenses such as team fees, competition entry fees, travel, or even the more arbitrary opportunity cost of being an athlete in the first place. Who knows where you would be financially if you never began sport as a mere kid. Sure, sports are fun games and spending money to partake in an activity that brings you joy is a worthy enough reason to do it (if you have the finances in the first place) but competing at the top of the food chain is expensive. Just like the stock market, you don't invest hundreds or thousands of dollars for little to no return. You invest your money to make more money. Investing in gear, membership fees, staff and any other line item is an additional, more concrete layer that contributes to our further solidified dedication to being an athlete - and being a successful one.

Idols

As we continue to ride the spike to the top, we learn who the best athletes are in our sport. They become our idols and we watch them in amazement, vicariously experiencing their performances and wins. Rafael Nadal, Serena Williams, Michael Phelps, Simone Biles, Cristiano Ronaldo, Katie Ledecky, Tom Brady, Lebron James, Tiger Woods, and Derek Jeter are just a few of the amazing athletes that perform(ed) at the top of their game. We love to love these athletes because they can do unthinkable feats of heroic athleticism. Have you ever seen Nadal chase a tennis ball so far off the tennis court that he is almost in the bleachers only to hit a perfect backhand that grazes the line for a point? Have you ever seen Tiger Woods hit a hole in one from hundreds of yards away, inciting the fans to go crazy and jump wildly up and down? We love to see the jaw-dropping moments of sport that our heroes open our eyes to witnessing. The benchmark of excellence is set so high, and we love chasing that benchmark. We see what is possible (or to us seemingly impossible) and with that excellence gauntlet thrown down we want to see where our own performance might land.

One More Thought. . .

I mentioned Tony Robbins earlier and his statement that progress equals happiness. When we move toward a goal and tangibly see growth, we feel accomplished. Because we feel accomplished, we feel good. Happy. In sports, we learn the rules of the game, we become the strongest version of ourselves, and we chase after the coveted #1 spot proving to the world the amount of progress we made. We garner attention for our accomplishments and pride ourselves on the amazing things we can do. Dopamine is everywhere, adrenaline is everywhere, and our ego eats up every last lick. From the ground up - learning a new game, bonding with teammates, loving our uniform, setting goals, dedicating time, idolizing the greats, and tasting victory - these elements create the mold that we then pour ourselves into. Our commitment, confidence, warrior self-image and teammate support system build the lens in which we view ourselves and our life. This unique, athlete lens sets the tone for everything, and our athlete identity only dives deeper the more we play. This is why, without a blink of an eye, we so easily fall into our own hero's journey, distracted by nothing but the thrill of standing atop a podium with a gold medal and running away from the fear of mediocrity. Nothing else matters but the pursuit of gold. We are athletes.

Chapter 6 Endnotes

1. Murray, K., & Hampton, D. (2021, March 24). *Addiction and the Brain: How Drugs Impact the Brain.* Addiction Center. https://www.addictioncenter.com/addiction/addiction-brain/

2. Gay-Rees, J., Martin, P., Todd, S. 2019-2021. *Drive to Survive.* Netflix.

3. Mcleod, S. (2020). *Stanford Prison Experiment | Simply Psychology.* SimplyPsychology. https://www.simplypsychology.org/zimbardo.html

4. Schrotenboer, B. U. T. S. (2012, October 11). *USADA releases massive evidence vs. Lance Armstrong.* USATODAY. https://eu.usatoday.com/story/sports/cycling/2012/10/10/lance-armstrong-usada-reasoned-decision-teammates-doping/1624551/

5. Moffitt, P. (2021). *Dancing With Life: Buddhist Insights for Finding Meaning and Joy in the Face of Suffering by Phillip Moffitt (2008–04-15).* Rodale Books.

6. Drevitch, G. (2018, September 20). *Why Self-Confidence Is More Important Than You Think.* Psychology Today. https://www.psychologytoday.com/us/blog/shyness-is-nice/201809/why-self-confidence-is-more-important-you-think

Chapter 7

Internal Patterns

Now, let's look at some of the defining thought patterns and internal beliefs that characterize the athlete identity.

Perfectionism

An athlete's greatest curse, best friend and worst nightmare is perfectionism. Perfectionism is the tactical specificity athletes rely on to win first place, pitch a no-hitter, stick the perfect landing for a 10/10, and beat everyone else all the time. Perfectionism is exactly what athletes rely on to push themselves beyond comprehensible limits and perform some of the most unbelievable sports performances to date. Being perfect makes everything make sense. Agassi puts it – "I like the feeling of hitting a ball dead perfect. It's the only peace. When I do something perfectly, I enjoy a split second of sanity and calm." (Agassi, 2010, p. 29).

A perfectionist is someone is who has a "a disposition to regard anything short of perfection as unacceptable."[1] We're all familiar with the standard qualities of an athlete - hardworking, strong attention to detail, dedicated, committed, persistent, tenacious, ambitious, etc. Every single one of these traits stems from the desire to be perfect. To be so good that no one else could possibly compete. When things go right and you find yourself standing atop the podium spraying champagne with a first-place trophy, perfectionism is an athlete's best friend.

Perfection, even when "achieved" still shines light on room for improvement. Don't be fooled by a first-place finish. Although an exemplary result, exemplary is not synonymous with perfect. What if you didn't slip on the start, clocked in .20 seconds faster and broke the all-time record? That would be truly perfect. What if your team completed every pass and beat your opponent by 21 points instead of 3? That would be truly perfect. These margins seem trivial. But you, as an athlete, can probably relate to analyzing the minutiae of your performance to identify where you could have been stronger, better, faster, smarter. Where you could have been even more perfect. David Hart, writer and podcaster, explains when talking about Nina the ballerina in Black Swan, "Perfection, as a goal of human development, is more than a bit tricky, and the striving for it can even lead to psychological disorders."[2] With perfectionist athletes, you're shooting for the moon. Even if you miss, you land among the stars, but you can't let go of what life might be like if you did in fact land on the moon. And the moon always seems to orbit just out of reach. Always out of reach.

The dark side of the moon (imperfection), when someone beats you or if you tear your ACL on a play or when you ultimately decide to retire and hang up the cleats for good, is the battle between unacceptable inadequacy and your perfectionist mind. It's enough to break your brain. Defeat, injury and retirement are moments that fall short of perfection. In these moments, athletes find themselves in the greatest struggles along their athlete journey. These moments in time expose athletes to the highest emotional vulnerability and their greatest fear, imperfection. This side of perfectionism is what creates many of the mental struggles athletes face both during competition and in a life post-sport. To your perfectionist mind, defeat, injury, and retirement are far off impossibilities not worthy of time spent preparing for. When these moments do inevitably happen, your brain's compass spins sporadically not knowing where or how to navigate through unplanned turmoil. When you're trapped in a species known for imperfection but dedicate your life to sports requiring perfection, it may seem impossible to reconcile your perfectionist curse with the reality of being a human being.

Your perfectionist mind loves to beat you up for being human, as being human is never sufficient. Your perfectionism secretly loves when you participate in self-hate thought patterns because it hopes that this internal dialogue will add further fuel to your perfectionist fire, pushing you to work even harder and strategize better for the next opportunity to achieve absolute perfection. When human error or subpar performances inevitably happen in sport, as they do for every single athlete, perfectionism waits patiently on the sideline ready for internal torture. It is a vicious, never-ending cycle. Modern athletes are cursed.

The frustrating thing about an athlete's perfectionism is the fact that this thinking is necessary to perform to the best of one's ability. The desire to be a perfect athlete inspires everything athletes do - when to wake up in the morning, what to eat at meals, how to identify oneself, what choices to make, who to surround oneself with, and quite poetically how to spend existence on planet earth (which is mostly attending practice). Modern sport and elite competition, where you can win or lose by .01 seconds, requires an intense level of precision. For example, not only is it what you eat but when you eat. In Loren Cordain's book, *The Paleo Diet for Athletes*, he recommends not only the food contents of every meal but the precise windows of time to eat.[3] This is the hyper-level of focus essential to achieve athletic perfection.

Without the desire to perform at perfect levels, the actions of the athlete would look much different, resulting in subpar performances not worthy of a podium. An athlete without perfectionism may exude behaviors such as skipping practice, not fueling one's body with proper nutrition or surrounding oneself with people misaligned with the life of a training athlete. These actions will not result in wins. While perfectionism feels harsh, critical, and draining, it is a double-edged sword having both favorable and unfavorable consequences.

As young athletes grow and form their own thoughts, beliefs, opinions and identities, this poignant desire to perform flawlessly roots itself deep in the mind. It runs so deep within us that we know nothing else. Sometimes it feels like our body was laid upon Frankenstein's table and a mad scientist opened our brains, inserted a microchip of perfectionism, and sewed us back up. When we bolt up and rise, we know nothing else but to aim for perfection.

Black-and-White Thinking

Another major distinction in an athlete's mind is black-and-white thinking, which overlaps with our perfectionist mindset. Dr. Sacco, PhD, says "black-and-white thinking is common among athletes. They think, 'If I don't do it perfectly and get it exactly right, then it's a failure'… This kind of thinking can lead to the strong drive for success that you see in elite athletes. But being so rigid in your psychological thinking can make it difficult to recover when something unexpected happens."[4] A great example of black-and-white thinking comes from professional tennis player Andre Agassi. In Agassi's autobiography he details the very first time he lost in the juniors at the age of nine - "…I'll now have a loss on my record - forever. Nothing can ever change it. I can't endure the thought, but it's inescapable: I'm fallible. Blemished. Imperfect. A million balls hit against the dragon [ball machine] - for what?"[5] As a little kid, a nine-year-old, he already views his record as tarnished, describing himself as "blemished" and expressing the emotional difficulty of moving forward with a loss. He was only nine years old when he said this.

Dr. Sacco is right, this intense perfectionist thinking is largely what drives athletes to reach the top one percent in their sport. However, black-and-white thinking also contributes to the incredibly harsh inner critic inside all elite athletes, often taking a toll on your self-worth. After a race or game and before any coach or teammate could offer feedback on your performance, you've already torn it apart a million times and know full well what could have been better. Agassi puts it - "I've been cheered by thousands, booed by thousands, but nothing feels as bad as the booing inside your own head during those ten minutes before you fall asleep." We are our own worst enemy. One misstep or one wrong turn eats you alive because your mind categorizes an error as the worst thing that could possibly happen. If it wasn't perfect, it was a failure. Black-and-white thinking is a key marker for an athlete's mind and contributes to emotional difficulties when our performances feel subpar or reality doesn't meet our expectations.

Athletes may find confusion and frustration outside of sport where black-and-white thinking is not applicable. Black-and-white thinking creates mayhem in the normal world where most things exist in a gray area. Real life situations and scenarios aren't as clear cut as wins and losses. With sport, the rules of the game are clearly defined, referees and officials are available to ensure fair play and you can't argue with a stopwatch. In the real world, however, there are entire college courses and corporate executive teams dedicated to clarifying "ethics". Is the entire legal profession not based on clarifying right and wrong and advising clients on complex matters? The real world, including hot topic issues such as abortion and same-sex marriage have so many differing opinions, caveats, and ripple effects that clear "yes" and "no" answers are almost impossible to generate for all parties. As athletes, we desire definitive answers, rules, guidelines, and benchmarks so we have certainty around what we can and cannot do. But the sports environment that cultivates black-and-white thinking doesn't seamlessly translate to the real world, often creating headaches for athletes when they enter a post-sport life.

Irrational Motivation

Training 20+ hours a week is not rational. Voluntarily putting your body through physical pain is not rational. The lifestyle and daily habits we create for ourselves, such as incredibly strict dietary plans, seem intensive to the point of crazy to a non-athlete. We do this, though, because we are motivated to win. We are motivated to do better. We are motivated to participate in irrational behaviors if that's what grants us the best shot at achieving our goals. Motivation is defined as "the reason or reasons one has for acting or behaving in a particular way."[6] Our reason for our objectively irrational behavior is to win.

Underneath the general consensus that athletes are incredibly motivated individuals, there are three different potencies of motivation. First you have the basic, default form of motivation of achieving a goal. Breaking a record, clocking a certain time standard, winning a gold medal, and beating a particular opponent are all basic forms of motivation. These are straightforward goals you can cross off. Motivators like these are default, commonplace North Stars that provide a general basis of inspiration to go to practice every day. Every athlete has been motivated by a goal that could be categorized as a basic layer of motivation.

The next level of motivation, the mid-grade if you will, is when an athlete has something to lose. A defending champion has greater motivation to keep the title than if he was another random opponent on the roster. A track athlete with one more shot at making the team is much more motivated to perform well in that race than if he/she already secured a team spot. Situations where the athlete has something to lose create higher stakes. If the athlete loses, he or she may feel a ripple effect of losing additional benefits (team spot, regarded title, prize money, etc.) and the threat of losing those sharpens the athlete's motivation sword more than simply entering competition with nothing to lose.

The highest and most potent form of motivation is having something to prove. This type of motivation is considered gold. The indescribable, burning fire within when you have something to prove is a level of motivation that can't be matched. Ronda Rousey explains that she is "more motivated by proving people wrong than fulfilling everyone's expectations."[7]

Your ex-girlfriend said you could never make the team? You're going to do everything you can to prove her wrong. Your coach constantly puts you at the bottom of the lineup? You're going to do extra reps on top of practice to improve and show him wrong. The reason proving something, to ourselves and others, is such a strong motivator stems from an athlete's reliance on validating worth based on capabilities. Seiko Shirai, a renowned psychotherapist, explains the underlying psychology of why the need to prove ourselves can be such a large driver in our behaviors. She says, "we don't want to feel a sense of unworthiness or we don't want to accept that we are unworthy, the urge of wanting to prove ourselves tries to protect us from the most vulnerable feeling of unworthiness."[8] When you have something to prove, you have everything you need to win.

Although an athlete's training schedule and competitive life may look objectively irrational, there are layers of motivation underneath those behaviors driving the athlete forward. We want to win; we want to protect our long-standing title and we want to prove to the world that we can do it. With these motivators, we are willing to do whatever it takes to win, despite how irrational it may seem.

Belief

Athletes are one of the few groups of people that blindly refuse to acknowledge reality. We believe in ourselves against all odds. We *always* believe we can win. If 200 athletes enter a 100-yard-dash, 199 don't think they will lose even though that is the actual outcome of the race. Only one person can clock the fastest time and with only one winner, 199 of them will place second or worse. Knowing those realistic odds and outcome of the race, it doesn't mean athletes enter the race and acknowledge they have a 1 in 200 chance of winning. Athletes don't consider the possibility of defeat. We just don't. All 200 racers genuinely think they have a shot at gold despite the reality that 199 will ultimately lose.

There is no alternative to this chain of thought. If an athlete doesn't truly believe they are capable of winning the race, they defeat themselves before the clock even starts and forego any chance of winning in the first place. Athletes have no other choice but to turn a blind eye to realistic outcomes, and we intentionally play mind games of belief against the odds so that we have a shot at winning. Have you, as an athlete, ever entered and won a competition believing the odds were stacked against you, thinking you were going to lose? Very rarely do athletes win without total belief they can do it.

The romantic part of our blind belief is knowing we are capable. We fall into a Hercules-complex, easily inspired by our own talents and hard work. We believe, no we know, we can go the distance. Doesn't it feel good to say, "I can do it"? Believing that we can rather than thinking we can't, for any pursuit sports-related or not, is empowering and when you believe in yourself, you develop an attitude of certainty. And what do humans love? Certainty. We latch on to the comfort created in our mind when we know that we can hit the 3-pointer, knock the ball past the fence and nail the landing. That empowerment creates certainty and comfort, and nothing can get in the way of those beliefs.

The belief in ourselves truly "sets" within us when we are totally alone. When you slide into a hot tub by yourself. When you lay in bed at night. When everyone leaves the locker room and you're the last one. Quiet space alone gives you the opportunity to let the belief in yourself really sink in. No one else is around to influence or distract your thoughts. There is no additional environmental stimulation preventing you from reflection. Everything sinks in. You may say "damn, I'm unstoppable" or "wow, I really did that". Lonesome reflection is like putting a newly sculpted piece of clay in the kiln to form and harden. In these moments all alone your athlete identity secures itself, manifesting in your soul in a way that even yourself cannot dispute.

Self-Importance

Selfish thinking and selfish behavior, although not very becoming, is simply a byproduct of being an athlete. Our focused, sometimes selfish thinking isn't to be pretentious or self-righteous. It comes from a place of surrendered dedication to do anything it takes to be the best. Selfish decisions and behaviors are necessary to appropriately focus on what athletes need to focus on to improve. Not hanging out with friends may seem like you're ditching the crew, but you're skipping the late night hang out to wake up early for morning practice. Not eating your sister's angel food cake may seem like an insult, but you're dedicated to top-of-the-line nutrition to fuel your body. Similar to my family's Fourth of July celebration, I skipped out on family time so I could sleep in the car in the parking lot to make sure I got enough rest for morning practice. I wasn't trying to be rude or anti-social. I wasn't telling my family I didn't want to hang out with them. Nothing could distract or deter my focus from doing whatever necessary to improve my training and swim faster.

Our success is dependent on ourselves (sure, there is a team and support system but even with those things in our environment we ourselves still have to make the choice to go to practice and compete). My body. My focus. My effort. We are in control (mostly) of our destiny, and it is up to us to go as far as we want. It is up to us to get to practice. It is up to us to race in the meet. It is up to us to make heat-of-the-moment decisions in the thick of the game to win. It is up to us to stick 100 more landings until it's perfect. It is up to us to stay late for hours after practice to nail our free throw. It is up to us to make decisions every single day that allow us to compete to the best of our ability. So, we live in a way that others may deem self-centered, but we live this way because we have to. The insane level of focus required to be the best possible athlete is simply what it takes.

Almost every decision an athlete makes is based on if it serves their performance. Is this helping me become a better athlete? What food to eat, who to hang out with, what movies to watch and more are all carefully considered. Kobe Bryant once said in an interview -

> Basketball, for me, was the most important thing. So, everything I saw, whether it was TV shows, whether it was books I read, whether it was talk shows, everything was done to try and learn how to become a better basketball player. Everything. Everything. So, when you have that point of view, then literally the world becomes your library to help you to become better at your craft.[9]

Behaviors and choices that athletes make, because of their infinite focus to their craft, might come across rude and self-serving, but this self-focused dedication is simply what's required of athletes to compete with the best of the best.

Rationalization & Overcompensation

Because of our athletic success, we rationalize inadequate parts of our life with the exceptional success we have on the field. We find that no one questions other parts of our lives as long as we perform well in our sport. I failed my biology exam? Oh well, I'm number one in the state. I got into a big fight with my best friend? At least my coaches love me because I'm the best on the team. When we're breaking records and winning gold, no one questions us.

Pockets of our life that don't measure up to what we wish they would be are often cast aside and, as an effect, our main life focus grows stronger on our sports success. Family trouble, friend drama, bad grades in school, money troubles, romantic relationships turned sour, whatever it happens to be in your life, we find comfort in the safety that our sports success envelops around us. We don't have to answer to other struggles, insecurities, fears, or mistakes when we're winning. We learn that we can avoid those uncomfortable topics altogether the better we are in our sport. Our sport, then, becomes our crutch to lean on. Our stellar performances lead the way and form the core of our identity while other aspects of our life fall to the wayside to be dealt with later. Our focus doubles down on that sports goodness as our subconscious fear about facing life without this crutch grows stronger. We may not even realize it at the moment, but we fear the day when we don't have our crutch to lean on and must face all parts of our life, the good and the bad, without our so-called painkiller. We fear the day when we have to try and be loved for who we are and not what we can do. How do we even do that? Who are we without sport?

Athletes face trouble when the crutch they so heavily leaned on to over-compensate inadequacies is kicked out from underneath them, such as experiencing defeat, injury or retirement, all moments where our sports success isn't there to prop us up. Because athletes have never had to confront the uncomfortable topics, we lack coping skills and social abilities to navigate and heal the avoided issues. Our diverted focus to our sport was a coping mechanism to turn away from insecure or inferior portions of our life. Rationalizing other aspects of life with sports success is a landmark trait of an athlete's mind.

Elitist

The more progress we make, the better performances we have, and the more opponents we beat leads to an elitist perception of ourselves and our capabilities. We love the fact that our bodies and minds can do things ordinary people can't even dream about doing. We are proud of how strong we are, and our identity indulges in the fact that what others cannot do, we can. Even our own competitors and teammates, who may train just like us, can't always match our performance. With our name on the record board, with our coaches using us as an example for everyone else, with the mere fact that we win games, our ego pieces together moments of accomplishment and, over time, constructs an elitist sense-of-self based on our extraordinary performances. If it were easy, everyone could do it.

Coach Ian held an annual 12-hour swim practice known notoriously as IHOP (Ian's House of Pain). The practice always took place around the holidays, where we had enough carbs around the house to help us survive. The 12-hour practice consisted of a 3-hour swim followed by a 1-hour break (x3) where we would lay down on the pool deck (and cry). In the last 3-hour session, my teammates and I were required to race from the starting blocks every single race offered at a real meet:

50 free
100 free
200 free
500 free
100 back
200 back
100 fly
200 fly
100 breast
200 breast
200 IM
400 IM

Thank goodness we were spared the 1,000 and the mile otherwise I might have actually died. After completing a grueling, exhausting 12-hour practice, it is next to impossible to walk away not feeling like you could take on anyone. We were phoenixes rising out of the ashes. My teammates and I could feel, really feel, our muscles growing stronger, our stamina strengthening and our speed increasing. Pushing crazy physical limits and accomplishing them grows our attachment to an identity belief that we can do things others can't. We start to cling to our self-view of being different and better than everyone else. In front of your very eyes, you've watched yourself clock faster times, bench heavier weight and throw passes you know your teammates couldn't make. Performing better, seeing tangible progress, and beating more opponents makes it incredibly difficult to not associate our identity with being an elite, strong, better-than-you athlete.

Fear

Everyone, athlete or not, is driven by fear. Fear of being a bad parent, fear of seeming stupid, fear of not being strong enough, fear of being the weak link, fear of being "weird", fear, fear, fear. If you haven't spent some time uncovering the fears in your own life, take a look at the choices you make every day. Think about what the ultimate driver for those decisions is. What is it that you are running away from and desperately trying *not* to be? For me, some of my fears are being out-of-shape, getting too old that I can't move around, seeming unintelligent and being unskilled at things. These fears drive me to exercise every day, take care of my nutrition and health to maintain longevity of my body, and proactively continue lifelong learning of topics interesting to me.

Athletes' biggest fear is mediocrity. Not being good. Not breaking the record. Getting beat by an opponent. Working day in and day out to be average. That is an athlete's nightmare. Can you even think about that in your own life? What if you never made the roster? What if your times weren't fast enough for the team? What if you practiced and tried but could never master hand-eye coordination? Imagine where you would be in your life today if you were bad at sports - scary thought, right? Patrick Mouratoglou, one of the most prominent tennis coaches in our era, talks about why some tennis players "choke" or give up in the middle of a tennis match they aren't winning:

There is one thing [players] are sure about - they have talent...There is one thing that they don't want to lose, is that (talent). So now what happens when you're a very talented player and you play a player that is not that talented, and you start to lose? Maybe that means that you're not that talented. You're not going to take that risk. You prefer to give up. And you can always say, I tanked, I didn't try. And that's what they do… it's the fear of losing the only thing that counts for you, your talent.[10]

His thoughts detail exactly why athletes do anything to avoid a possibility of being mediocre. That they aren't as good as they thought they were. Athletes would rather give up and lose than give their best effort and lose. The latter option forces the acknowledgement that you are not as good as someone else, an athlete's biggest fear and something we never want to face. The fear of not being good, not being the best is one of the biggest, quiet drivers for athletes to push beyond limits in practice and games to do everything they can to quash that fear.

Now that we've uncovered internal aspects of our self-view (selfishness, elitist attitudes, strong belief, black-and-white-thinking, rationalization, fear), let's look at some of the ways external factors impact our identity.

Chapter 7 Endnotes

1. *perfectionism.* (2021). The Merriam-Webster.Com Dictionary. https://www.merriam-webster.com/dictionary/perfectionism

2. Hart, D. (2018, March 11). *BLACK SWAN AND THE SEARCH FOR PERFECTION - David Hart.* Medium. https://medium.com/@pccasestudy/black-swan-and-the-search-for-perfection-9a874a840327

3. Cordain, L. P. A. J. F. (2021). *Paleo Diet for Athletes A Nutritional Formula for Peak Athletic Performance.* Rodale Books.

4. *motivation.* (2021). The Merriam-Webster.Com Dictionary. https://www.merriam-webster.com/dictionary/motivation

5. A. (2015, August 2). *Ronda Rousey Quotes -.* Quotesmeme. https://www.quotesmeme.com/quotes/ronda-rousey-quotes/

6. seikoshirai.com. (2020, April 3). *Changing poison into medicine.* Psychotherapy For Emotional Freedom. https://seikoshirai.com/2017/12/24/the-urge-to-prove-yourself-to-others/

7. G. (2020a, October 15). *How to Mentally Come Back From a Sports Injury.* Cleveland Clinic. https://health.clevelandclinic.org/how-to-mentally-come-back-from-a-sports-injury/

8. Agassi, A. (2010). *Open: An Autobiography* (Reprint ed.). Vintage.

9. *Bigger Than Basketball - The Legacy of Kobe Bryant.* (2020, February 4). LinkedIn. https://www.linkedin.com/pulse/bigger-than-basketball-legacy-kobe-bryant-david-angstadt/

10. Netflix. (2020). *The Playbook.* Boardwalk Pictures, Delirio Films, SpringHill Entertainment.

Chapter 8

External Factors

Even when we think we have a strong understanding of who we might be, under different circumstances we change and showcase different aspects of ourselves, sometimes bringing out parts of us that we didn't know existed. Intense competition has a knack of bringing out elements of our persona, such as spite, jealousy, and superiority, that we may not have experienced to such a magnitude outside of this environment. Let's look at some of the external factors at play in comprising our athlete identity.

Coach-Player Relationship

Note: It is sad I even feel the need to put this note here, but in this section I'm only talking about good coaches. Not the ones caught up in psychological abuse. Emotional abuse. Sexual abuse. Any other form of abuse. For our purpose here I'm only referring to good natured coaches.

Summarizing coach-player relationships is challenging because there are so many different personality types and styles of communication for both athletes and coaches. The same coach may have different strategies to motivate a particular athlete than another one. The same athlete may perform much better under the guidance of one coach than another. With a grain of salt regarding the endless permutations of coach-player relationships, let's look at some of the core characteristics from the athlete's view.

Athletes depend on coaches to help optimize his or her own talents. Coaches, in the most literal sense, coach the athlete on how to effectively train and compete to perform to the best of one's ability. Could an athlete do it alone? Maybe, but probably not. In the Tokyo 2020 Olympics, American swimmer Bobby Finke won both the 800-meter and 1500-meter races by sprinting the last lap, recording an astonishing time split for the end of a distance race. In his post-race interview, he credits his strategy to his coach saying, "I texted my coach after the 800, telling him he has no idea I had him yelling at me in my head to switch gears for that last 50. That's where I got it — my coaches constantly yelling at me to come home."[1] Think about your own athletic journey. Where do you think you would be today if you never had a coach? Would you have made it as far as you did? Coaches are wells of knowledge and support helping you become the best athlete you can possibly be. How nice that they're there to help you. Guide you. Support you. Train you. Good coaches are so precious to an athlete.

There is a poetic beauty in partnering with someone to achieve glory. Imagine one of your friends approached you with an elaborate plan to rob a bank. After 20 minutes of explaining the intricacies of the robbery, your friend looks you straight in the face and asks, "You in?" You take a second to think. You look back to your friend. "I'm in." You're both committed to a mission and to each other. You want to rob a bank (or win a gold medal) and your friend (coach) is all-in to support your mission. Although a bank robbery is a much more nefarious project than winning gold or breaking a record, a coach's commitment to help you pursue your dreams is a unique, emotional bond hard to replicate elsewhere. It feels like the end of the 1986 movie *Stand By Me*. The main character all grown-up sits at his computer desk and reflects on a younger, adventure-packed summer where he and his friends "go on a hike to find the dead body of a missing boy and confront a bully."[1] After that summer of trouble, venturing far from home and growing up, the adult Wil Wheaton sits at his desk and types the final sentence in his memoir writing, "I never had any friends later on like the ones I had when I was twelve. Jesus, does anyone?" Athletes never have a bond with others like they do with coaches when they're striving for gold. Jesus, does any athlete?

One characteristic distinction important to highlight in athletes is the tendency to grow roots into a subservient, mentee, student role. It makes sense. When a coach is constantly telling you what to do on a daily basis, you fall into the student role. Being coached from someone you respect and trust creates a reliance on that person's feedback, opinion and views over time. Athletes grow accustomed to constantly checking in with the coach's reaction or feedback to determine their own thoughts. In some cases, coaches "baby" or "parent" the athlete so much so that the athlete becomes dependent on the coach's instruction. They know their coach is always there to keep them in check. The athlete knows exactly how to push the coach's buttons, where the boundaries are drawn and how to please. It is a perfect recipe for an athlete to attach themselves confidently to a student role, relying on instruction from others to know how to be successful.

Athletes, when they retire, may find the adjustment challenging to make decisions with no one else's input but their own. There is no coach standing on the sidelines of your life guiding you in adulthood. Once athletes leave that mentor-mentee relationship the athlete may not know how to make decisions for themselves without the constant guidance they had from a coach. Doubt can creep in as the constant feedback you received from your coach when competing is now gone and you might wonder if you're making the right decisions.

Pressure

In the 1953 play, *The Crucible*[2], "playwright Arthur Miller employs a fictionalized account of Massachusetts Bay colonists accused of witchcraft in 1692 as a metaphor for government persecution of suspected communists during the mid-20th century."[3] To recall some of my high school reading material, an entire community of conservative Puritans in Massachusetts ended up participating in a heated finger-pointing, blame-game out of fear. Fear of possible witchcraft within their Puritan community (something against their religion and beliefs), and fear that if they didn't point to someone else as a suspect then fingers would point toward themselves. If that happened, the result was persecution. Once fear of witchcraft crept in, the environment cultivated intense pressure, paranoia and the highest of stakes (death), leading the characters to behave and think in ways that they may not have chosen if these factors did not exist. A community that started out as a very quiet, unassuming town rapidly flipped to showcase behaviors of outward blame, incredulous fear and even persecution. The Crucible is a great example of how incredible pressure from the environment transforms an individual's habitual behaviors and thoughts.

How in the world does this relate to athletes? In an athlete's world, unimaginable pressure and surmounting expectations set the stage for how athletes behave, think, and view themselves. Athletes largely exist in our modern society to compete, perform, and win. The pressure of constantly delivering on those expectations generates enormous amounts of stress. Michail Antonio, a West Ham United footballer puts it, "Imagine you had a bad day and then you had thousands of fans telling you you're terrible…There is a massive stress in the game when you have to constantly be your best."[4] The crucible that is sports competition – constantly performing at peak levels – affects athletes in ways that might not have surfaced if they weren't feeling the pressure of sports in the first place.

The presence of pressure can lead to performance anxiety and very real, physical side effects. Pressure "makes your heart rate speed up, makes you struggle to breathe. Thinking clearly becomes difficult, you may lose some control of your physical and mental abilities and your capacity to execute your skills."[5] What if I don't stick the landing, don't score points, lose my spot on the roster then lose my scholarship? Stressful thoughts. The more attached you are to the outcome of your performance, the more pressure you will feel. Pressure to win millions in prize money may cause a player's game to be "tight" with missed shots. He may refuse to shake hands after the match if he ultimately lost, a decision he may not have chosen had pressure not been involved.

Pressure has the capability to compress our mind, negatively narrowing our actions and thoughts. Maybe we are so amped up about the game this weekend that we snap at our significant other. In the absence of pressure, we would have never behaved that way. Maybe with intense pressure weighing on our career we strategize with our team to make decisions that allow us a better chance of winning even if not playing totally fair. The presence of pressure can also create converse, positive effects as some athletes thrive under pressure. Some people need imminent deadlines and tight constraints to perform their best. With so many eyes on your performance, pressure to perform well can be exactly the push you need to win. It can be the cherry on top to your performance.

In one of my screenwriting courses in undergrad, my professor gave us an assignment with strict, limiting guidelines. We had to write a scene with only one character, in a single room with one object. Some students wrote about a woman in her bedroom with a hairbrush. I wrote about a scientist in a laboratory with a test tube. My initial thought about a limiting assignment such as this is that it would be incredibly difficult to come up with a compelling storyline for the scene with so little to work with. What my classmates and I found to be true, though, was the opposite. My classmates were able to write even more clever ways of conveying emotion in the scene because of the constraints. When forced to write "inside the box" you're pigeon-holed to think of interesting, creative strategies to complete the assignment as opposed to limitless instruction which can be counterintuitively suffocating. This is the same philosophy when it comes to athletes who thrive under pressure. The constraints of the do-or-die mentality can be exactly what an athlete needs to find their fifth gear and win as opposed to competing in the absence of pressure.

There is an upside to this pressure once an athlete goes on to live a life post-sport. Over time, athletes (hopefully) grow tolerant to these high-pressure environments that a meeting with the CEO feels like a low-stakes hangout compared to performing on the Olympic stage with millions of eyes watching every single move. One reason many athletes find themselves working in sales post-sport is likely due to the ability to thrive under pressure, among other qualities that translate from sports to performance-based working roles. The behavioral changes and inspired thought patterns rooted in the presence of pressure contribute to an athlete's self-view and, consequently, the decisions and actions carried out. These thoughts and behaviors further identify the athlete.

Attention

Humans, whether athletes or not, crave attention from the day we are born. As babies we cry, as kids we throw tantrums, and as adults we may do stupid things that seem out of character just to elicit a response. We want to feel heard and noticed so our "belongingness" in Maslow's hierarchy of needs pyramid is met.[6] "When others pay attention to us, [their attention] connects us together, expanding our sense of identity".[7]

Athletes generally receive positive attention. The very simple psychology behind positive attention is that when people see us, listen to us and value us, it feels good. We feel important. We feel accepted. Have you ever met someone for the first time, explained you're on the volleyball team, and they responded, "Wow, that's awesome!" You feel special, cool, or elitist when others react to your position on the team with such positive affirmations, as most people do react to athletes. Your ego eats this positive attention right up, affirming that you are a special somebody based upon your sport. Andre Agassi talks about his back-and-forth thinking about attention: "The way they [fans] watch me and ask for my autograph, the way they scream as I enter an arena, makes me uncomfortable, but also satisfies something deep inside me, some hidden craving I didn't know was there. I'm shy - but I like attention. I cringe when fans start dressing like me - but I also dig it."[8]

The sheer volume of attention is unique to athletes. Hundreds if not thousands of people scream your name and praise your skills when you score a goal. Not only are there so many eyes on you as an athlete filling up your attention cup, but athletes receive constant feedback from coaches, trainers, and other team members. Athletes simply cannot be ignored.

Think of all the practices, meets, games and tournaments you attend, giving you countless opportunities to demonstrate your skills and receive attention. At practice, your coach constantly critiques, offers feedback, and shares strategies with you on how to optimize training and competing. Maybe you win the championship game, and your sponsors buy you a bucket list item. Maybe you broke a record, and the local newspaper shares your achievement with the entire community. When you're putting yourself out there and competing at such a high frequency, the level of positive feedback is abnormally high compared to the normal human being. We become accustomed to being noticed - positively noticed.

The hyper-detailed, constant level of attention we give athletes builds a pattern of expectation. Athletes adapt to a homeostasis that includes a constant spotlight, growing an acclimation to never-ending attention from people watching their every move, tending to their wants and needs, and constantly curious about them. Even as kids we observe our parents or coaches devote themselves to our success. We have no problem, then, taking the stage assuming the main character. I'm the best. I'm doing something great. I'm the center of attention. We feel our journey is truly worthy and we are doing something incredible based on the frequent and abnormally large amount of attention that reinforces those thoughts. Our ego becomes inflated, as you can probably note in several world class athletes. We feel like the new, cute puppy dog that everyone wants to pet and hold and love. Constant positive attention from multiple sources cues our minds to build a story about who we are - a story reliant on others to deem us worthy and feed our eyes and ears with praise.

Being incredibly good at your sport can also be polarizing and attract negative attention. When you're at the top of your game and incredibly good at your sport, it becomes very easy to be well-liked by everyone except your opponents. While your family is proud of you and your achievements attract positive attention, your competition begins to hate you. With a field of strong athletes vying for the top spot, your position in first place puts a target on your back for jealousy and resentment. I wish I could say this jealousy is more prominent with younger athletes that haven't matured or learned the sportsmanship skills despite the anguish of defeat, but there are adult competitors under incredible pressure that still deliberately refuse to shake hands. This jealousy and frustration can externalize beyond simply not shaking your hand and can evolve into hurtful actions against you. Hello, Tonya Harding.

When unsportsmanlike conduct happens to you or, heaven forbid, opponents take action against you, it can feel incredibly ostracizing and hurtful. After all, it is simply your performance as an athlete that creates a fissure between you and your opponents, not necessarily the person you are. Being treated this way can cause you to retreat from your competitors in fear of further beratement, leaving you to double down on your focus on being the best athlete you can be. Your sport becomes less about camaraderie and enjoying the journey and more about being and maintaining your #1 position. The pressure increases monumentally as you pour your heart into the one thing that can keep you at a safe distance from mean competitors - being unlike any of them in first place. This further solidifies our identity as a top athlete and perpetuates a cycle of wanting to win. Whoever said that it can be lonely at the top is right.

Self-Worth & External Validation

Gymnastics is such a beautiful sport, but if you think about it from a very young age, from the time I was 2 years old I started gymnastics and from that young age I was taught that my results or my worth in the sport is based off of what other people think of me. So, at the age of 5 if I did a beam routine I would look over and look to my coach, I would look at my coach for approval and I realized in my regular life outside of gymnastics I do that too. And I found myself, even after interviews, I would call my mom or call my friends and be like 'How was that? Was that good?' A lot of people would say 'Well it really depends how did you feel? Did you feel that was good'.[9]
- Aly Raisman, CBS Interview for World Wellness Break Day

Self-worth is one of the largest psychological components in building or deconstructing an athlete identity. The sports world deems value based not on characteristics of your personality, such as having a good sense of humor or your love of cooking, but on the number of points you can score in a game or the number of gold medals you can win. Athletes don't have the luxury of relying on their personality traits to accrue favor. Athletes are seen as who they are and awarded trophies based on capabilities alone. Roger Federer, although a handsome spokesperson for Gillette, would not be *the* Roger Federer if it weren't for his 20 Grand Slam titles. This begins the correlation trail of "I'm worthy if I win and if I win, I'm worthy."

This externally validated self-worth isn't limited to athletes - runway models, musicians, artists, and performers create similar mental habits of depending upon the approval of others to feel like they are truly "good". We learn that winning is equated with being liked and losing is equated with shame. Athlete or not, it is simply human to run toward acceptance and avoid shame at all costs. This structure of "good" and "bad" athletic behaviors becomes *the* framework we use to seek validation, leaving us as athletes to rely on our accomplishments and capabilities to feel liked and accepted.

What deepens this reinforcement is the fact that our entire environment promotes this thinking. Actually, our environment conditions us to base our worth on our accomplishments. Psychologically, this is positive reinforcement in full effect. By definition, "positive reinforcement involves the addition of a reinforcing stimulus following a behavior that makes it more likely that the behavior will occur again in the future. When a favorable outcome, event, or reward occurs after an action, that particular response or behavior will be strengthened."[10] Basically, if you run the fastest and earn a ribbon, you are being conditioned to repeat that behavior because of the ribbon reward. If you score more touchdowns than the other team and win a ring, you are being conditioned. I don't think positive reinforcement could get any clearer in sport – compete, win, earn a reward, repeat.

After enough reinforcement, our self-worth becomes inseparably correlated to the accolades we garner as an athlete. According to Barbara D. Lockhart, EdD, "research indicates that the more an individual identifies with athletic performance (high athletic identity), the less stable their individual identity and self-esteem."[11] That makes sense. If the physical capabilities of our bodies become *the* source of our worth, how do we feel good about ourselves when we inevitably lose a match or tank a game? If we're pulling our self-worth from one source, of course it is going to be unstable. In those situations where we aren't always top of the pyramid, we may begin to feel inadequate, unaccepted, and maybe even disliked. We struggle to deem ourselves worthy. We struggle to deem ourselves good. This is a harsh, undiversified, and dismal way to live your life.

The dark side of being conditioned to base your self-worth on your accomplishments is when you are taken out of the context of sport. As Aly Raisman describes, she struggled seeking approval and validation from others when she was no longer competing. She struggled feeling worthy without a peanut gallery constantly providing that validation. When you are no longer able to seek validation through sport, especially during injury and retirement, it's incredibly challenging to build self-esteem and confidence when you have never learned alternative methods of filling those buckets. We'll dive into this later in Chapter 17.

Basing our worth on external validation is not the athlete's fault. In an environment that conditions us to feel worthy based on the things we accomplish, it only makes sense to succumb to the deep impact of positive recognition. When we crush it at a tournament, when our coach pays more attention to us, when we land a new brand deal, and when our teammates want to beat us at practice because we got that much better, we lay in bed at night with a blanket of reinforcement that everyone views us in a positive light because of our athletic accomplishments. We love this approval. Performing well in our sport becomes the sole criteria we use to base our worth, and, thus it becomes a defining characteristic of the athlete identity.

Chapter 8 Endnotes

1. Day, M. (2021, August 1). *Bobby Finke Comes from Behind Again, Wins Gold in 1500m*. RSN. https://www.nbcsports.com/philadelphia/tokyo-olympics/bobby-finke-comes-behind-again-wins-gold-1500m
2. Miller, A. (2000). *The crucible*. Penguin Classics.
3. *The Crucible: Study Guide*. (2021). SparkNotes. https://www.sparknotes.com/lit/crucible/
4. *3 Types of Psychological Stress Affecting Athletes In-season - Firstbeat Sports*. (2021, March 16). Firstbeat. https://www.firstbeat.com/en/blog/3-types-of-psychological-stress-affecting-athletes-in-season/
5. Boulter, S. (2018, May 9). *Performing Under Pressure — 9 Ways Great Athletes Make It Count, When It Counts Most*. Medium. https://medium.com/@thesimonboulter/performing-under-pressure-9-ways-great-athletes-make-it-count-when-it-counts-most-b271619f17e3
6. Mcleod, S. (2020b, December 29). *Maslow's Hierarchy of Needs*. Simply Psychology. https://www.simplypsychology.org/maslow.html
7. *The Need for Attention*. (2021). Changingminds.Org. http://changingminds.org/explanations/needs/attention.htm#:%7E:text=People%20may%20even%20self%2Dharm,as%20worthy%20of%20their%20attention.
8. Agassi, A. (2010). *Open: An Autobiography* (Reprint ed.). Vintage.
9. Dokoupil, T., King, G. (2021, May 1st). *Olympic Gymnast on Importance of Mental Health, "World Wellness Break"*. CBS News. https://www.facebook.com/watch/?v=2916426025244842
10. *Positive Reinforcement Can Help Favorable Behaviors*. (2021). Verywell Mind. https://www.verywellmind.com/what-is-positive-reinforcement-2795412
11. Pinalto, C. (2021, March 22). *Creating a Healthy Identity Beyond Sports*. Sidelined USA. https://www.sidelinedusa.org/resources-blog/2018/6/19/becoming-sidelined-creating-a-healthy-identity-beyond-the-game

Chapter 9

Identity Foreclosure

With all these internal and external factors contributing to an athlete identity, it makes total sense why athletes throw all their eggs in one basket of being an athlete. Stir the cauldron of setting goals, dedicating time and resources, competing, seeking attention, external validation, fear, rationalization, winning, pressure and out pops a purebred athlete with barely any room left for additional spices. This double-down, singular life focus of being an athlete is what researchers call "Identity Foreclosure". Identity Foreclosure describes a category of individuals that "have committed to an identity without having explored the options."[1]

Commitment

		Present	Absent
Exploration	Present	Identity Achievement	Moratorium
	Absent	Identity Foreclosure	Identity Diffusion

2

Having little to no room to pursue being a musician, a chef, or even a gamer, athletes foreclose on their identity. There isn't much space for new friends, hobbies, or other pursuits, preventing us from exploring other parts of life. Imagine how different your whole personality might be today if you never put on a pair of cleats in the first place. Who knows who you may be in an alternate universe. Here's an excerpt from an interview with retired Austrian swimmer, Dr. Markus Rogan, who competed at the 2004, 2008, 2012 and 2016 Olympic Games:

> When we're teenagers, a normal teenager asks themselves, 'who am I? What is good about me? What is not good about me? What is socially acceptable? Not socially acceptable? Unappealing?' These are painful questions of identity. Athletes in general, but good athletes especially, get a ready-made identity handed to them. Oh, you're a good swimmer. Case closed. (In my experience) I have great social connections, I could become part of groups just by being a great athlete. Athletes don't have to go through the painful teenage process of finding their identity because they have an identity that's handed to them in the form of achievement. But achievement is more than just, you're good at something. It gives you a full picture. Of course, you do get a little – you're great, I'm a swimmer, I don't have to worry about what's my sexuality, what's my gender identity, what's my motivation for living, what's my motivation for dying – all these painful, uncomfortable, awkward questions that I never had to have. But then of course, the questions don't go away. They linger, and then while the other teenagers figure it out by their mid-20s, we're getting medals, we're getting money, we're not going to listen to those questions. We've got more medals to win and more money to make. Then the questions catch up to you. And you see this all the time. Why do grown men, like 30-year-old athletes, behave like teenagers? Because that's where they are.[3]

Without having the experience of exploring other facets that make up the very person we are, all we know is being an athlete and being an athlete is all we know. This identity is further cemented across different environments over a long span of time. We aren't an athlete only in the gym. We are an athlete at home with family, at school and in other environments. Our attachment to the athlete identity spans years if not decades. Being an athlete across different environments over long periods of time leaves us with a deep-rooted self-identification of being that athlete, foregoing other opportunities to build additional labels of who we are.

Martyr Complex

The objectively irrational total commitment to our sport looks a bit crazy to those who aren't doing the same thing. How odd is it to shut down the rest of your life as a human being to be an athlete and win? Why do athletes secretly take pleasure in the grandiose gesture of casting everything aside for the gold? Particularly in the athlete context, a martyr complex is described as "the belief that the martyr has been singled out...because of exceptional ability or integrity."[4] As athletes, we feel as though we are "the chosen one". We are the ones who can make it to the top. We are willing to sacrifice friends, family time, grades, relationships, everything if it means we will become the best. We are willing to let other parts of our life die - making us a martyr to our sport - if it grants us the desired legendary aura and status we crave so much. The only other group of people this might sound remotely normal to are musicians. Musicians are the most similar to athletes in terms of life journey, dedication levels and performance attachment. Both groups spend hours practicing. Both groups work on a team (or band/orchestra). Both groups perform in front of crowds. Both groups have a hierarchy of talent (first chair, second chair / first string, second string). Both groups learn skills that become so marginally intricate. Both groups train under a coach or conductor. The major difference between the two groups is society's higher value on sports than arts - you'll find more audience members at a professional basketball game than a symphony concert. But both athletes and musicians are dedicated, overly dedicated, to becoming the most skilled in their respective crafts so much so that they might even be willing to sacrifice themselves if it means a perfect performance.

In the 2014 film Whiplash[5], an ambitious jazz drummer barely makes a spot in an elite band and must deal with an overly perfectionist band leader. Albeit this is a movie about music and the main character is a drummer, you could swap out the movie's environment and characters with the situation of any athlete and the story seamlessly fits. After an entire season of ups and downs, it's time for the final show. On the way to the show, the drummer gets into a car accident, just minutes away from the venue. He hops out of the car, running to the concert venue to perform his solo. Bloody, dripping in sweat and out-of-breath, he sits at his drum set and performs an unbelievable solo to close out the concert. The lights go out on the band leader's last cue, but the drummer continues to hammer on the drums for an amazing solo performance. It is one of the best movie endings of all time. The young drummer in the movie exemplifies a martyr complex based on his absolute commitment to performing. Only someone with a surrendered commitment and a martyr complex would walk away from a car crash, run to a concert venue and continue to perform in that condition. Nothing else matters and everything can be sacrificed for the chance of doing something great. Both athletes and musicians showcase an objectively irrational commitment to their identity, almost sacrificially, reflecting a martyr complex.

Love

While identity foreclosure feels dark and serious (which, it is), there is a poetic, silver lining in choosing one pursuit to dedicate yourself to. Each day you have 86,400 seconds of life. Those seconds cannot be transferred. They don't rollover. Dedicating your most precious, valuable, and non-transferrable resource – your time – to your sport is the most beautiful form of love.

I think about marriages that have lasted 35 years or 50 years and I can't think of a higher form of respect and love than to share your journey on this planet with another human being. Same with choosing your sport. You could have chosen a million other activities to pursue. Cooking, gaming, writing, acting, linguistics, juggling, singing, dancing, chemistry, politics, anything. You could have solely dedicated your interests to anything else on this planet, but you chose your sport. That is a beautiful form of love.

In 2015 Kobe Bryant produced his animated short film "Dear Basketball" as a farewell letter announcing his retirement. In his 5-minute video, Bryant poetically details his love for the game saying "I knew one thing was real. I fell in love with you. A love so deep I gave you my all. From my mind and body. To my spirit and soul."[6] A total athlete identity. A total love for the game. I can't think of another profession where an expert or professional would offer similar sentiments of love. Would a surgeon write a love letter to surgery? Would a lawyer write a love letter to the law? This expression of love feels unique to the athlete profession. Bryant's short film is a beautiful piece of art sharing the love we feel as athletes toward the games we spend so much time playing.

One more thought...

Now that we've explored, uncovered, and dissected what it means to be an athlete, we can use our strong understanding to practice healthy coping skills when times get tough. Learning why athletes are the way they are - with irrational motivation, overly competitive desires, and fear of inadequacy among all the other characteristics and thought patterns we mentioned – grants us the awareness needed to build effective mental strategies. Remaining ignorant to the deeper psyche of why you, as an athlete, are the way you are only perpetuates unhealthy patterns and demands extraneous amounts of energy on your part to navigate life's road bumps. Identifying and recognizing who we are as athletes sets us up for a light, clear, healthy mind, which is quite the opposite if this work is left unchecked.

Chapter 9 Endnotes

1. Arduini-Van Hoose, N. (2020, June 1). *Identity Development Theory | Adolescent Psychology*. Lumen. https://courses.lumenlearning.com/adolescent/chapter/identity-development-theory/
2. Harris, Paul & Pusser, Brian & Kelly, Darren & Hull, Michael & Gates, Phil & Desmond, Rachel. (2018). Identity Promoting Identity Development in Student Athletes: There's An App for That. 2. 34-55.
3. International Swimming Hall of Fame / Swimming World. (2021, January 28). *Out of the Pool: Markus Rogan on Performance Psychology and Finding Identity*. Swimming World News. https://www.swimmingworldmagazine.com/news/out-of-the-pool-markus-rogan-on-performance-psychology-and-finding-identity/
4. Wikipedia contributors. (2021, July 28). *Martyr complex*. Wikipedia. https://en.wikipedia.org/wiki/Martyr_complex
5. Chazelle, D. (Director). (2014). *Whiplash* [Film]. Bold Films, Blumhouse Productions, Right of Way Films.
6. Bryant, K. (2015, November 29). *Dear Basketball*. The Players' Tribune. https://www.theplayerstribune.com/articles/dear-basketball

Half-Time

Level-Setting

"Everyone is going through something."
—*Kevin Love, NBA Basketball Player*

Chapter 10

What is Certain for Every Athlete?

Three things are certain for every athlete:

1. **You will face defeat.**
2. **You will injure yourself.**
3. **You will retire.**

We don't like to hear about defeat because we always believe we can win. That is the point of the game - score the most goals or run the fastest time to beat your opponent. Performing in a way that is superior to your competition has defined "sport" dating all the way back to the Ancient Greeks. But, despite our winning beliefs, we won't place first every single time. We may have amazing winning streaks such as Roger Federer holding the world's number one ranking for 237 consecutive weeks or Michael Phelps winning eight gold medals in a single Olympic Games, but even they sometimes drop a match or finish second place. It is inevitable that on some days, someone will be faster. Someone will be stronger. Someone will be more prepared. Sometimes, you will be that someone dominating the field. The fact of the matter is you won't win every single time and it serves our mental health to calibrate our expectations with reality.

This may sound counterintuitive, or even shocking, to athletes because part of our training is to visualize finishing first and believe with all our might that we will be the victor. The mindset of believing you will win despite all odds is necessary to perform at your highest level. What is important to hold a shred of awareness around, though, is that sometimes (even if incredibly rare) we will lose. Stuart Heritage, writer for The Guardian states:

> Failure is much more common than success, but less often discussed. Indeed, with sport - which is built upon a teetering narrative of victory against all odds - there are many more failures than victors. One team might win the Premier League every year, after all, but 19 do not. Their stories are never heard, because the spotlight always swings around to the winners.[1]

As long as we can acknowledge on the very backburner of our brain that our sports journey will be speckled with a loss here and there, we can better manage those situations when they do arise.

The second certainty is injury. Injury comes in varying degrees, from minor bruises and fractures to major head injuries or even paralysis. Sometimes death in more extreme cases. I still remember when freestyle motocross driver, Jeremy Lusk, crashed his landing on a jump in 2009 ultimately ending in his death. Somber, devastating, and rare as this side of the injury spectrum of sports is, it does occasionally occur. Rest in peace to those athletes of all sports who have died too soon. The rest of the injury spectrum includes every varying degree of ailment the human body can succumb to. Some requiring surgery while others might just require some ice.

Suffering an injury in sports makes so much sense. Sounds weird to say, right? Think about it. Whatever sport you play, you push your body further and harder. Weightlifting, sparring opponents, endless repetitions, hours-long practices, grueling training schedules, competitions most weekends, competition risk, it goes on and on. It makes total sense that sometimes the bodies we throw into this intensity sometimes break. It isn't anyone's fault. No one wakes up and says, "I can't wait to injure myself in practice today." But on the sole basis that we are humans with the potential to succumb to illnesses and break bones and pull muscles, we sometimes get injured. Add the layer of being an athlete where physical activity is at an exorbitant level compared to your average Joe, the chance of injury is much higher. The fact of the matter is all athletes face injury of some degree at some point.

The final certainty is that, as an athlete, you will one day hang up your goggles or cleats or racket for the last time. You will eventually decide that your life is moving on, or your body isn't as strong as it once was. Maybe you crossed off all your goals and are ready to call it quits. Maybe you suffered an unexpected injury that ended your career. However retirement shows up on your journey, we all face the daunting transition into normal life that most athletes are unprepared for. This transition can often be termed as some form of an identity crisis. Really, how does one go from being an elite athletic machine to a regular person shopping at the grocery store? In Olympic Swimmer Katie Hoff's book, Blueprint, she eloquently describes entering retirement - "It was hard to make the transition from a career of winning races, setting records, and being well compensated, to how elegantly I had structured an email. That type of transition plays with your head."[2]

While it may seem as though these certainties are negative (no one likes to confront the possibility of losing, breaking their body or going on without sport), having a grain of awareness around these topics benefits our mind to navigate through them when they do arise. I may lose a soccer game and be so upset with the way I played for weeks to come, antagonizing my own wellbeing. Or I can adopt new perspectives and frameworks - like always doing my best regardless of the outcome - that put losses like that at ease in my mind and allow me to move forward as a stronger person and athlete. Approaching these tougher moments on our athlete journey with an open mind can protect ourselves from falling into darkness and frustration after defeat, injury, and retirement.

Preemptively thinking about these hurdles in an athlete's career is not intended to defeat yourself before you start or to think negatively about sport, but to realize certainties of the sport that affect aspects of your mental health. Mind over matter is what they say and imagine competing with a mind trained as tough as your body - the results could be incredible. Your ability to improve your physical specimen in the game is beyond commendable, especially for the level you're competing. Apply that same capability of improving yourself to your mind, and you might amaze your own self how mentally strong you can become.

Now that we've grown awareness around the inevitable pitfalls we face along our athlete journey, let's uncover strategies to effectively cope through them. How can we reduce emotional distress in times of defeat, injury, and retirement to better thrive for tomorrow? Let's tackle some of the toughest moments along our journey with acceptance that while defeat, injury and retirement are inevitable, the strength we can build in those moments is limitless.

Chapter 10 Endnotes

1. Heritage, S. (2019, April 4). *Winners are boring! The genius Netflix doc that celebrates losers*. The Guardian. https://www.theguardian.com/tv-and-radio/2019/mar/01/winners-are-boring-the-genius-netflix-doc-that-celebrates-losers
2. Hoff, K., & Bader, R. (2020). *Blueprint: An Olympian's Story of Striving, Adapting, and Embracing the Suck*. CG Sports Publishing.

Chapter 11

Two Spoonfuls of Sugar

Here is a bit of immediate comfort regardless of what you're going through, athlete or not. We often hold these two misconceptions about periods of struggle in our lives: I am alone, and I should not feel this way. We believe no one can relate to what we're going through, and we judge our own human condition. Let me offer a spoonful of wisdom to combat those thoughts and instantly provide relief to help the tough moment pass a little easier.

Misconception #1: I am alone.

No one can understand how I feel or relate to my situation. Why am I the only one to be hurt like this? Because of the magnitude of pain or change, we feel as though no one ever in the world has experienced what we are going through right now. Nothing anyone could say or do can help. We are in the thick of it and stubborn to believing anyone could possibly relate - how in the world could they? They don't know the situation from my view. They don't know how I'm feeling. Maybe we feel wronged, guilty, or overwhelmed to such a magnified degree we can't possibly begin to show compassion to the situation. We are trapped in our own self-loathing or self-pity party, thinking the world is cruel to us and only us. The mistake here is that that is simply not true. Pain is universal of varying types and degrees, so even though it feels new, fresh, and painful to us does not mean it is new to the world.

Think about how long humans have existed, and thus how long emotional pain has existed. Archaeologists have found fossils dating about 2.1 million years ago in Africa.[1] Our species looked a lot different way back then, but those homo sapiens had their own set of struggles, likely more dire as their direct survival depended on the stresses that impacted their daily lives. Fast forward 2.1 million years to today and you have centuries of the human condition where every shred of emotion, good and bad, has been experienced in some way, shape or form. The presence of darker emotions is quite normal and common for humans when you look across the entire history of our species.

The history of human pain goes to show you are not alone in your suffering. I will say that again. You are not alone in your suffering. Drawing comparisons to eras over the history of time is a broad view that really makes your pain feel insignificant. But even in today's modern sports world, every athlete experiences the trials and tribulations of pushing oneself daily to be the best. You may resist that acknowledgement because your heart tells you that no one else in the world sees the situation from your view, so how can someone else be feeling a similar pain or possibly relate? Yes, the details of the situation are different from person to person, but your feelings of pain are universal across humanity. We are a species of emotional highs and lows and neither end of that spectrum discriminates who experiences them. We all go through it.

Don't believe me? Google what you're going through. Google how you're feeling. I wouldn't put too much merit into medical suggestions, especially if they are not from an accredited medical website, but you will find blogs, articles, and websites covering the topics that are boiling inside you right now. You can seek advice, connection, shared pain, and stories from others that have gone through it before you. The internet is a double-edged sword so proceed with caution, but you can find tangible commonalities between you and other people that truly reinforce you are not alone in your pain. Missing the homework assignment sucks when the teacher singles you out and embarrasses you. But if half the class also missed the homework, then you don't feel so bad.

Misconception #2: I should not feel this way.

When life hits us hard, many of us judge ourselves for the negative emotions we experience. We might default our thinking to "I shouldn't feel like this" or "Other people get through their life situations just fine, why is this crushing me". As if the pain itself wasn't bad enough, we foolishly add to our torment by judging how we feel about the pain. Why do we do this? This isn't how we approach broken bones. Teal Swan, International Speaker and Best-Selling Author, offers the following view:

> Physical humans expect themselves to heal from things instantaneously on a mental and emotional level. Have you ever noticed that? They don't tend to have the same type of expectation of physical injury. Right? It's not like when you get in a high speed car accident and there are multiple bones broken, and now you've got to be in physical rehab nobody comes in and says "god, something is seriously wrong with you. I don't know why this is taking so long." You don't wake up with sixteen bones broken and be like "what is wrong with me? I can't run today." But this is what you are doing to yourself emotionally...For some of us it's going to be a longer road.[2]

Negative feelings are totally normal for human beings, but we often judge ourselves for experiencing emotions on the darker end of the spectrum. When we feel disappointment or confusion or apathy or depression, which are natural and normal emotions for a human being, we judge our own condition. Society trains us to always be okay. Don't show weakness. Never cry. Every time someone asks you, "how are you?" your response is always, "good" or "fine". We've been trained that anything lower than "good" isn't supposed to be there. They'll say: don't feel those feelings and definitely don't talk about them. The lack of normalization of expressing our true states exacerbates our internal pain because not only are we struggling with the traumas of our situation, but our judgement toward our darker emotions encourages avoidance, delaying our path to healing. The price we pay is suffering mental health and a continued suppression of unwelcome yet totally normal feelings.

Think about social media for a second. Why do we only post baby announcements, marriage proposals or job promotions? Modern society treats negative experiences like the plague, such as losing your job, failing an exam, or losing a friend. Avoid anything and everything bad and do anything and everything to be happy and good and smiling all the time. Going back to our athlete identity, the conditioning to always be good and never show weakness takes on an extreme form, for athletes are expected to be a perfect, robot machine constantly adding gold medals to the collection.

Here it is, folks: It is okay for the shocks in our life to be above our adaptive range. It is okay if we feel like we can't carry the burden, we can't figure out how to feel better, or we don't know where we can turn. That is okay. That is human. If the contrary were true and we were generally unphased by life's personal events (which probably sounds nice and peaceful right about now), we would have no grasp of our identity, no barometer for the happy moments, and life would fly by leaving us dead before we knew it.

The worst thing we can do is think that however we feel is not acceptable. Because it is. However you feel right now – you may have hate, jealousy, guilt, shame, fury, confusion, despair – it is normal. It is okay. Do not judge yourself for simply reacting to events that occur. If a lightning bolt strikes the Earth 100 yards in front of you, your eyes will likely widen, your heart might skip a beat, and you may jump back a foot – or five. Would you judge yourself for this? Would you say, "gosh, why did I let my eyes open that far?". No, you wouldn't. You were naturally reacting to an event that occurred, so how can you look at yourself and say your emotional reaction should be any different? PsychCentral's leading tip is to simply observe your emotions to prevent judgement. Their example is to acknowledge to yourself, "I'm feeling hurt that my friend chose to go to the concert instead of spending time with me. I'm having worry thoughts about what this means for our friendship. I'm feeling like I want to cry — my throat is tightening up. Now I'm noticing that I'm starting to judge myself because I don't want to cry. This is uncomfortable, but I'm OK; I can tolerate this."[3] Observe the emotions and nothing more. No judging.

Lest we forget we are also human. By nature, we have strong feelings and emotions that kick up when strong events happen in our lives. Resisting a natural effect causes more tension and pain. Believing that you shouldn't feel frustrated or sad or emotional invalidates your natural pain and attempts to close up a wound that hasn't had a chance to heal. Have you ever shaken up a soda bottle and then opened the top only to have it start to explode but you quickly twist the top back on? Twisting the top back on that soda bottle is what you're doing to yourself when you perpetuate the thinking that your feelings aren't appropriate. Letting yourself unscrew that soda cap and releasing the effects of events around you will grant you healing opportunities to reach a place of calm and understanding. Let things out to let things in.

Don't judge yourself for how you feel. Don't judge yourself for the magnitude or depths at which you feel those feelings. You're a human being, responding naturally to events in your environment. Let the waves crash over you, feel them, lean into them, and offer your soul grace for whatever comes up.

Chapter 11 Endnotes

1. Nature Editorial. (2018). *Tools from China are oldest hint of human lineage outside Africa.* Nature.   https://www.nature.com/articles/d41586-018-05696-8?error=cookies_not_supported&code=4983e568-74dc-430a-a185-fc88a8543465

2. Swan, T. [@_tealswan]. (2021, July 10). *#spiritualtiktok #tealswan #motivationmonday* [Video]. TikTok. https://vm.tiktok.com/ZMd3eqoxg/

3. Tartakovsky, M. M. S. (2014, September 30). *How to Sit with Painful Emotions.* Psych Central. https://psychcentral.com/blog/how-to-sit-with-painful-emotions

THIRD QUARTER

In The Thick of It

"I never thought of losing,
but now that it's happened, the only thing is to do it right.
That's my obligation to all the people who believe in me.
We all have to take defeats in life."
—*Muhammad Ali*

Chapter 12

Why We Hate Defeat

AAAAAHHHHHHH. I FUCKING HATE LOSING.

Even a sentence like that doesn't express the maddening heartbreak and absolute agony of losing. I FUCKING HATE LOSING.

Defeat feels as if, in an instant, the earth splits from underneath us and the core belief that we are capable and deserving of winning cracks open like a coconut. Our greatest fears are exposed - your hard work wasn't enough, your talents aren't all that, your mastery is average or worst of all, maybe this is as good as you will ever be. Losing solidifies that your skills, talent, and hard work simply do not measure up to someone else. Your opponent's skills, talent and hard work are of a higher quality that you could not match. When athletes lose, they are required to acknowledge inferiority - one of the most unnatural concepts for athletes to process. After all, you have pushed yourself to incredible limits to reach the extremely skilled level of athleticism you are performing at today. It feels hard to imagine someone else could have a stronger drive, more dedication, more talent or harder work ethic than you.

Athletes think about losing the same way people think about death - we don't. Chris Bosh explains, "You don't work for a whole season, fight all the way through the playoffs to the finals and really imagine that you're ever going to lose. It just doesn't enter you mind."[1] Everyone faces death one day, yet until that day arrives, we live in complete oblivion that death will one day fall upon us. Me? Not me. Only when we're faced with dying on our death-bed do we recognize that, indeed, death does happen to us. We feel the same way about losing. Everyone else loses but me. We never enter a competition expecting to lose. We don't even think about losing as a possibility. Death and defeat are far-fetched scenarios barely registering in our peripheral vision, never grabbing our attention until we're forced to look them in the eyes.

When defeat happens, nothing feels worse. Nothing comes close to the crushing agony of defeat - an exposing, public confession of inferiority. Whether it's a blown lead, a last chance, a major upset, or a blowout, defeat is the 180-degree opposite result you're working so hard for every single day. You don't spend hours training for second place. You don't voluntarily subject yourself to physical pain (or what coaches call "training") or diligently study your opponents' weaknesses for the result of losing. Sure, there are worthy life lessons and teachable moments in the game of sports, but we're kidding ourselves if we say the point of the game is not to win. Every athlete wants to win. So, when our desired result of winning escapes us and we're left with defeat instead, looking up at somebody else tasting gold, it absolutely sucks. Andre Agassi ruminates on defeat in his book, *Open,* - "How can losing hurt so much? How can anything hurt so much? I walk off the court wishing I were dead." Katie Hoff also describes the excruciating pain of defeat, saying "I think about defeat to the point of unhealthy obsession. The rational me should look for the positive in defeat, should look for what's to be learned from losing. But in the moment of defeat, the rational me has vanished. I wonder how long the pain will last. I wish I could be someone else."[2] Pardon the colloquial language, but losing SUCKS.

Losing - just like winning - is simply part of competition. You cannot have one without the other. To crown the champion, there must also be a non-champion. Imagine if this contest structure didn't exist in the world of sports. Let's say The Patriots play against The Falcons in a Superbowl, but there is no score tallied. The game then becomes 60 minutes of running, throwing, and tackling with both teams shaking hands and grabbing beers when the clock runs out. Since there is no end goal of supremacy in this hypothetical situation, there is no final determination of winner and loser. Winning and losing, in this example, simply does not exist. While we certainly don't enjoy a loss, the structure of winner and loser is what makes sport "sport" at the end of the day.

Since losing is inevitable, but hopefully not too frequent of an occurrence, let us dive into the layers of why defeat hurts so much. Let's uncover why it is sometimes incomprehensible, excruciating, and wildly infuriating to lose and free ourselves from the blunt intensity of defeat. As Anthony de Mello says "What you are aware of you are in control of; what you are not aware of is in control of you. You are always a slave to what you're not aware of. When you're aware of it, you're free from it."[3] How can we grow our awareness to uncover why are we so affected by not winning? What is so threatening to our ego that we negatively fixate on the loss? What makes us ruminate on "everything we could have done differently" until we start to hate ourselves? How can we understand the impact defeat has on our mind, so that we can better move through the pain? To reference the philosophy underlying the insights in this book, when we can understand the "why" behind defeat we can process the loss and move forward with a stronger, lighter mind.

Threat to Identity

The very first layer is the painfully obvious answer. We didn't win, so by default we lost. What? How can that be? We never prepare for losing. That simply isn't part of being an elite athlete. When it happens to us, we feel shock. That isn't who we are. We don't lose. We are the fastest, the strongest, the smartest, the best. To compete with top athletes, there is no room for straying beliefs other than "I am the best". Unless you catch an athlete in an extremely sour mood, they usually don't enter a race or game or tournament expecting to lose. If they did, why would they want to compete in the first place? It would be self-defeating, and they would have zero chance of a fight before they even walked up to the starting blocks. Henry Ford concisely illustrates this thinking with an old quote, "whether you think you can, or you think you can't - you're right."[3]

Athletes visualize finishing the race in first place. Athletes visualize scoring the most points. Losing to your opponent blindsides us after we've set our own expectations and visualized ourselves winning. When we lose, our identity feels threatened and our brains expend energy rectifying reality with what we thought was true about ourselves. Losing goes against everything we live and feel and do every day. It goes against who we are.

You don't have to be an athlete to experience the shock of facing a harsh reality check about who you are. People often attach themselves to beliefs about their identity that are not always true. Think about yourself; in your biased view you might think you are a great employee, but you've clocked in late three out of five days this week. You may think you're a great friend, but you've canceled on your friends the last two times. It is natural and human (and often subconscious) to selectively remember the positive moments in your life and discredit the mistakes. This is a cognitive bias showcasing the natural human "tendency for people to give themselves credit for successes but lay the blame for failures on outside causes."[3] Our mind takes with it the accomplishments and positive merits while disparaging errors and shortcomings. Thus, we form a rose-colored self-view of who we are. Sometimes people think they are funny when they're not. Sometimes people think they are selfless when they're not. Have you ever thought you were a great conversationalist only to meet a new person whose social skills blew you out of the water? Have you ever thought there's no way anyone could beat you in the long jump, your best event, but then one day someone does? It's a harsh reality check leaving you feeling insecure and exposed when you experience moments that debunk the beliefs you genuinely feel are true about yourself.

These attachments and beliefs are created from environmental cues and our own internal desires. Sometimes they are true and sometimes they are not, but what remains the same is *we believe what we believe.* If a comedian genuinely thinks he is funny, he genuinely thinks he is funny. When those beliefs are called into question and proved inaccurate, it is incredibly uncomfortable to admit that the beliefs he built about himself aren't reality. No one likes to admit that they didn't even know something about themselves, that they were wrong. "The three most difficult things for a human being are not physical feats or intellectual achievements. They are, first returning love for hate; second, including the excluded; third, admitting that you are wrong."[2] How tough is it, then, for the comedian to admit a wrong self-view when he believed standup comedy was his future career?

For athletes, we attach ourselves to the belief that we are the best. To believe you are the best comes with already believing you can beat everyone else. No one is as good as us. Holding this belief is as important as going to practice every day. Even going up against all-time greats, the stiffest competition, you still hold a shed of belief that maybe this game will be different. Then, at the end of the game or match or race if you find yourself with the loser trophy, you're left with the harsh reality check that you are not the best. All the thoughts your mind used to hype you up and believe that you can do it feel like lies.

When we think to ourselves "I'm inferior" because of a loss, we reflect negatively on our shortcomings. If only I was a little bit taller. If only my legs were a little bit stronger. If only I adopted a race strategy like hers. This internal, self-critiquing chat with ourselves spurs us to internalize the loss as solely our fault. We contemplate everything *we* should have done differently, as if winning is entirely dependent on ourselves and not also our opponents. Have you not ever asked yourself, "if only I kicked harder after that flipturn" or "if I only jumped one more inch." Whatever the thought happens to be about your performance, the burden of the loss rests entirely on your shoulders.

But what about your opponent? As much as it hurts to say, couldn't the loss be attributed to the fact that they simply had a stellar performance better than yours? What if there was nothing else you could have done to secure the win? Absorbing the loss as a result entirely within our control weighs heavy and is not always true. Because our identity is threatened and our fears are exposed, we grasp for control and take on the loss as solely our own doing because that feels more reassuring than admitting we don't measure up. Taking on the responsibility of the loss gives us hope that we can do something about it rather than suffer helplessly in the shadow of someone else's superior skills.

In all the ways we've discussed how we build an athlete identity with winning/perfection as the ever-elusive carrot dangling in front of us, the act of losing strikes at the foundation of who we are. Losing exposes our emotional vulnerabilities about our talent, skills, and work ethic. Losing is a rude reality check forcing you to calibrate a rose-colored identity with reality. It is uncomfortable. It is shocking. It is incredibly difficult to accept something that goes against our beliefs about us as a winner.

The World Values Winning, Not Losing

What makes defeat hurt even more, outside of simply losing, is that our surrounding environment places total emphasis on gold. The world prizes winning, especially in America - be on the Wheaties box, make the Olympic team, collect the Superbowl ring – and we shun the losers. I guarantee you've felt exactly what I'm talking about. You've probably won a race or game or match and afterward handfuls of different people congratulate you and want to touch the trophy. On the flipside, when you don't win and walk sluggishly past people in the halls or locker room their eyes dart down in avoidance of having to console the sad dog. If there isn't a more classic example of positive reinforcement - applaud the good and ignore the bad.

We see and hear and read about heroic sports legends, and the fables inspire us to replicate the dream for ourselves. If he can do it, if she can do it, then I can do it. If you've ever noticed after an athlete wins a medal or breaks a record, we're always burning to know their secret. How did they get there? What did they do to win? What do they eat before they compete? It's as if we are asking for the recipe so we can go home and bake the bread ourselves.

"How many calories in a day does Michael Phelps eat?"
"How many hurdles does Lolo Jones jump during practice?"
"What is Rafael Nadal's pre-match ritual?"
"What's inside Agassi's 'Gil Water'?"

We are desperate to know exactly what it takes to be #1 because we ourselves want to be there. Our society conditions us to believe winning is *the* goal everyone should pursue, and anything less than first place or gold is unworthy. As Ricky Bobby would say "if you ain't first, you're last."[3]

On a more micro level, our immediate environment reflects the same notions about winning and success that are praised at the macro level by society. Our parents give us more attention when we win, our coaches smile and pat us on the back when we win and our friends think we're the coolest kid on the block when we win. It is a drastic, opposite response to winning than it is to losing. Subconsciously observing the reaction to our winning pursuits programs us to love winning, desire winning and dream about winning. The flipside is that we learn to despise losing, fear losing and have nightmares about losing. Such heavy emphasis and praise on winning makes losing that much more intense. The larger societal importance of winning make losing unbearable at times. Winning is good. Losing is bad.

Winning and Losing are Public: Everyone Knows

Wouldn't it be nice if the times you failed, the times you fell flat on your face, no one was there to witness it? Have you ever realized a booger was hanging out of your nose and darted your eyes around the scene to make sure no one else saw before you picked it? Just me? Awesome. Part of the excruciating pain from defeat is the fact that everyone knows you lost. Fans, coaches, other teams, friends, and the media all watched and witnessed your loss. Mass attention on sports competition is a double-edged sword, we revel in the glory of winning but suffer the public embarrassment of defeat. Either way, everyone knows.

Outside of the embarrassment or humiliation you feel that everyone knows you lost, worst are the comments and feedback everyone feels so entitled to make. Don't they know you're your own worst critic already? Don't they know you're analyzing your game wondering where things went wrong 100x more than any spectator? Don't they know losing sucks in and of itself and you don't need additional comments from outsiders? Don't they know!? Reporters and the media are the absolute worst. A headline from 2012 referencing the then basketball team, Seattle SuperSonics, reads "Sonics advance to Finals, oh wait"[5] , referring to the immediate success the team had after they relocated to Oklahoma City. I'm sure the team was already feeling bad about not securing much success before the relocation and now they must hear the jabs and puns in the newspapers and press conferences. Why kick a dog when it's down? Humans can be savages.

Because of the attention-grabbing arenas of crowds that watch sports, a coliseum style of awe dating back to the Ancient Greeks, there is no avoiding the fact that both wins and losses are very public events. You can't cover up your mistakes or pretend all is well and swell. When everyone knows you lost, each pair of eyeballs feels like another shake of salt on the wound.

Time, Effort, Resources Required

In Chapter 6 we talked about the time, effort and resources required that contribute to our athlete identity. This is another reason we hate losing - simple input versus output. Training takes time. Massive amounts of time. Upkeeping aerobic capacity and strength to be able to perform at the levels that meet our goals requires hours every day. We attend practice daily, compete in tournaments on the weekends and bolster our training programs with additional weightlifting, yoga, or cross training sessions. You can begin to calculate how much of a time commitment this is. The larger the chunk of time spent focused on improving, the better result we expect. A painter doesn't spend years on a portrait for it to ultimately look like a stick-figure. Athletes don't spend years improving their bodies and game strategy to ultimately lose the championship.

Hours alone aren't the only input, for hypothetically you could spend the same amount of time but be simply going through the motions. You could show up at practice, throw the passes, stretch the quads and finish the reps. This may result in good performances, but it won't result in the best performances. Swimming 8,000 yards at practice is one thing. Racing 8,000 yards, pushing intervals, springing off the starting blocks, exploding off the wall, squeezing your arms on the streamline and giving your maximum effort is much different. Outside of the hours required to practice, it is the effort we put forth to be the best that feels infuriatingly futile when we don't get the winning outcome we work so hard for.

Lastly, there are the tangible resources required to compete. Expensive gear, team memberships, competition entry fees and travel expenses accrue over time and require a substantial investment to be able to compete with the best in the field. When you spend money, small or large amounts, you expect something in return. If I buy an $80 ribeye at a restaurant, I expect the taste and value of the steak to reflect the $80 I spent. For competition gear and the dollar investment required to train and compete, I also expect my result to reflect the money I put forth. Sports can be expensive especially at the elite level, and when we pay up, we also expect the payout.

When we put forth grandiose amounts of time, effort, and resources to train and become even better than we were yesterday, it can be devastating when your sports performance doesn't match that expectation. After hours of exercise, after numerous conversations about strategy, after upgrading your equipment to the latest technology, you may feel as though there could be no other outcome but to win. However, for some reason it didn't work out in your favor. A dismal output after a monumental input can be one of the most frustrating things to accept for an athlete.

But I did it in practice...

We build expectations based on data - practice. In practice, we do amazing things. Maybe we stuck our landing on a complex vault routine. Maybe we touched the rim on a dunk. Maybe our scrimmage team made a triple play. We see ourselves in practice growing our competency and performing some of the more awe-inspiring skills in our sport, sometimes for the first time.

I can remember my own swim practices closer to the championship meet. Our coach asked us to slip our fins on our feet and swim a mock race. We knew our times would be much faster than reality because, after all, we had an extra foot of feet thanks to our fins. We would awkwardly step up on the starting blocks with our fins hanging over the edge. Then our coach would hold out his stopwatch and time a race as we swam 50 or 100 meters as fast as we could. When we finished into the wall, he would call out our times, shocking us with how fast we swam. Sure, we had fins on to help propel us through the water, but this was an exercise to envision our goal times and feel what it was like to swim that fast. The hope was that by the time we were racing in the championship meet, our taper, rest and racing suits would make up the exaggerated time drop.

After seeing ourselves perform at levels never reached before in practice, we so desire to replicate the performance where it truly counts - in the arena. If Michael Jordan played amazing basketball during practice but then fell short during the actual games, he wouldn't be the legend he is today. The sad truth is we don't always perform in the arena how we perform in practice. Have you ever heard of athletes playing "tight" or having "match stress"? The environment, the opponents and the circumstances are totally different in a true game versus practice. Not everything we do in practice to prepare for competition automatically copies over to the race. We are human beings, after all.

This can be one of the more frustrating pieces of defeat - when we know that we can make the shot, we have seen it with our own two eyes, yet that capability eludes us completely during the time when we need it the most. Hopefully this happens once or twice and you can learn how to play your best despite the stressors of a real time game, but for the more complex skills it can be tough to replicate those successfully at the meet. It is not every day a gymnast performs a Produnova vault. It is not every day a track star jumps 8.9m in the long jump. It is not every day the quarterback throws a 99-yard touchdown pass. When we fall short in competition, knowing full well we performed the skill at practice, it can be infuriating.

Technical in Nature

Because sports are technical in nature, we retrospectively evaluate what we could have done differently with our bodies to improve our performance. We think about bending our elbow more on our freestyle stroke, shifting our weight to the opposite leg on a forehand swing, reaching our arm just a couple inches longer to grab the football. If the margin is close enough, we believe loss could have been avoided if we had only done XYZ. It brings a wave of maddening frustration attached to the desire of changing the outcome even though we know we aren't capable of time travel. We can't go back in time, yet we fixate on what could have been, analyzing the minutiae of the game looking for any error on our part to criticize.

Have you ever thought back on a performance and told yourself over and over, "I would have won if I didn't _____"? Fill in the blank. Your mind is stuck on that one error, repeating the video in your head, and coming up with all the ways the error could have been avoided. Then you think about what winning would look like if that slip didn't happen. Before you know it, you're sliding down the rabbit hole of "what ifs", torturing yourself over something that can't be changed. Because sports are technical in nature, by default we beat ourselves up analyzing every degree, inch or choice made during the game. Thus, we come to hate defeat.

Tiny Margin of Error

If an opponent totally crushes you, it might feel easier to accept the loss than if you were close enough to securing gold that you could taste it. A large margin between competitors proves that whoever won was truly the better player in that moment regardless of what the loser might have done differently. There is nothing the loser could have done to cover that much ground. Self-berating, then, becomes futile because even if you could go back in time and change your performance, it wouldn't make up for the wide gap between first and second place.

Now, what is genuinely frustrating is when the margin of error is so small it is practically nonexistent. How can you sit back and accept a loss if the difference between yourself and first place is barely distinguishable? I remember watching the 2008 Beijing Olympics when Michael Phelps was swimming the 100-meter butterfly in the lane next to Milorad Čavić from Serbia. Phelps was on his way to win his historic eight gold medals, but this particular race was medal number seven. The race, which was only two laps, started with a bang and Čavić took off. At the halfway point, Čavić was ahead of the entire field - including Phelps - by a half-body length which is not common especially at the Olympics and especially for a shorter race. It was not looking good for Phelps. With 10 meters to go, Phelps was catching up but still trailing Čavić. Five meters left. Two meters left. Boom! They touch the wall at seemingly the exact same time and immediately look to the scoreboard. Michael Phelps smiles. He won, squeaking by with a last-minute half-stroke to pound the wall one hundredth of a second (.01) before Čavić. This is the smallest margin that exists in the sport of swimming. Again, this is the smallest margin that exists in the sport of swimming. Anything smaller than .01 is a tie. (If you've never seen this race, I highly suggest checking out the videoclip on YouTube. Unless you have high blood pressure. Then don't.).

Losing in a race by the smallest margin that exists, literally .01 seconds, is a much harder pill to swallow than losing by 10 seconds. At this level of precision, your brain gets stuck in the "where did I go wrong" analysis, shredding every technical movement to pieces to find where you could have been just a smidge better. Just a smidge! That is all you needed. You know fixating on the small margin won't change the outcome, but you beat yourself up thinking of the "what ifs" that would have placed you ahead of your opponent by a mere fraction. Talk about agonizing.

Losing by a small margin can also crush your soul when you were in the lead the whole time. You've been there - your opponent is in the palm of your hands and there is no way they could possibly catch up. You're playing the best you've played and you're already imagining the post-match celebration party. But, little by little your opponent inches past you or makes 10 great shots in a row. You become concerned and refocus on what you're doing but by then it's too late. Right in front of your eyes, your opponent managed to squeak by and capture the win at the last second, leaving you in disbelief. How can they possibly have won when I was in the lead the entire race? I was so far ahead there is no way they could have come back and beat me. This must be a mistake.

I bet this feeling of disbelief is how the French men felt in 2008 during one of the greatest Olympic swimming relays of all time. The U.S. and France were in side-by-side lanes for the 400-meter freestyle relay, Phelps' second opportunity for a gold medal on his quest for eight. The U.S. trailed behind France with a gap that seemed impossible to make up. Going into the final 100-meter leg of the race, the U.S.'s Jason Lezak dove into the water behind France's Frederick Bousquet. Inexplicably and superhumanly, Lezak swam lights out to catch up to Bousquet in the final 15 meters of the race, winning for the U.S. by .08 seconds. It was a comeback Wikipedia describes as "the greatest the sport has ever seen."[6] The French team, having the lead on the

United States the entire race only to lose in the last few meters probably left them in denial looking up to see "2nd" on the scoreboard.

Over the recent decades where sport has become so advanced, skilled and elite, the margin of error continues to get smaller and smaller. When a loss does happen and the difference between winning and losing is a margin shorter than a blink of an eye, it hurts to feel so close to gold but not win.

Pressure to Not Disappoint

We all know far too well that while our athletic abilities are the core driver of our career, we wouldn't have made it as far as we have without the support of our team. Our coaches, our family, our teammates, and our friends are with us, supporting us, every step of the way. Whether we succeed or fail, our team backs us up encouraging us to keep on fighting. With their undying support, it can be devastatingly painful to come home with a loss. We want to make our team proud and show them that not only can we do it, but we can be the greatest there ever was. It's like letting down the mean bully at school versus letting down your best friend at school. If you let down the mean bully, you don't care because you don't like him or her. You're probably happy that they're disappointed and suffering. But when you let down your best friend, a whole other level of empathy fills your heart because you so deeply care. You never want to see your best friend hurt or upset. It crushes you. We feel the same way toward our supporting team when we don't measure up to the accomplishment we want to give them in return for their unconditional support.

Once you become established as a leader in your sport it can be incredibly pressure-inducing to maintain that status. Every competition or game you enter, a target is placed directly on your back. Not only do you feel that you must perform at the highest level every single time you walk on court, but your fans (or family or teammates or whomever is in your sphere) also expect you to maintain the status quo of winning. When you lose with the weight of this external pressure, it is humiliating. It can feel like the whole world is solely focused on the shortcomings of who you are. Michael Bentt, former world heavyweight boxing champion, quickly won his matchups in the amateur rounds. However, he was knocked out during his very first professional match. Bentt describes the emotional impact a highly public loss had on his psyche, saying "I was beyond depressed after the fight. I was suicidal. It was like having your heart broken by a woman you love and I wanted to cover my head in shame every day. People had reason to judge me as a loser and I started to see myself as a loser. I had a broken spirit. My confidence as a boxer was shattered."[7]

When we lose, it feels like we let our supporting team down. We let ourselves down. Especially at professional levels where prize money or sought-after trophies are on the line, experiencing a loss in those circumstances can be beyond devastating. It is hard enough to let ourselves down, and it feels even worse to let others down. Mounting pressure, public endorsements and everything on the line is a recipe for heartbreak when they're followed by defeat.

High Stakes

If the stakes are low, the agony of defeat feels less intense than if there are millions of dollars of prize money on the line. Or if the winner earns a coveted spot on the leaderboard. Or if the win breaks a long-standing record. Or if there are bragging rights involved. If the loss separates you from achieving or obtaining something beyond the win itself, the pain runs so much deeper because you feel as though you've missed out on something important. No one cares if you lost a scrimmage game. It doesn't count. No one cares if you lose a race in practice. It doesn't count. The competitions where it counts, where winning matters and high stakes are involved, the feeling of something being taken away from you when you had the full opportunity to earn it can be excruciating. So close yet so far has never felt truer.

One More Thought. . .

When we set expectations to perform to the best of our ability and win, any other result leaves us unsatisfied. We know what we are capable of, and we choose to enter every race with a winning attitude to give us the best chance of a great performance. However, reality reminds us that there can only be one winner and when that winner is not us, despite the expectations we laid forth, we often find ourselves devastated.

Regardless of why you lost, it sucks. Your brain is flooded with feelings of shock, disappointment, embarrassment, insecurity, and absolute frustration. For all the reasons we've uncovered - the small margin of error, the stakes involved, the desire to give your team a win, feeling you deserve a good result after the time and effort you've put forth - it is incredibly difficult to wrap your brain around the reality check that, at least in this instance, you aren't as good as you thought you were. For athletes, having built a solid, core belief in themselves that represents everything phobic to losing, defeat is possibly the most painful experience an athlete will face in his or her career.

Recognizing why defeat crushes us is not the hard part. The hard part comes next - figuring out how in the world to get through it. Will the pain ever stop? How in the world can you accept the loss? How in the world can you move forward? How in the world can your mind even open space to learn lessons from an experience that brings so much negative energy to you? These are exactly the questions we are going to answer to help navigate through the turmoil and come out even better on the other side.

Chapter 12 Endnotes

1. Hoff, K., & Bader, R. (2020). *Blueprint: An Olympian's Story of Striving, Adapting, and Embracing the Suck.* CG Sports Publishing.
2. DeMello, A. (2021). *Awareness: The Perils and Opportunities of Reality by Anthony De Mello (1990) Paperback.* Image Books.
3. *Types of Cognitive Biases That Distort How You Think.* (2021, January 20). Verywell Mind. https://www.verywellmind.com/cognitive-biases-distort-thinking-2794763
4. McKay, A. (Director). (2006). *Talladega Nights* [Film].Columbia Pictures, Relativity Media, The Apatow Company, Mosaic Media Group.
5. Depta, L. (2017, October 3). *Best Sports-Related Newspaper Headlines.* Bleacher Report. https://bleacherreport.com/articles/2471874-best-sports-related-newspaper-headlines
6. Wikipedia contributors. (2021b, March 6). *Swimming at the 2008 Summer Olympics – Men's 4 × 100 metre freestyle relay.* Wikipedia. https://en.wikipedia.org/wiki/Swimming_at_the_2008_Summer_Olympics_%E2%80%93_Men%27s_4_%C3%97_100_metre_freestyle_relay
7. Staff, B. N. (2019, May 19). *Michael Bentt: 'I started to see myself as a loser. I had a broken spirit. I was suicidal' -.* Boxing News. https://www.boxingnewsonline.net/michael-bentt-i-started-to-see-myself-as-a-loser-i-had-a-broken-spirit-i-was-suicidal/

Chapter 13

Living With Defeat

"When things go wrong, first you need to be honest with yourself. Learn from the bad things, and if you need to cry, you cry. But learn. Make the mistakes. Trust in your talent. Trust in your ideas. Trust in the way you want to do things. You suddenly start to think in a different way on a few things, and then you are changing your approach. You change as a person, you know, and then suddenly, you make a step in your career. You must try to analyze and then turn the page, fully committed, fully concentrated in the next race."[1]

—Carlos Sainz Sr., (Spanish rally driver and father of Formula 1 Driver, Carlos Sainz Jr.)

It Just Hurts

The very first step is to simply feel the pain. This part is the worst. But resisting uncomfortable, negative emotions won't help you move through them. In fact, "one of the main causes of many psychological problems is the habit of emotional avoidance."[2] We can't move forward with improvements in our thinking until we let ourselves feel the feelings, and this includes pain.

After all, we are sentient human beings. So, more pain to cure pain. Let your heart break. Cry. Punch your pillow. To feel better, you might need to feel worse. Whatever you do, don't avoid, resist, or ignore the way you feel in the thick of defeat. Here is Psychology Today's metaphor for emotional avoidance (and their suggestion to accept, feel and acknowledge your emotions):

> Swimmers who are caught in an undertow and feel themselves being dragged out to sea often panic and begin to swim against the current with all their might. Often, they fatigue, cramp and drown. To survive, such a swimmer should do the opposite—let go. Let the current take him out to sea. Within a few hundred yards the current will weaken and the swimmer can swim around and back to shore. The same with a powerful emotion: pushing against it is futile and possibly dangerous. But if you accept the emotion, it will run its course while allowing you to run yours.[2]

So how can you let go? How can you accept and release those emotions of disbelief, frustration, disappointment, embarrassment, and everything else that may accompany losing? Acknowledge them head on. We talked about the power of acknowledgement in Chapter 3. Journaling, talking to yourself or talking to a trusted friend are super effective methods of relieving those feelings by simply recognizing they're there. That is the first step. For me, I respond really well to verbal processing (yes, you will often find me talking to myself in the car) and I love to use the Voice Memos app on my smartphone to talk out my emotional state. I do this with zero intention of acting or creating a plan (yet). First, I simply recognize the way I'm feeling about what's going on without judgement.

I feel discouraged....
I'm absolutely frustrated...
I'm shocked...
I feel embarrassed...
I feel insecure...

Then, after some time has passed, I can listen back to my audio recording and maybe even pick up on observations or insights I didn't know were there. This acknowledgement exercise loosens the power that your charged emotions have on you, and here's why: The simple concept behind the power of acknowledgement, behind saying out loud exactly how you feel, is that when you confront the uncomfortable head-on you take away its power. Charged, painful emotions grasp your mind and can incite a number of unhealthy behaviors and feelings: ruminating on the negative, fixation, self-berating, lashing out, self-torture, self-loathing, anger or even thoughtless decisions. Why does the girl who just found out she was cheated on slash his tires? (Well, he probably deserved it.) But, in the thick of the pain, in the shock of defeat, we may feel inclined to act fast to alleviate pain. We may lash out against loved ones, honk our horns out of anger rather than danger or, like Agassi, smash every single one of our trophies (Agassi, 2010, p. 223).

We find ourselves "swinging into action simply to get rid of [our] negative feelings…coming from guilt, anger, hate; from a sense of injustice or whatever."[3] It is normal to feel the adrenaline and intensity of these emotions, especially because you care about your performance, but what good does it do to "substitute one cruelty for another, one injustice for another"?[3] That's where the work comes into play when we're hung in that moment of deciding what to do next. Punching the wall is easy. Sending the mean text is easy. Taking a moment to breathe, cool down and process is hard. It requires awareness and practice. You wanted to win so bad, and you can't believe how your opponent beat you. It hurts. It sucks. Say it out loud. "This sucks."

If you aren't used to managing your mind in this way, it is going to feel incredibly unnatural. We pretend to be sophisticated beings with total control of our actions and thoughts and feelings at all times but we still punch walls. We still raise our voices. We still send someone to break the legs of our archnemesis (Tonya Harding). Strengthen your mental muscles of choosing the healthier way to respond to negative experiences by practice. Start with the smallest of events. If the barista got your coffee order wrong, it is perfectly okay to say in your head "I'm frustrated, I'm disappointed that my coffee didn't turn out the way I wanted to drink it." It sounds pretentious as I'm writing this example, but you get the point. Acknowledge exactly how you feel as life unfolds, and you'll notice those emotions leave your realm just as quickly as they entered.

Once you're able to reach stable ground, then read on. Once your charged emotions don't feel so sharp, then read on. Don't skip over this step of acknowledging your emotions. Let yourself feel, then read on.

We All Lose (and it's much more common than winning)

Failing is a fundamental part of life, especially if you compete in sport. Defeat is a certainty every athlete will experience in his or her career. If you can name one professional athlete that never lost a single time, then put this book down and collect your refund. We all experience defeat. Michael Jordan famously recounts the 9,000 basketball shots he missed and the 300 games he lost.[4] Even he, a basketball legend that will forever mark the sport and beyond, experienced defeat.

Pointing out the fact that every athlete experiences losing is not to shame athletes or take on a misery-loves-company attitude, but to instead objectively showcase that defeat happens to everyone. Ronda Rousey, one of UFC's greatest female fighters, lost in a shocking upset to Holly Holm in 2015. Jordan Spieth, former world number one golfer, crumbled with a 5-shot lead and lost the 2015 Masters Tournament. "The careers of record-breaking sports greats Michael Jordan, Serena Williams and Peyton Manning all have one common element: failure."[5]

Indulge a bit of comfort in the fact that defeat is much more common than winning. For every game, every tournament, every championship, and every race there can only be one victor. For example, in a tennis grand slam tournament there are 128 entrants. By the end of the tournament, after each opponent either advances or drops out, only one lone tennis player raises the trophy above her head in the championship final. That means 127 other tennis players, 127 of the top athletes in the sport, lost. 127 tennis players did not win the ultimate match. I'm no math guru, but 127 is a lot more than one. An entire documentary series on Netflix called "Losers" exists solely to showcase athletes or coaches and their public, crushing losses. Losing, simply due to the structure of winner-loser sports, is much more common and frequent which should help root your perspective and offer comfort that everyone goes through it.

Accept the Loss

When you argue with reality, you always lose – but only 100% of the time.
—Byron Katie, Author

In the 2020 Men's U.S. Open Tennis Final, Dominic Thiem sparred against opponent Alexander Zverev in a three hour, 42-minute championship final. It truly came down to the wire in a fifth-set tiebreak, both men barely able to stand on their own two legs. Zverev hit a shot just wide of the sideline, giving Thiem the 2-point lead necessary to declare a winner. I'm not sure about you, but after almost four hours, winning the first two sets then losing the next two sets, going to a tiebreak, and then losing the tiebreak by the smallest of margins would have me on my knees in disappointment. I would feel so close to the finish line and then overcome with anguish seeing the trophy swept right under my feet. Zverev, however, showed classic sportsmanship and congratulated Thiem on the win with a handshake and hug. Zverev then sat down on his designated bench and stared off into the distance for several minutes. I'm no telepathic guru, so I couldn't tell you exactly what was going through his brain, but I'm sure he was coming to terms with the match and accepting his defeat, albeit with disappointment. As much as it hurts, as much as we feel shocked that we lost (who me? I lost?!) accepting that it wasn't our day to win closes the loop on what happened and better sets us up to move through it.

Acceptance is incredibly difficult because we have to overcome the friction of agreeing with an outcome that we believed to our core was impossible. Saying "I lost", "I am not a champion", "I did not win" are some of the most unnatural, undesirable words that will ever come out of an athlete's mouth.

That, however, is the very key to truly practice acceptance. Saying those words out loud to acknowledge the result of defeat roots yourself in reality, paving the way for acceptance and ease. If you can't say those words out loud, you haven't fully accepted the loss and will continue to feel stuck in turmoil. This turmoil, or disagreement with reality, leaves you ruminating on everything about your performance that could have, would have, should have been changed. Backwards thinking on the loss will forever prevent you from practicing acceptance, and since we all know we can't time travel we might as well accept the loss sooner rather than later.

Much of how we can accept what just happened and begin to grow from defeat depends on where we put our focus. Are we focused on everything we didn't do during the race? Are we focused on how we couldn't stop the opponent? We tend to focus on the negative, what went wrong and why we didn't win, preventing us from having any chance of stepping toward processing the loss. Rather, shifting our focus to the positive once the sharpness of the pain doesn't feel so sharp allows us to swallow the medicine with a little bit of sugar, knowing we are going to turn a negative into a positive. How am I going to learn from this? How can I use this loss to add fire to my motivation for next tournament? Focusing on areas of growth can help ease the pain of the shark bite and allow you emotional space to recover.

Katie Hoff points out that "failure is just part of the process, and it comes with its share of pain, tears, and moments of despair. Once you accept this, and embrace it, the suck may not go away, but it begins to lose its power over you."[6] Calibrate expectations with reality and acknowledge that today was not your day; acceptance, then, will wash over you with ease.

Always Do Your Best

> The best players, in general, are motivated by performing their best and the result takes care of itself, so focus on performing your best and not necessarily the result.
>
> —Shawn Foltz-Emmons, Ph.D. (Former WTA touring professional and Appointed Member of the USTA's Sport Science Committee).

Comfort can also be found in adopting the framework of always doing your best. It sounds common sense, but it is worthwhile to highlight and reinforce. There is a simple yet profound book by Miguel Ruiz known as *The Four Agreements,* offering pillar principles on how to live an enlightened life. The Fourth Agreement is "always do your best".[7] I highly recommend every athlete buy this book and read this chapter in particular. This mindset is so relevant to athletes because if we know that we performed to the best of our ability and "left it all in the pool" or "left it all on the court" or "left it all on the field", how can we not be satisfied with our performance even when we do get beat?

Ruiz goes on to say "if you always do your best, there is no way you can judge yourself. And if you don't judge yourself, there is no way you are going to suffer from guilt, blame, and self-punishment. By always doing your best, you will break a big spell that you have been under." For athletes, absorbing this perspective into our competition mindset relieves unnecessary pressure we place on ourselves. Before a game, we can cease nerves and jitters by knowing we will do what we can do and that is all we can do. Post-game, whether we are defeated or not, we're satisfied that we did everything in our power to perform to the best of our ability.

No matter how fast we swim or hard we kick the ball, we have zero control of our opponent. We don't control how much they train, we don't control what skills they learn, we don't control who their coach is, we don't control what competitions they enter. Everything they do inside and outside of a competition is totally up to them. Professional Tennis Player Naomi Osaka's coach, Wim Fissette, reinforces this attitude with his advice to Osaka after she lost in the 2020 Fed Cup. In Osaka's words, she explains his advice: "He just told me my life won't change if I lose, it can only get better from winning. That's something that I can't really fully control, but as long as I try my best, my percentages or my odds of winning will increase."[8] It seems simple, but this mindset is often lost on many athletes. Always do your best for what's within your control and eliminate unhealthy thought patterns of wishing reality is different.

Discounting Negative Feedback

It's not the critic who counts; not the man who points out how the strong man stumbles or where the doer of deeds could have done them better. The credit belongs to the person who is in the arena. Whose face is marred with dust and sweat and blood; who strives valiantly … who at the best knows in the end the triumph of high achievement, and who at the worst, if he fails, at least fails while daring greatly …[9] -Teddy Roosevelt

Just before the 2021 French Open, Naomi Osaka announced she would skip all press conferences despite hefty fines, saying, "I've often felt that people have no regard for athletes [sic] mental health and this rings true whenever I see a press conference or partake in one…We're often sat there and asked questions that we've been asked multiple times before or asked questions that bring doubt into our minds and I'm just not going to subject myself to people that doubt me."[10] Most athletes supported her decision, but the media criticized her. Why would an athlete want to put them in a position to be torn down, doubted, and interrogated? News reporters poking and prodding at athlete's when they're vulnerable has gotten out of control. Not treating athletes as human beings has gotten out of control.

People who want to make a snide comment or remark about a loss should immediately be cast aside. Here's why: it is easy to sit back, relax with a bucket of popcorn and watch athletes fight to the death. It is easy to work a 9 to 5 job, earn a salary and buy a ticket to the basketball game. It is easy to watch your favorite team lose, grab your phone and take to social media and comment how stupid a particular player was. There's nothing remarkable about being a spectator. It is so easy a caveman could do it.

What is hard is the work you do as an athlete. What is hard is grinding day in and day out to be the best. What is hard is to enter every match or competition with your ultimate game face almost ready to kill your opponent. What is hard is risking all your effort, training and being to win. What is incredibly hard is to lose in front of a crowd of people after everything you've been through. *That* is hard.

Imagine the pipsqueak in the audience posting to Twitter about "hOw MuCh tHe tEaM sUuUcCcKksSssss" doing what you do every day. Ha! Imagine him running the drills at practice. Imagine him sticking to your nutrition plan. Imagine him having even the slightest ounce of motivation that could remotely compare to the fight inside you. You don't see me writing this, but I'm cracking up. Athletes are a different breed - gladiators, warriors, fighters - and to think of your Average Joe attempting to participate in the life of an athlete is incredibly funny. He wouldn't last a single minute.

Unless someone has been in your shoes and knows exactly what it takes to fight as an athlete, their opinion is worthless. The passive aggressive tone of their question in the press conference is worthless. Don't take it from me; take it from Teddy Roosevelt himself. Let the haters have their jabs because that is all they have. How sad is that? How pitiful that there are people out there ready to criticize at the drop of a hat when they don't even know the half of what your glory path looks like. It must be a sad existence, so let them have their shallow, fleeting moments of satisfaction by bringing another human down. Your life is not only on another level, but it is on an entirely different planet.

Practice Sportsmanship

Have you ever lost a game and then acted in a way of such poor sportsmanship that it haunted you for days after, or maybe still does to this day? I have. You were caught up in the moment, endorphins running high and stressed over the fact that you couldn't quite capture the win. You may have said something rude to your opponent, thrown your racket across the court, launched the basketball to the ceiling, or done something else stupid in the heat of the moment. Adversity reveals character. Nothing feels quite humiliating, humbling and distressing than acting poorly after defeat. Learning how to accept the loss and respect the winner creates a healthy environment for all involved. Shake hands. Congratulate your opponent. Not only is sportsmanship classy and healthy, but it is simply the right thing to do.

You of all people know how difficult it is to win. Even when you yourself don't secure the win, you have to give credit where credit is due. After all, he or she beat you, so they must be on their A+ game. Poor sportsmanship takes the moment away from the winner, which is ugly, bad karma and stressful. Think about the behavior of Serena Williams in the 2018 US Open when Naomi Osaka defeated her. Osaka, likened to a 20-years-younger version of Williams, outplayed Serena in what reporters described as a contentious match leading to chaos and Williams calling the umpire a thief. Not to discount Williams' feelings of frustration but acting in such a way that draws the attention to your shortcomings and insecurities (not to mention receiving illegal coaching) pulls away the positive attention that Osaka should have been given for her amazing performance. Osaka, crying during her trophy speech, felt the need to apologize and comfort Williams as well as the crowd for winning. This may be my own personal view on the situation, but the poor sportsmanship from Williams took away from the positivity of Osaka winning her very first grand slam title.

This is not to say we should suppress how we feel. Sometimes a loss can sting incredibly bad, and we may want to crawl under a rock and cry forever. It is okay to feel that way; we care about our performance. What is not okay is to externalize those feelings into harmful actions, both to our opponents and to ourselves. We want mutual respect from our competitors regardless of who wins the trophy. If your opponent wins, respect them. If you win, hope they respect you. Congratulating and respecting the winning opponent is not only the right thing to do, but it prevents us from acting unskillfully by saying hurtful words, refusing to shake hands, or other stupid decisions we might make out of frustration.

To help yourself survive these heated, chaotic moments of defeat in a healthy way, develop a mantra for yourself that can remind you to show respect for the situation and the opponents. When you're grasping for air immediately following a loss keep this mantra in your head (or write it on a notecard and keep it in your bag).

Say to yourself:

"I did my best and I'm proud of my best."

"I could control what was in my control."

"It's not my day but that doesn't mean I can't win next time."

Whatever works for you, create a mini ritual during your tough moments to help remind yourself how to behave healthy and positively during painful defeats. When you create a ritual, your mind can perfectly fall back on the routine you set forth when there is no additional mental energy to expend such as in the moments right after defeat. The alternative is risking poor actions or words after you lose that could create sleep-depriving anxiety, stress and maybe even enemies. Positive sportsmanship creates healthy sports, healthy athletes, and healthy minds - all things the very games we love to play deserve.

Appreciate the Fight

Even when Lebron James has a mediocre game (which he rarely did), his performance is still something not many basketball players could replicate. It must be nice to have an off day and still crush it. The sheer talent and skill of high-level athletics is beyond amazing, and it is why so many fans congregate to watch matches, games, and races from the best performers in the world. The power behind hitting a homerun, the flexibility required to perform complex gymnastics routines, and the aerobic capacity needed to race 1,500 meters is awe-inspiring. Not only can one athlete perform like this, but there are heaps of athletes that have trained to compete at peak levels, setting new records and continuing to push the boundaries of excellence. As a collective athlete unit, this time in history has more top-performing and record-breaking athletes than ever before. We should be proud of all we can do!

When we are defeated, we often lose sight of what we have accomplished. Competing at such a high-level warrants self-recognition for the absolute amazing level of skill, talent, and hard work, even if we lose. We may have performed our best routine ever but still trailed behind first place. It is a bittersweet moment - we're sour because we still wanted to place first but we're sweet because we recognize the amazing results of our hard work. It can be easy to lose the sweet side of the moment when we get too wrapped up in the sour side. Just because we lose doesn't mean we are a loser and encouraging ourselves to offer gratitude for what our bodies can do for us is necessary to maintain a healthy view of loss even at the highest of competition levels.

Part of our gratitude for ourselves is simply appreciating the fight, appreciating the amount of effort we gave until the very last second. There is something poetic about embarking on a journey, going to war, giving everything you have, and feeling proud of putting yourself out there regardless of the outcome. There is something gratifying about fighting, feeling sweat pour off your head. Even if the movie ends on a sad note, how amazing was the journey? When I used to play softball as a kid I loved when I finally got home, exhausted, and stepped in the shower watching all the dirt from my hands and legs turn the clear water brown and spiral down the drain. I loved that feeling of being in the fight. I slid into second base. I dove for the ground ball. I was part of the action and loved that the dirt on my body symbolized my commitment to fight. Looking back, I don't remember the scores of the games, but I do remember how I felt being an impelled fighter. It's not always easy, but practicing gratitude for what your body is capable of and how you continue to trek along your own athlete journey is something to be so proud of and deserves our appreciation.

Learn & Plan

Learning from our defeat is critical to overcoming loss with a healthy mindset. Niki Lauda, renowned Formula 1 Race Car Driver puts it, "really, you should always discuss the defeats because you can learn much more from failure than from success."[11] I want to state very clearly that healthy learning in these moments focuses on both areas of improvement and things well done. When we only focus on the shortcomings, we don't give ourselves an opportunity to positively reinforce the good aspects of our performance. This subconsciously trains our minds to direct our attention to only the negative and quickly turns into a vicious, draining cycle of negative self-talk. After enough time of critiquing and never congratulating, strengthening our neural pathways to normalize this thought pattern, we start to review all life's events with a hyper-critical, praise-phobic way.

Even after athletics, the ordinary events of life such as conversations, parties, and business meetings never feel sufficient because we have trained ourselves to retroactively critique, calculating that everything in life can be improved next time (which stems from our perfectionist attitude). So, for every bad, state a good. For each low, find a high. For every time you wish you kicked the ball just a tiny bit harder, also recognize how you psyched out the other player when you dribbled right around their body.

Once you've constructively reviewed the good and bad of your performance, create a plan to change behaviors which should then change your results. Creating a plan feels so good because it gives us hope. It gives us an outline, a treasure map if you will, illuminating exactly how to get where we want to go. We feel excitement and new energy thinking about our destination and how good it will feel to be there. If you couldn't time your baseball swing quite right and ended up contacting the ball late every hit, schedule two more weekly batting sessions to practice your batting skills. A small change, sure, but this new plan incites feelings of hope that your new actions will deliver new, better results.

Building an actionable plan is a totally underrated practice every human, athlete or not, should incorporate into his or her life. Even if the plan never sees the light of day, simply committing to action shifts our entire energy forward. It is natural for modern humans to seek improvement or knowledge in areas of life interests: cooking skills, workout regimens, social skills, history, pop culture, cars, virtual reality, etc. When you take the time to devise a structured framework, even something so simple, that progresses your knowledge or skills in a particular area it offers excitement and happiness. Remember, progress = happiness. Conversely, not creating a plan leaves us feeling helpless, uninspired, and stagnant.

Since we can't go back in time and change the outcome, we might as well take an undesired result of poor performance and repurpose that experience to grow even stronger for the future. After a loss, focusing our attention on both improvements to be made and positive aspects of our performance reinforces a healthy feedback loop we can engrain in our minds. Then, we can use that feedback to create an actionable plan for the next time we compete. This learning and planning cycle softens the harsh blow we sometimes feel after defeat and gives us a glimmer of hope that next time can be better.

Trust the Process

Process is defined as a "a systematic series of actions directed to some end".[12] Notice how this definition doesn't include adjectives like 'good' or 'bad'. The process of improving as an athlete and becoming the best you can possibly be (the "end") includes the good, bad and everything in between. It includes the wins, the defeats and every other daily decision made along the way. It is the collective of everything, day in and day out. Even when losing feels crushing, zooming out to a bird's eye view and filing the loss as one event along your journey opens up the perspective to see the whole process of your "becoming", hopefully diluting the pain of the loss.

Part of participating in the process, or journey, of being an athlete is leveraging the negative moments of defeat to inspire, teach and motivate you to reach even higher levels of competition than ever before. Speaking from my own sports experience, the toughest losses and absolutely disappointing races were the very moments that generated the energy in me to push training harder than I ever had to avoid the same outcome. In an "ad released by Gatorade titled 'The Secret to Victory,' the star athletes (Michael Jordan, Serena Williams, Peyton Manning) agree that overcoming defeat is the essential ingredient to achieving career success."[13] Sure, losing isn't our desired outcome, but it could be the very ammunition you need. As much as losing hurts and as much as you may not want to hear this if you're in the thick of defeat, failure is exactly the fuel needed to light a fire within you to emerge stronger. Failure is the "can't live with it, can't live without it" component of the process.

Steve Jobs, co-founder of Apple, gave Stanford's 2005 commencement speech, which is one of my favorite YouTube videos.[14] In his speech, he shares a piece of wisdom illuminating how you can make sense of the events in your life. Jobs says that you can't connect the dots looking forward, you can only connect the dots looking backward. I can't think of a more perfect depiction of trusting the process than to think about it this way where you must let go of wondering why things are happening (like, why did I lose?) and trust that one day when you look back it makes sense. Letting go of the wonder, letting go of control, letting go of the desire for outcomes to be different feels so much easier when you view life in this way, where you can one day connect the dots looking backward.

I often think about Elizabeth Pelton, world champion swimmer with a running list of accomplishments and accolades. If you just look at her

Wikipedia page, it details how over the course of a couple years "she set the American record in the 200-yard backstroke, then bested her own record again at 2013 Pac-12 Conference championships (1:48.39), then breaking the national, U.S. open record at the 2013 NCAAs with 1:47.84... [she earned] 2013 NCAA Swimmer of the Year, NCAA Swimmer of the Meet, Pac-12 Swimmer of the Year, Pac-12 Freshman of the Year and Pac-12 Swimmer of the Meet honors."[15] She was one of the top American female swimmers. Her heartbreak came at the 2012 Olympic Trials, where a swimmer must place either 1st or 2nd place in an event to make the Olympic Team. Pelton placed 3rd in two separate events, barely missing a chance of becoming an Olympian not once but twice. I can't imagine what that must have felt like for her - to be so good, so competitive, and fully deserving of a spot on the Olympic team but to fall short by milliseconds. Twice. In her case, coming so close to the Olympics but not making the team, I would say trusting the process becomes a survival technique. How can you make sense of not making the team by the tiniest of margins in two separate events? You can't. Only after time has passed and more of her story has been written can she look back and understand. Only after time has passed and your life plays out can you turn back around and connect the dots to make sense of the pain.

If We Never Lost

"Without failure you have no barometer to succeed."
- Robert Dover, equestrian Olympic coach.

When we think about a career without a single loss, we may think that would be one of the coolest things in the world. Sure, it is nice to dream about an alternate universe where we are undefeated. However, what we miss in a world of zero losses are the fulfilling milestones of progress and the fierce level of competition that make up the sport we love so much.

When we lose against another team, we return to practice to push ourselves on our technique and skills to hopefully beat them the next time. The loss gave us drive, ambition, and further motivation to improve. Maybe your opponent was able to pitch curveball after curveball, striking out most of the lineup. So, at practice your pitcher learns new techniques, consults with coaching staff and trains for extended hours to nail his own version of the curveball. Then, at the next game your pitcher shines and pitches a no-hitter. This gratifying progress milestone would not have come about if it weren't for the previous loss against the other pitcher. The previous loss uncovered an area of weakness that we could then go back and refine to become an even more skilled player on the next round. Being able to take defeat with learning lessons and grow those lessons into your own athletic capabilities are moments during your athlete journey you will always appreciate, despite being born out of defeat.

This sounds a little weird to say, but sports would not be as fun or thrilling if you beat your opponents every single time you competed. Some games may be close, and others may be blowouts. Either way, the lack of a challenging opponent would create boredom over time, and you would lose interest in competing. Getting beat can be good for us. Yes, I will say that again. Getting beat can be good for us. It teaches us a lesson we needed to learn, it proves areas we could focus on, and it keeps our ego in check. Plus, think about the high level you perform. You would say you are a pretty good athlete and can do some amazing, strong things with your body, no? Is it not cool in the least that someone else out there has similar or better talents than you that drive you to become even better than you were yesterday? Is that not part of the thrill on your journey of becoming the best you can be? Opponents that defeat us challenge us, motivate us, and check us - the very things we need to fuel our own fire. Losing hurts, yes, but it is better to take losses with evolved ambition for the next competition than to never experience defeat and grow boredom with unfulfilling wins.

Overcoming adversity, such as losing, prepares you for later experiences in life. When you can learn how to cope and thrive with loss in a safe environment such as sport, you can adopt these same coping skills when you face adversity as you get older or grow out of your sport. What can you take with you from the loss to make you 10x better for the next time? How can you use a negative experience to make a positive one? The adage "when life gives you lemons you make lemonade" rings true here. Instead of letting a crushing loss leave a negative mark on you, take what you can to make yourself even that much better in the future.

One More Thought. . .

Defeat is never fun. Excuse me, DEFEAT FUCKING SUCKS. Although it's one of the more difficult moments we experience in our athlete journey, now you have expanded your mental tools and strategies to help swallow defeat with a spoonful of sugar, processing the loss a little easier. Remember, it happens to every athlete. It is okay and normal to feel the array of negative emotions. Finally, trust the process because this moment of defeat is serving you in some way, and you can only connect the dots looking backward.

Chapter 13 Endnotes

1. Gay-Rees, J., Martin, P., Todd, S. [Producers] 2019-2021. *Drive to Survive.* [Series] Netflix.
2. Shpancer, N. (2010, September 8). *Emotional Acceptance: Why Feeling Bad is Good.* Psychology Today. https://www.psychologytoday.com/us/blog/insight-therapy/201009/emotional-acceptance-why-feeling-bad-is-good
3. DeMello, A. (2021). *Awareness: The Perils and Opportunities of Reality by Anthony De Mello (1990) Paperback.* Image Books.
4. *Michael Jordan Quotes.* (2021). BrainyQuote. https://www.brainyquote.com/quotes/michael_jordan_127660
5. Connley, C. (2017, July 7). *Michael Jordan, Serena Williams and Peyton Manning agree this is the secret to a winning career.* CNBC. https://www.cnbc.com/2017/07/06/top-athletes-agree-that-this-is-the-secret-to-a-winning-career.html
6. Hoff, K., & Bader, R. (2020). *Blueprint: An Olympian's Story of Striving, Adapting, and Embracing the Suck.* CG Sports Publishing.
7. Ruiz, D. M. (2021). *Don Miguel Ruiz Toltec Wisdom Series Collection 3 Books Set,(The Four Agreements: Practical Guide to Personal Freedom, The Mastery of Love and The Fifth Agreement).* Amber-Allen Publishing.
8. Tennis Magazine. (2021). Naomi Osaka's most underrated weapon. *Tennis Magazine, 32.*
9. Duxbury, C., Duxbury, C., Duxbury, C., Duxbury, C., & Duxbury, C. (2011, January 18). *It Is Not the Critic Who Counts.* Theodore Roosevelt Conservation Partnership. https://www.trcp.org/2011/01/18/it-is-not-the-critic-who-counts/
10. Miller, K. (2021, May 27). *Naomi Osaka to Skip Press Conference at French Open to Bring Attention to Athletes' Mental Health Concerns.* Health.Com. https://www.health.com/condition/mental-health-conditions/naomi-osaka-press-conference-french-open
11. T. (2021c, May 27). *Top Niki Lauda quotes that make more sense in everyday life.* Racing Trend. https://www.lautosports.com/2020/10/top-niki-lauda-quotes-that-make-more.html#:%7E:text=Really%2C%20you%20should%20always%20discuss,me%2C%20I%20take%20it%20on.
12. *Definition of process | Dictionary.com.* (n.d.). Www.Dictionary.Com. Retrieved May 28, 2021, from https://www.dictionary.com/browse/process
13. Connley, C. (2017, July 7). *Michael Jordan, Serena Williams and Peyton Manning agree this is the secret to a winning career.* CNBC. https://www.cnbc.com/2017/07/06/top-athletes-agree-that-this-is-the-secret-to-a-winning-career.html
14. Stanford University. (2017, June 12). *Text of Steve Jobs' Commencement address (2005).* Stanford News. https://news.stanford.edu/2005/06/14/jobs-061505/
15. Wikipedia contributors. (2020, December 29). *Elizabeth Pelton.* Wikipedia. https://en.wikipedia.org/wiki/Elizabeth_Pelton

Chapter 14

Injuries Suck

When Olympic skier, Picabo Street, sustained significant leg and knee injuries in March 1998, she battled significant depression during her recovery. She stated: "I went all the way to rock bottom. I never thought I would ever experience anything like that in my life. It was a combination of the atrophying of my legs, the new scars, and feeling like a caged animal." Kenny McKinley, a wide receiver for the Denver Broncos, was found dead of a self-inflicted gunshot wound in September 2010 after growing despondent following a knee injury. He had undergone surgery and was expected to be sidelined for the entire season. He had apparently made statements about being unsure what he'd do without football and began sharing thoughts of suicide.[1]

When athletes suffer an injury, it feels as though you've been placed in purgatory. All of a sudden you go from an elite athlete, an able-bodied person, a record breaker, an invincible player, to someone with a bandage on the bleachers. That hurts, and I'm not even talking about the physical pain. Injuries uproot your identity and your role in the world and replace those comforts with dark clouds of the unknown. You're not in heaven and you're not in hell, you're just somewhere you know you don't want to be. Michael Jordan describes his periods of injury saying, "My body could stand the crutches but my mind couldn't stand the sideline."[2]

While we're mostly talking thoughts and feelings during an injury, it goes without saying that the physical pain of a broken body is enough in and of itself to create inner turmoil, frustration, and stress. Depending on the severity of harm done to your body, you may live every day with ibuprofen and gentle movements. Maybe you struggle completing daily tasks because your arm is in a sling, or your foot is wrapped in a boot. One small twitch of a muscle could send a lightning bolt of pain up your spine. The pain could be unbearable at times, sucking up all your mental focus just to alleviate what hurts. It is a monumental task to not only manage the mental stress and frustration of an injury, but to manage the agonizing physical pain of an injured muscle or bone.

I'm here to acknowledge that injuries suck. They're physically painful. They're mentally painful. It is an unwanted situation that takes a lot of time, effort, and patience to move through. Let's dive in and unravel why injuries suck. You guessed it, when we can better understand the "why" we can intelligibly move through the struggle.

Uncertainty & Stress

Uncertainty is the long pole in the tent that plagues our injured period. Uncertainty about how your body will heal and how long it will take to heal creates frustration over our lack of control. Uncertainty about your career, your body, your team and really, your life, creates a less than ideal rehabilitation process where not only are we healing our bodies but healing our minds. The wave of uncertainty that an injury brings to shore creates a perfect breeding environment for stress and anxiety.

When injured, there seems to be an endless cycle of existential stress and uncertainty, crippling states of being for humans. Being the action-oriented creatures that we are, uncertainty plagues our ability to make decisions, act, and live a life with peace. When we don't know what might happen or could happen, we fear any type of action as if to avoid making things worse and thus we drown in helplessness. Researchers have actually discerned through sophisticated experiments that "uncertainty is more stressful than predictable negative consequences."[3] We would rather know with a full guarantee that the hurricane will demolish our house than glue our eyes to the radar wondering if our home will be there tomorrow morning. This dates back to human beginnings in our caveman days. Certainty meant a higher likelihood of survival. If we knew where to find our food, where our predators lived, and how to build a fire, we would be okay. These were factors we could count on, rely on, that made surviving another day more likely. We would have the best chance of living when we knew things for certain. Take away the known factors and that leaves a caveman on chronic high alert, which in our modern times we would classify as an indisputable cause for exhaustion and overwhelming stress.

When injured, some of the stressful uncertainties could be:
- When will I be able to play again?
- Will my body fully heal to pre-injury condition?
- Is my coach going to replace me?
- Will I be able to catch up to my teammates once I'm healed?
- Who am I without playing my sport?
- What if I re-injure myself?
- What if rehab/healing takes longer and I'm out for another season?
- What if I can never play again?
- Will I live with this injury my whole life?
- How are my teammates and coaches perceiving me?
- What is my other outlet for exercise and stress-relief?

If you're injured, I'm sure you can think of your own daily uncertainties to add to this list. It's like throwing a ball high in the air and when it reaches the apex of the toss time pauses. The ball simply stops, and everyone wonders what happens next, including you. It is a stressful period compounded by the fact that the very activity you rely on to relieve said stress - playing your sport - is eliminated. When you can't even play or practice or train or put your effort toward something, what outlet do you turn to work through emotions? What outlet do you turn to for relieving your stress? The place you sought validation, earned accolades and made worthy contributions is no longer available to fill up those cups and it can feel suffocating, especially when you've had virtually no practice relieving stress elsewhere because, frankly, you never had to. (You can jump to Chapter 16, Why is Retirement So Challenging?, to read more about the biology of endorphins and how to build alternative stress-relieving habits outside of sport).

Uncertainty cultivates mental states of stress, anxiety, depression, apathy and other debilitating thought patterns. Stress is helpful for us in short bursts, alerting us of potential danger and keeping us alive, but prolonged stress has real, adverse effects on our bodies and minds. Chronic stress, such as waking up every morning and wondering how much longer it will take to heal your injury, can lead to a number of exhausting and harmful symptoms: aches and pains, decreased energy, difficulty sleeping, disorganized thinking, fatigue, feeling a loss of control, feelings of helplessness, frequent illnesses and infections, gastrointestinal complaints, headaches, irritability, muscle tension, nervousness and anxiety, trouble concentrating, and upset stomach.[4] To broaden your perspective on how stress affects humans as a population, it is estimated that between 60-80% of the general population's primary care visits are due to a stress-related component.[4]

This is part of the reason why humans love certainty. Certainty eliminates stress. Certainty is easy. It requires less mental effort. Have you ever driven a few minutes out of your way to go to your favorite grocery store simply because it is familiar? Maybe you shop at the same store even if it's out of the way because you know exactly how to navigate the parking lot. Maybe you are a customer of Amazon Prime because you love the certainty of knowing your package will appear on your doorstep in one day. Maybe you are in an unhealthy relationship because it is familiar and even though you know it's not good for you, the uncomfortableness of forging a new, uncertain path is a lot scarier than staying with a person that hurts you. Even if they hurt you, you know exactly what to expect. It's safe and you can survive. In short, we often mistaken comfort with happiness.

In our modern world, it is this mindset of staying safe that keeps us in jobs we dislike, in relationships we know we shouldn't be in, and with friends that aren't really our friends. Even though these situations don't serve us, the fact that we know exactly what we're getting feels better than the uncertainty of doing something different. Even if what is different is actually better for us, our brains latch on to what we know out of survival and comfort. The agonizing curiosity of what will happen in unchartered territory vanishes when we have certainty. And we love that. We want the unknown and the uncertainty to stay as far away from us as possible.

Suffering an injury is like pulling the safety blanket that envelops our world right out from underneath us. It removes all certainty we once had about the thing in our life most important and identity-forming for us - our sport - and painfully drops a basket of crippling stress at our door. The list of questions such as "will I be able to play again?" or "who am I without sport?" is just the starting point of uncertainty that our minds will indulge. We don't know for certain if our body will fully heal, if our career is actually over or if people will think of us differently because we're injured. Our life feels on pause, and the painful waiting game of physical therapy mixed with the uncertainty about our outcome stifles movement toward peace.

Lack of Control

As athletes, we hold a belief that we are unbreakable. We are special. We are invincible. Our teammates might get injured but never us. My body is stronger than *that*. Our mind indulges in the belief that injury can't happen to us, but this belief totally ignores the simple fact that we are just another human being like everyone else before we are an elite athlete. Unless your body is made of bionic parts and not flesh and bone, there is no other option but to let go of the notion your body is impervious to injury. Serena Williams twists her ankle every now and then, Tom Brady hyperextended his thumb during a play, and Michael Jordan fractured a bone in his left foot leaving him on the bench for six weeks. Injuries happen, they are outside of our control and resisting the possibility that injuries can happen to you creates unnecessary suffering.

The lack of control we have over the healing process can be crippling. In the 1953 Disney classic film, *Peter Pan*[5], Captain Hook ties Wendy's hands behind her back and directs her to "walk the plank". With her hands tied behind her back, we watch as she walks to the very end of the plank dangling over the treacherous ocean below. I envision Wendy as the metaphor of our sports career when we suffer an injury. Our hands are metaphorically tied, our athletic capabilities vanish and if nothing saves us then we know the impending doom that awaits when we jump off the plank - death. As Wendy walks out to sea, she must feel helpless, frustrated, and scared. We feel like Wendy when we are injured - we don't have any other option but to walk the plank and attempt to heal. We can't turn back and unless Peter Pan (or a fully healed body) saves the day then it's all over.

We feel frustration over the lack of control we have over our bodies. We can't simply rub out a strained hamstring or fuse broken bones back together. As an able-bodied athlete, we are accustomed to telling our bodies what to do and having our bodies comply. We add 20 more pounds to the bar, we push another 200 yards at the end of practice, we throw 100 more free throws even when we feel like we can't lift our shoulders. We are accustomed to controlling the very tool that makes us who we are - our body. Now, as an injured person, the control we so heavily leaned on vanishes and we free fall in a world of no control. Our body can't listen to us right now, and when we aren't feeling heard we indubitably feel frustration.

On top of not being able to control the very tool you've used to get you where you are in your sport, there is the uncomfortable uncertainty of not knowing how long it will take to fully heal. Wouldn't it be great if your doctor reviewed your broken bone and said "okay, looks like you will be able to play again in exactly three weeks and two days." But, not knowing a definite rehab timeline puts us in that infuriating limbo of helplessness. We don't know how long it will take to heal or how our bodies will perform once we do reach a full recovery. It is a perfect storm for anxiety to grab a stronghold on us. When we are vulnerable during this injured phase in our life, anxiety welcomes us with open arms, ready to sink its teeth into our soul. Anxiety sniffs our frustration a mile away. Having certainty on how long it will take to heal would offer some relief to know when the cloud of doom will float away. Referencing our earlier hurricane/house example, we would rather know things for certain even if they are negative outcomes because certainty is much less stressful. But, human beings heal at different rates and not only is every part of the body different in terms of healing rate but each individual heals at his or her own pace as well. Could it take six months? Could it take a year? Longer? The agony of different timeline possibilities makes it difficult to plan, schedule and hold onto hope for the actual day you can play again. Unlike Excel spreadsheets or time ticking by, things that are exact, it is impossible to know the exact day when you will wake up and be fully healed.

Another layer of helplessness, and frustration relates to our lack of control of our career. This injury could be career-ending, and you had no say that the wrong move on the field tore your ACL and took you out of the game. Forever. It's not like you told the forward on the other team to run full speed right into you. You had no say over having an injury in the first place or over the severity of the injury. It feels like you came home from school one day and your parents told you that you're starting boarding school 1,000 miles away and your flight leaves tonight. What gives your parents or your body the right to make decisions or do things to you without you even having a seat at the table when the decision is being made? *That* feeling is the feeling of injury.

Putting our career on hold for six months, giving up a team spot we trained years for, or even ending our career altogether are difficult pills to swallow. Not only are you frustrated with your physical body, but you are frustrated with the consequences this injury has on your actual career.

Timing of when the injury occurs is another heartbreaking layer. What if you shatter your pelvis the night before your biggest competition yet? Talk about bad timing. It is one thing to hurt yourself in the off-season when you have a little more wiggle room to heal. It is an entirely different level of pain and disappointment to injure yourself right before competition. It's not like you can schedule your injury around your season. Because the injury itself as well as the timing of the injury are outside of your control, your feelings of frustration are multiplied because you have no choice but to sit back, heal and watch how skills and stamina you've spent years building swirl down the drain.

When we can't fix our body or have certainty around rehabilitation and what it means for our career, we feel helpless. We feel frustrated. We feel stuck. The action-oriented, able-bodied athlete we depend on doesn't apply here. It crushes our soul to peel us away from the driver's seat and plop us in the passenger seat. We want to press the accelerator; we're used to steering the vehicle and we thrive on successfully completing fast turns. When we no longer have that control of our path and simply hold on in the passenger seat, natural feelings of frustration and stress over our lack of control become the new norm.

Self-Worth & Identity

When one of my friends was injured with a severed nerve during her collegiate basketball career at a Division I college, she viewed herself as completely worthless. To try and reconnect the nerves in her neck back to her shoulder, she attended two physical therapy sessions every single day over the course of a year. At a Division I college, you can imagine the top notch level of care she received. However, after a year of intensive therapy from some of the best sports medicine doctors in the collegiate scene, my friend was told there wasn't much more they could do to help her. A new set of x-ray scans revealed her nerves had made little progress during rehab, leaving little hope for a complete recovery. Devastated, she walked to her car in a daze and sat paralyzed (figuratively) in the driver's seat. She couldn't bring herself to insert the keys into the ignition and drive home. She was in shock. How could she drive home? She was just told her injury was likely permanent, cementing the fact that she would never compete on the elite level she used to play. In this moment, sitting in her car, she was faced with the realization that the next part of her life would have to be one without sports. Everything that she had built inside herself, reinforcing her basketball player identity, was crumbling down in front of her eyes. How could she accept that her journey to becoming the best basketball player she could be was over? If she started the car and left the parking lot, that meant she was on board with the trajectory her life would be taking. And she wasn't on board.

Over time, my friend learned to shoot her free throws left-handed but never was able to capture the potential she used to possess on her right side. She thought about playing in Europe like some of her teammates, but her injury stifled her performance levels and held her back from being recruited. Eventually, she retired from the sport entirely and was left with a crippled identity, forced to come to terms with her perceived shortcoming of an athletic career.

This story is all too common. Many athletes over decades of sports eras can relate to my friend's story in some way. A common challenge during periods of injury is figuring out who we are without sports and, consequently, how to fill our self-worth bucket. We experience the same self-worth crisis when we retire, leaving our sport for good and eliminating our "validation outlet". The context we use to build our lives (our position on the team, the number of points we scored this season, our race times from last meet, the number of meters we jump) vanishes. All the things that make us feel worthy and grant us confidence are gone. Without the option to use our sport for validation, we doubt our worth and question who we are.

Who am I without my sport? Who am I if I'm not "Kim the Swimmer"? The sense of who we are and what we offer to the world is called into question when the activity we've rooted our identity in is not available to us during a period of injury. The very definition of self-esteem is "confidence in one's own worth or abilities" and if your abilities are gone because you physically can't play, self-esteem drops. We've categorized ourselves as valuable because of the things our bodies can do and when we can't do those things, how do we feel valuable? This identity shock can be so devastating and, sometimes, even more so than retirement because of the uncertainty. Unlike retirement, where you know for certain you're wrapping up your sport for good, injuries bring along that cloud of "what's going to happen" with the possibility you can play again creating all the negative stress we talked about. The big question mark and consequent doubts we have about our value, our worth and who we even are as a person when we can't compete spin us out into this world of low self-worth and contemplation on our identity.

Some injuries are so severe or timely that they end a career. It is one thing to prepare for your retirement, deliberately choosing the end of your career, but it is a whole other mindset to be blindsided by the end of your career due to injury. (If you are retiring due to injury, please also see Chapter 17: How to Retire). In these circumstances, it is sadly poetic, like a heartbreak story of fatal attraction. The very body that launched you to euphoric levels of success is also the very body that suffered an injury and led to your retirement. This is lack of control at its finest, and we'll dive into how we shift our perspective on this in the next chapter.

Regardless of whether an injury causes a single benched season or your official retirement, you are forced to face life without your sports identity. During rehab, which could potentially last years, your teammates and competitors continue to strive for gold while you're left behind. It can feel like you've been cast aside, a broken toy placed back on the shelf for repair. Who am I without my fully capable body? You have validated yourself based on past athletic performances, and your sports persona has become a core part of who you are. If you suddenly fracture your ankle or suffer a concussion or tear a ligament, almost instantaneously your driving purpose vanishes. It's like trying to conduct a space launch with a broken rocket ship. Launch day is delayed, you're unsure about when the rocket ship will be ready, and when it finally feels ready to launch the ship might explode again anyway. The uncertainty could kill you before the launch does. You sit there by your rocket ship, and you cry. Do I give up on making it to the moon? Is the effort to put this broken rocket ship back together worth the risk? Maybe I'm just meant to be on Earth.

One More Thought. . .

While I'm making observations and referencing data points in a matter-of-fact way, I don't want to gloss over the very real and serious impact being injured has on an athlete's mental health if not paid attention to properly.

Not only is the injury in and of itself difficult to accept, "adding the sudden end to an athletic career into the equation is what often pushes some people into depression and anxiety."[6] According to an article in the British Journal of Sports Medicine, in a "study of Division I football players, 33% of injured athletes reported high levels of depressive symptoms...compared with 27% of non-injured athletes."[7] While it's not great to see high levels of depression in non-injured athletes, it is clear that depression increases among athletes who suffer injuries due to a number of agonizing factors rooted in uncertainty and perceived threats to the athlete's identity.

Regardless of the body part that is injured, the sport you're pulled away from or the level of competition you compete at, injuries are infuriatingly stressful times. Unfortunately, there are many factors that contribute to angst we feel when injured, such as our friends moving on without us or our coach's perception of us, but the root of our problems during injury stems from uncertainty. Uncertainty is the seed that is planted and the leaves that sprout are stress, lack of control, frustration, low self-worth and confused identity. When we didn't want the injury in the first place but have to follow the rules of human nature, it leaves us feeling like a passenger in our own life. We don't have any other choice but to focus on healing and do the best we can for the things that are within our control.

Chapter 14 Endnotes

1. *Mind, Body and Sport: How being injured affects mental health.* (2017, July 11). NCAA. Org - The Official Site of the NCAA. https://www.ncaa.org/sport-science-institute/mind-body-and-sport-how-being-injured-affects-mental-health#:%7E:text=For%20some%20student%2Dathletes%2C%20the,and%20substance%20use%20or%20abuse.

2. *Michael Jordan Quotes.* (2021b). BrainyQuote. https://www.brainyquote.com/quotes/michael_jordan_114789#:%7E:text=Michael%20Jordan%20Quotes&text=Please%20enable%20Javascript-,My%20body%20could%20stand%20the%20crutches%20but,couldn't%20stand%20the%20sideline.

3. Lewis, M. (2018, February 14). *Why we're hardwired to hate uncertainty.* The Guardian. https://www.theguardian.com/commentisfree/2016/apr/04/uncertainty-stressful-research-neuroscience

4. *Management Techniques Are Important If You Have Chronic Stress.* (2020, December 7). Verywell Mind. https://www.verywellmind.com/chronic-stress-3145104

5. Geronimi, C., Jackson, W., Luske, H. (Directors). (1953). *Peter Pan* [Film]. Walt Disney.

6. Editor In Chief. (2017, March 22). *Knocked out: the dark side of quitting a sport post injury.* The Eyeopener. https://theeyeopener.com/2017/01/knocked-out-the-mental-health-effects-of-quitting-a-sport-post-injury/

7. Putukian, M. (2015). The psychological response to injury in student athletes: a narrative review with a focus on mental health. *British Journal of Sports Medicine, 50*(3), 145–148. https://doi.org/10.1136/bjsports-2015-095586

Chapter 15

Injury Coping Skills

Now that we have a baseline understanding of the factors that make injury so challenging - mostly its relation to uncertainty - let's take a look at a number of helpful methods to help the hurt, hurt less. Many challenges you face when injured overlap with challenges during retirement, such as finding a new outlet to relieve stress, validating worth outside of your sport and growing patience when things feel tough. Please also refer to Chapter 17 to glean further insights on how to thrive when your sport is no longer accessible.

The Whole View of Injury is Flawed

First, zoom out and let's think about this from a realistic standpoint (which, if you haven't caught on by now, I love grounding in reality). I'm going to give you a bit of my tough Irish love and say that despite the circumstances of your injury, injury is a risk you take when you are an athlete. It comes with the territory of elite competition. We've established how injury feels like purgatory. But, in a sense, you signed up for it. You hate me for saying this. But imagine for a moment you were the world's best chess player, sitting at a computer all day and clicking a mouse (which, in that case maybe you get carpal tunnel syndrome). Playing safely from the comfort of a computer desk and chair, you don't run the risk of running head on into another player. You don't ever blow out your shoulder. You don't ever twist your ankle on a landing or break a bone. You click and sit. Click and sit. Your body stays healed and whole.

On the contrary, as an elite athlete playing modern sports, you're out on the field sliding in the turf. You're diving below the water. You're smacking another player with your stick. Your body is in the thick of the action and thus subject to getting hit. Your body is not only pushed to extremes amid competition but also during training. Your body, or your tool, is pushed beyond normal pressures to achieve aerobic capacity, flexibility, and strength. When you're constantly (and I mean constantly) pushing a flesh-and-bone tool made of shoulders, backs, knees, skin, tendons, nails, hair, cartilage, arteries and 206 skeletal bones to achieve insane athletic accomplishments, it is rather natural for injuries to occur. I might even venture to say it is expected. Or at least it should be. But it's not. Which is partly why injuries suck that much more.

Injuries are viewed as an avoidable, undesired tragedy. We think we can prevent injuries. Ha! Injury prevention…do you think you're a God? We think injuries are heartbreaking. We view injuries as some sad surprise. This couldn't be more inaccurate or unrealistic. Injuries are, in fact, unavoidable and expected. Should we continue to kid ourselves and live in a fairytale reality that while *other mere peasants* suffer injuries our bodies are impeccable and infallible? Injury should be viewed as part of sport no different than wiping down your counters after you cook or putting your toys away as a kid. Just like a Formula 1 car pits during a race, your body also pits during your own athlete journey. You burn out your tires. You overuse your shoulder. You snap your Achilles tendon. You tear your ACL. Although undesired, it's natural. Looking at the circumstances and probabilities of your extremely physical life, it's expected.

You can eyeroll me for saying this. I'm not saying injuries don't suck. I think we have already established the suck and challenge of being injured. But continuing to act blindly surprised when an injury does occur, as if it were never even slightly considered as a possibility, is not serving the sports community. Updating our perspective to view injury as a natural part of sport considering the circumstances we put our body through can help soften the blow of feeling like you could have avoided the pothole. Because the truth is you can't. And sometimes you must drive over the potholes, blow out a tire and do your best to repair it. Yes, it makes your route longer and more stressful, but it is a risk you take driving a car. Now let's zoom back in.

Counseling

Seek the help of a counselor to help you process the uncertainty of the situation. The invaluable benefit of working with a counselor includes getting specific with the details of your own situation (as opposed to listening to a generic podcast episode or YouTube video or even this book). The help of a counselor can help you talk through exactly what you're experiencing and provide a safety net when things feel really hard. Particularly if you are feeling symptoms of depression, anxiety, or other severe mental states, reach out to a counselor to help shed your emotional distress and learn specific coping skills. Refer to Chapter 17: How to Retire to uncover further benefits of counseling and alternative options if counseling is too expensive or not a viable option for you.

Accept & Acknowledge

A common theme in this book (and in life) is practicing acceptance for the way things are exactly as they are right now. Acceptance that injuries happen outside of any athlete or coach's control is a great first step to set the stage in your mind of how to healthily navigate the uncertainty. Running the play over and over in your head and thinking about all the ways the injury could have been avoided will only further your frustration and stress. Just as Olympic Skier Picabo Street or Pro Football Player Kenny McKinely suffered injuries, it can happen to you too. Injuries can happen to any athlete. When it happens, facing the uncomfortable truth head on and acknowledging that you have an injury removes a bunch of bullshit your mind will want to indulge. And here's why: referring back to Chapter 3, when we acknowledge uncomfortable truths, uncomfortable emotions and uncomfortable experiences we remove their power. Practice saying these out loud:

- I am injured.
- I could not have avoided this injury.
- Sometimes bodies break and right now my body is broken.
- I won't play in the next game(s).
- I am so unhappy right now.
- This is one of the most frustrating things to happen to me.

Such phrases may be difficult to recite out loud because there is discomfort in admitting you are not the able-bodied, badass athlete (for the moment). Saying "I am injured and cannot play" goes against what you believe. It goes against your purpose. It goes against who you are. Acknowledgement has the power to neutralize and defuse emotionally charged situations. It may seem simple but sometimes our complex brain patterns need the simplest of methods to control the mayhem. Once you accept the situation and can acknowledge not only what is happening but how you feel about what is happening (I am disappointed I won't be able to play the rest of the season, I am fearful all my teammates will get much better than me while I'm healing, etc.) you're clearing your emotional capacity to manage your mind amid the most uncertain and frustrating of times. Take a moment to acknowledge exactly how you feel right now. Say it out loud.

Gratitude for Health

Calibrate your perspective with gratitude for the health and life you do have. In 1984 Olympic Swimmer Melinda Harrison's book, *Personal*

Next, she details how one of her interviewees, a Professional Rower, suffered an injury and had no alternative but to quit the sport if he wanted to live.[1] Frustrated with his predicament, he ended up retiring and held frustration over how his career ended. Six months later, a teammate of his with a similar condition ended up dying. A harsh example for sure, but even with an injury hold space for gratitude that you have your life. Health is wealth and should not be taken for granted.

Your health should be your primary focus at this point in your life. Yes, it is going to be difficult to see your friends and teammates score record-breaking goals. Yes, it is going to be uncomfortable to watch your team perform well without you. Yes, it is not going to be fun to watch everyone else go on while you're sitting in the sports medicine wing. But no game point, no race time, no match, no winning streak, no record, no nothing should trump your health. Your focus is not on all the things you feel like you're missing out on. Your focus is on healing your body regardless of if you play your sport again. I can't stress enough that the health of your body trumps everything else in your life, and it doesn't serve you to spread your focus to areas that generate negative emotions or anxiety. Be selfish right now and direct your energy toward the things you *can* do to heal your body.

Things Aren't Always in Your Control

Sometimes it is hard to hear pieces of wisdom or life perspectives when you're really going through it. When you're hurting, stressed out or just feel totally down and someone recites a quote from Pinterest to you, like "everything happens for a reason", you probably want to punch that person in the face. What I'm about to say might also incite similar feelings, but it is a worthy reminder to highlight regardless of what hurdles you face. Life is a mix of things you deliberately choose and things that happen to you. For everyone. No one can avoid this truth, and I'll repeat it. Life is a mix of things you deliberately choose and things that happen to you. The outfit you're wearing right now - that is a deliberate choice. That is part of the free will you have as an individual. The food you eat, the strategy choices you make in a game and the team you decide to train with (depending on the sport) are all choices within your control. A snowstorm so rampant that snows you in your home for five days? Out of your control. Unless your name is Mother Nature that is something you have zero control over. The death of a loved one, someone blindside tackling you and being cut from a team after you gave your best shot are all events out of your control. Michael Jordan was cut from his high school basketball team after tryouts. He played his best, but making the team was a decision the coach made. A decision Jordan had no control over. The journey that is your life, athlete or not, is made up of those choices you deliberately choose as well as events that occur outside of your control. As athletes, we're often ignorant to this life-mix thinking we can control all our outcomes.

An injury is an event outside of your control due to the pure fact that you're a fallible human being. Every human being is susceptible to injury, athlete or not. Kids get scrapes, the elderly fall and athletes, subjecting themselves to extremely physical activities, have higher chances than most of suffering an injury. Just as an army soldier has awareness that his life is at risk, athletes, too, should hold space for awareness that injury is a real possibility despite all preventative measures. Things happen. Human bodies break. Especially in games, races and practices where physical exertion is extreme and risks are rewarded you run the chance of injury. When it does happen, remember that it is an event outside of your control.

Progress

Again, progress = happiness. When you feel like you are improving and making strides, you feel so much satisfaction. How can you make progress when you're injured? You can't play, you can't perform, you can't practice, so how do you live a life that generates happiness based on the progress you're making? As an injured athlete, go out of your way to set aside the miniature goals for your healing and health. Write down on a piece of paper with checkboxes next to each item everything you will accomplish each week. Maybe it is to attend two physical therapy sessions. Maybe your goal for the week is to be able to stand without crutches. Maybe your goal is to throw one practice pitch without pain. Or maybe your goal is to simply listen to your body and give it the proper rest it needs to better heal. Whatever goal(s) you decide to choose, write them down every single week and cross them off as you achieve them. According to a sports medicine article reviewing injured athletes, "patients benefitted primarily from a concrete, problem-focused, behaviourally orientated programme which minimises uncertainty."[2] We talked about how uncertainty is the large rain cloud hovering over our injured period, so minimizing uncertainty through clear achievements reduces emotional distress.

Set aside weekly check-ins with your coach, a trusted teammate, or another support person in your life. If you feel comfortable, share your goals with him or her. Talk about how things are going and what you did that week. Let someone root for you. Let yourself feel supported. It may feel elementary to write down simple, weekly goals and share them with your support system, but structuring a progress tracker that includes support from others helps you observe your own strides, however tiny they feel, toward healing. It not only helps keep your physical rehab on track, but it will help you visualize that you are still making progress when it might not always feel like it.

Don't underestimate the power of your brain. We mentioned how practices like manifestation and visualization can bring thoughts to life. Lay in bed before you go to sleep and envision your future self fully healed. "Visualize yourself being healthy, going through motions of your rehab, and seeing yourself executing your sport with perfect form."[3] You have to dream the dream before you live the dream, so take advantage of the subtle yet powerful effect your mind has on creating the results you seek in your life.

Silver Linings & Self-Worth

What if this injury is the best thing that has ever happened to you? It sounds crazy, but think about it. What if, because of this injury, you ended your career early which led to you landing a job which led to you meeting your coworkers which led to you meeting the love of your life? What if this injury could have actually been 10x worse if it happened 1/10th of a centimeter lower? What if this injury was perfectly timed, giving you a season of rest, you desperately needed so that your body could bounce back to unforeseen levels of performance the following season? What if this injury is somehow teaching you an overdue life lesson? What if this injury is preparing you to help others when they also experience injury? To reference Steve Jobs again, we can only connect the dots and make sense of why things happened looking backward. We may not understand the purpose or reason of why things happen when we're in the thick of the pain, so hang tight until the fog clears and you can look back and say "It all makes sense now…"

Perks and silver linings of being injured:

- Get some rest from tough practices
- Build new/stronger relationships with trainers
- More time to play video games
- Much needed rest for your muscles (you have a good excuse to be lazy so take advantage of it)
- Improve stretching
- Connect with a community of others with similar experiences (organizations like The Sideline Perspective)
- Opportunities to observe your teammates and/or opponents to pick up new methods
- Temporary relief of no expectations

One of the most important ways to cope with a long-term injury is to find self-worth beyond the activity.[4] While our sport is on hold for the time being, what other areas of life can you dabble in to validate self-worth?

Here is a list of other activities:

- Read! Expand your knowledge by reading books like this one
- Learn a new skill (YouTube has a video for everything)
- DIY projects around your living space (also YouTube)
- Expand your friendship circle (your neighbors, internet friends, friends from other sports, etc.)
- Babysit - see the world through the eyes of a kid
- Help at least one person every day
- Do something you normally wouldn't do every day
- Learn to cook a new recipe
- Discover new music
- Practice daily affirmations

One More Thought. . .

Yes, injuries are not fun. Yes, injuries hurt. Yes, rehab is intensive and painful. Yes, it is hard to watch teammates and opponents play on without you. Yes, the uncertainty and frustration boils inside you. Yes, yes, yes. These circumstances are presented to you, just as they are presented to every athlete that experiences injury. How are you going to step up and proactively manage your mind during these challenges? You could sit back, not do anything and suffer. Anxiety could multiply. Frustration could boil over. But, if you're reading this book, then you're probably looking for ways to navigate the struggle. I'm not saying it is easy, but it is worth it.

Remember, your health is more important than anything else. You may want to rush the healing process to get back out there, but injuries don't discriminate based on who you are or what your sport you play or anything.

Imagine yourself not prioritizing your health and severely injuring yourself further and living with a rickety back for the rest of your life. Take the time, focus, energy, and effort to put your health on a pedestal and do everything you can, or at times do nothing at all and rest, to help your body take care of itself. I'll say it a million times over but no gold medal, no team championship, no sporting event could ever be more important than your health.

After you've prioritized the health of your body, take care of your mind. Shift your perspective to practice acceptance - injuries can happen to some of the best players that have ever participated in your sport and they can happen to you too. When you do face injury, acknowledge your experience. "This hurts. This sucks. I'm frustrated. My ankle is broken" - whatever the details of your situation look like say them out loud. Go ahead. Say it out loud. The power of acknowledging things that hurt or create sensitivity softens the influence they hold over you. When you're able to acknowledge your situation for what it is and how it affects you, then you can develop healthy, realistic perspectives through your uncertain time.

Chapter 15 Endnotes

1. Harrison, M. (2020). *Personal Next: What We Can Learn From Elite Athletes Navigating Career Transition*. LifeTree.
2. Smith, A. M., Scott, S. G., & Wiese, D. M. (1990). The Psychological Effects of Sports Injuries. *Sports Medicine, 9*(6), 352–369. https://doi.org/10.2165/00007256-199009060-00004
3. Staff, A. (2019, March 6). *6 Ways to Mentally Recover from an Injury*. Athlinks Blog. https://blog.athlinks.com/2016/08/05/6-ways-to-mentally-recover-from-an-injury/
4. Golden, D. (2019, November 26). *Beyond the Physical: How Sports Injuries Hurt*. The Recovery Village Drug and Alcohol Rehab. https://www.therecoveryvillage.com/mental-health/news/depression-and-sports-injuries/#:%7E:text=One%20of%20the%20most%20important,who%20have%20shared%20this%20experience.

FOURTH QUARTER

When It's All Said & Done

"Elite athletes are the only people who have to die twice."
—*John Murray, Sports Psychologist*

Chapter 16

Why Retirement is so Challenging

Up to this point, we've explored a number of factors that contribute to an athlete's identity - our quest for perfectionism, our irrational motivation, our relentless desire to compete and more. We've dealt with the wins and losses. The fight. The perspective. The life experience. Every component of our journey contributes to who we are as an athlete. Then one day, we turn the page and realize there are no more chapters. The book shuts and our sports adventure comes to a close. How do we walk away from something that constituted our entire life? Our entire identity? How do we validate our self-worth without winning games? How do we let go of perfectionism? How do we undo the years of adrenaline-driven elite athleticism?

Athletes don't plan for retirement. Focusing on anything other than winning the championship is discouraged. So, when the day comes and we fully step over the line into a post-sport life it can feel like we dropped into a new country. All of a sudden, we washed ashore to find strange people that speak a new language and eat weird food. There's a seemingly long road ahead of us on how we make sense of not only our environment but how we fit in. Overwhelm, ambiguity, confusion, low self-confidence, apathy, emptiness, and hopelessness are just some of the characteristics that paint the picture of how athletes may feel when entering retirement.

Most athletes are not able to withstand this vulnerable and uncomfortable evolution, often falling into a deep depression or distracting themselves sufficiently with adult responsibilities. Consciously or subconsciously, we avoid facing the deeper parts of our being beyond athletics. If these emotions go untended, a depressive state amplifies as the athlete may feel the glory days are behind them, like nothing will feel as exciting, worthwhile or gratifying as their athletic pursuits. Exiting a world where your self-worth is constantly validated by external accomplishments and entering a world where you no longer achieve those accomplishments feels abruptly harsh. Where do I fit in? How can I feel worthy? What am I good at now? Many athletes struggle to answer these questions. Unfortunately, this depressive state can become "all too encompassing and over the years, there have been a number of cases of athlete's committing suicide following their retirement from professional sport."[1]

It is not entirely the fault of the athlete for feeling confused, lost, or depressed during this transition. The athletic programs and systems that sports are built on don't quite have the awareness, capacity, and resources to offer guidance to athletes entering retirement. Even though every athlete walks off the field one last time, few resources are available on the topic. One helpful resource is BelievePerform, a mental health & wellbeing website with insightful articles from Emma Vickers, PhD Sport Psychology Student and England table tennis player.[2] What makes matters worse is that athletes grow up in an environment promoting "toughing it out" and "don't show your weakness". This leaves athletes with little to no experience in expressing struggle or diving deeper into helpful strategies to help during a transition. The sports culture that gave the athlete everything they needed to be successful when competing is simply not equipped or available in the way athletes need when they retire.

To give ourselves the healthiest mindset to navigate retirement, let's first look at *why* the retirement transition is such a struggle. Let's look at what retirement means on a physical, mental, and emotional level. Once we've dissected and understood the layers of the retirement transition, we can adopt coping skills and thought patterns allowing clarity and ease for our new chapter.

Basic Biology & Stress

Before we dive into our soul, let's look at our basic biology. Every day, sometimes multiple times a day, depending on your training schedule, you exercise and the brain releases endorphins. Endorphins are a group of hormones on the opiate receptors of our brain, meaning those hormones help reduce pain and increase pleasure. Even when your coach gives you an extremely tough set, you leave practice feeling that "runner's high" with endorphins released throughout your body comparable to mini doses of morphine.[3] When you retire and your workout schedule is severely reduced, you crash. Endorphins aren't flowing through your brain in quantities you've become accustomed to so chemically, you're depleted. It almost feels like the opposite as if pleasure is reduced and pain is increased.

Bill Cole, a world-renowned performance coach, notes how there could be a causal link between depression and an imbalance in serotonin levels. As Cole explains, "Athletes have had regular doses of serotonin daily for many years, when this is suddenly decreased or stopped outright, we see a huge upset to the chemistry of the body."[4] When we go from 10 workouts a week, competitions most weekends, and the exciting pursuit of being the best athlete to only handful of workouts a week, or maybe none, and a comparatively boring life we aren't able to achieve those same levels of chemical release we had grown accustomed to.

Not only does the new absence of chemicals create physical imbalances, the elimination of the very activity that served as our outlet for stress relief also vanishes. "Exercise is often an escape or coping mechanism for many athletes, so if injury (or retirement) occurs and they cannot exercise, it can result in a problematic response."[5] Have you ever had a bad day and went to practice just to blow off some steam? Or maybe you hit the weight room with your headphones on, blocked everything out, and squatted the heaviest you've ever squatted. It doesn't solve all your problems, but it helps. Even though practice doesn't automatically make what's going on off the field disappear (although it can feel that way temporarily) sports give us that safe and highly effective stress outlet. Releasing stress allows us to walk away from practice with a much clearer, calmer mind than when we walked in. Not having this sandbox readily available for when inevitable stressors come into our lives is stressful in and of itself. You might feel like a lab rat in a maze, stuck in a corner unable to figure out where to go next. You've never explored other coping mechanisms for stress because you've never needed to; your sport was always there.

Frankly, there isn't much scientific-backed research out there about the sudden drop in endorphin levels for athletes once they do retire, so we can do our best to grow our awareness that our bodies likely feel symptoms of withdrawal. At least understand that when it comes to the basic biology of the body, the chemical imbalance created from suddenly stopping your sport and the lack of having additional outlets for stress contributes to depressive moods and stress build-up before any thinking has occurred. By simply growing your awareness on chemical imbalances in retired athletes, you're already ahead of the curve because this scenario typically eludes us completely. Our minds typically go to everything wrong with us, with our own thinking, with our own feelings and not to the fact that sometimes the way we feel is a direct response to a biological imbalance, something out of our control.

Athletes Die Twice

In ordinary life, time passes, we grow older and eventually we reach the inevitable - death. All good things considered, we reach an elderly age and pass on. Everything in our life comes to a close and we never have to manage stress, anxiety or negativity again. There is no existential angst, depression, or frustration beyond a certain point. We are simply a biological organism resting in the earth (of course, depending on your religion or beliefs there could be an afterlife). I'm not glorifying death, but when a person dies at the end of his or her life that's the end. That person does not face excruciating turmoil such as an identity crisis nor is there any attempt to rebuild a new version of themselves. That person is simply laid to rest and the world moves on.

In our sports life, we also experience death. We eventually take off our jersey one last time. Maybe some finish four years in college and enter a post-sport life. Maybe others play professionally for a decade and end with a victory lap. Regardless of the how and why, every athlete eventually retires. Unlike death in our ordinary life, an athlete's retirement is a form of death we live on and deal with. We can't just lay in the earth and forget about everything. We continue to live for decades reconciling our past as an elite athlete with building a new version of us beyond sport, which is not an easy task to complete. The emotional impact of retirement is often underestimated as so many athletes struggle to effectively grow into a new chapter of their lives. This is exemplified by the number of athletes that come forward to share their own struggle transitioning into retirement – Michael Phelps, Aly Raisman, Apollo Ohno, to name a few. Simultaneously, you're forced to grieve and rebuild yourself which can be overwhelmingly emotional and confusing.

Untangling deep-rooted identities, forming different friend groups, and validating self-worth are, at times, seemingly impassable obstacles we may not be able to figure out on our own. We never planned for this new life, and it can feel incredibly heavy to navigate when you don't understand or know how to move forward.

Battling Perfectionism

Like we discussed in Chapter 7, our perfectionist thinking doesn't stop once we leave the field. We desire perfection at school, at home, with friends, with our body, at work, with our health, in our relationships and even with the small actions we take every day. Heaven forbid we spill a cup of coffee; that is not perfectionist behavior. We feel anything and everything has potential for improvement, spinning us on the hamster wheel of "it's not good enough". I should have spent 10 more minutes on the homework assignment. My house is nice, but I should have looked at a better neighborhood. I shouldn't have sent that last text to my friend. I wish I closed 2 more deals last month. Why did I eat fries for lunch? My biceps are gone. I don't communicate my needs enough with my significant other.

The constant feeling of inadequacy is an exhausting byproduct of perfectionist thinking. It feels as though nothing satisfies the inner critic who won't take anything other than "flawless" for an answer. Because we're so used to analyzing the smallest of details for improvement in the next game, we also criticize the smallest of details in our non-athlete life. Conversations with others, morning routines, traffic routes, dietary selections, time spent, anything and everything that could be criticized is criticized.

Perfectionism is an athlete's curse. Even when we've stepped away from being an athlete, years of reinforcement to achieve perfection can't be turned off like a light switch and we struggle with our habitual pattern of aiming for no errors but living as an adult in a species prone to errors. Where we struggle is getting stuck in the impossible attempt of putting a square peg in a round hole, attempting perfection over and over when there is no perfection. While perfectionism served us in our sports life it does not translate to ordinary, human life.

The North Star Fades Away

Our whole career, we are guided by an end goal (i.e., a North Star). This North Star may have been to compete at the Olympics, to play professionally, or to make the world championship team. Through the ups and downs on our journey we chase that North Star knowing all the blood, sweat and tears are worth it. The struggle is always worth making it to that end goal and even if we lose along the way, we get back up and view the loss as another stepping-stone on our journey of making it to the top.

Our career as an athlete is similar to a narrative story structure known as the Hero's Journey, in which a character ventures out to get what they need, faces conflict, but ultimately triumphs over adversity.[6] Movies such as The Lord of the Rings or Thor exemplify a clear and explicit Hero's Journey storyline. The toughest, heartbreaking moments along the journey are always worth the struggle because of the desire to reach what's waiting for the hero at the end. What happens when that end game is over? What happens after the One Ring is destroyed? The movie ends and the credits roll. What are we fighting for then? What is our inspiration? What is the ultimate point of our sacrifices? Losing this ever-flowing current of our purpose in life, our North Star, can crush us.

You may replace your North Star in sport with a North Star in your career or life, but there are differences in the glory and clarity of the path. Sports feel like glorious, prideful journeys of "becoming". Sending emails from your desk doesn't quite hold that same sparkle. Sports offer clear-cut milestones, benchmarks, and performance requirements to get you to the next level. You know the exact time you need to clock. You know exactly which opponent you need to defeat. You know exactly which tournaments, games and matches will land you on the podium. In other careers, the paths to reach your desired milestones are generally less clear, which is frustrating to someone foreign to an ambiguous environment. What is also dangerous for athletes is to immediately fall head-over-heels into another pursuit without reaching closure and peace with your sports career. If this pattern occurs, you're only compounding inner struggles which may feel even that much harder later in life.

With the North Star gone, with our clearly defined goals gone, we struggle to feel purpose and progress. We don't quite know what to look forward to. We don't quite know why we're doing what we're doing. What's pulling us, inspiring us, motivating us now?

Identity Crisis

With the North Star faded away and the sports journey over, a paradigm shift of identity brews inside us. Who are we without our sport? After decades of reinforcement we've wired into the circuitry of our brain about being an athlete and being a great athlete, you can imagine it's a bit difficult to immediately catalogue those as past tense and unglue them from our present identity. Especially as we grew to love who we are as an athlete, we may have a hard time embracing a version of ourselves that excludes high-profile accomplishments. I don't want to be average. For so long we validated and reinforced our goodness based on the results of our performance. Winning and competing at such a high level feels good and we design a view of ourselves based on that good feeling. Jennie Gow, a Formula 1 journalist, talks about the challenge drivers face when they retire, emphasizing that, "It is incredibly hard for drivers who spend their entire lives trying to be in Formula 1. Leaving that is almost like stepping away from an addiction."[7] Part of the challenge is that we're starting from scratch to flesh out other parts of who we are outside of athletics. When we talked about Identity Foreclosure in Chapter 9 we described how athletes close off exploration of other parts of their identity because sports require so much time and effort. We put all our eggs in one basket of "being an athlete". Walking away from that identity puts us at square one for literally everything else (unless you're superhuman like Elizabeth Beisel and can also shred notes on the violin and piano among skills like being an Olympic Swimmer). Do I like country music? Am I a good cook? Who am I a good friend to? What do I enjoy? Can I simply sit still and just be? Am I an honest person? What else am I good at? Do my sports skills translate to other activities? So many questions and parts of who we are may have not been thought about before. The confusion of knowing where to even begin on a self-discovery journey can be so overwhelming due to the intimidating factor of starting all over.

While all this confusion is happening inside us about what makes us "us", we also struggle figuring out how to validate self-worth when our usual validation sources (competitions, games, meets, tournaments, medals, podiums, coaches, etc.) are now gone. By design, athletes base their self-worth on their capabilities. Can you run fast or not? Can you swim fast or not? Can you score points or not? That worth is validated during competition without dispute; you can't refute the points on a scoreboard. After the athlete retires, the need for the external validation still exists yet there is no similar outlet to affirm and reassure the athlete of their worth as a person. The immediate feedback loop in practice and the instantaneous results from a game are gone. Leaving a sports world doesn't also rid us of our reliance on the immediate and limitless sources of external validation at our fingertips when we're actively competing. We continue to seek approval in the normal world which isn't as kind or generous with feedback, and so we struggle feeling worthy, good, and accepted.

An extreme example of an athlete's externally validated self-view in full form is captured by professional wrestler Ric Flair. If you don't know Ric Flair or have never seen his interviews, please spend a few minutes on YouTube looking up the very best clips of the heavyweight champion. You will not regret it; I promise. Even if much of his flamboyance was exaggerated due to rumored drug use and 80's lavish entertainment lifestyle, the way he speaks about himself is an epitomic example of someone who truly loves who they are based entirely on their performance. One hilarious and over-the-top line: "I've had more world championships than you've had women!"[8] His interviews consist of gloating chatter about all the things he can buy based on being the heavyweight champion - limousines, $600 snakeskin shoes, Rolex watches, and private jets. He built his identity, both as an athlete and entertainer, around being the world's number one and embellished that into every other aspect of his life. How can someone go from being a high-profile, high-achieving, highly successful athlete to then be your ordinary adult without major adrenaline achievements? How do you think Ric Flair would behave if he were Regular Ric shopping the aisles in a grocery store?

This (sometimes) suffocating feeling of having our validation outlets cut causes athletes to turn to unhealthy behaviors, almost out of desperation, to fill up their self-worth bucket. Relying on these new, unhealthy behaviors is like applying a dirty band-aid on a wound. It stops the blood temporarily, but the unhealthy behaviors infect the wound much worse than if the band-aid was never applied in the first place. These compensatory behaviors could look like total absorption in a career, overly sexual behavior, co-dependent relationships, or the constant need to be around other people. It could also include people-pleasing behaviors to garner favor and feelings of acceptance, such as never saying no, agreeing with others when you don't, over apologizing, failing to cope with any level of criticism or generally acting in ways that satisfies others but doesn't reflect your own values. We grasp, sometimes desperately, to feel remotely close to the levels of positive reinforcement we used to feel in sport.

Sea of Ambiguity

What athletes take for granted when actively competing are the clearly defined benchmarks and fully known landscape of the sports world. You know where you stand at all times of the day, week, and year. You know what you need to improve on - thanks, Coach. You know what you are inherently good at and which teammate is the Pippen to your Jordan. You know which opponents can beat you and which haven't yet. There is almost a caste system you become accustomed to - who makes the national team, who is a club athlete, who is branded with the Olympic rings tattoo, who is sponsored by the major brands like Nike. You know exactly where you and everyone else stands in the world of athletic hierarchy and when you leave that known environment and enter regular life lacking those clearly defined segments, there is uncomfortable ambiguity as to where you fit in. This furthers the internal identity struggle because you no longer have the smoke signals in every direction reinforcing who you are.

Sports are simply technical in nature. You can bend your elbow, stretch your quad, and squeeze your legs tighter to achieve better outcomes. It is relatively clear where you can improve or what constitutes a good job. You kick the ball into the net. You did a good job. Regular adult life doesn't quite have the level of technicality as your sport where you know for certain what's good or bad or needs improvement. You give a presentation at work. You think it was well received but you're not quite sure. Your boss doesn't offer feedback every single day like your coach might have in the sports world. Just about every single decision as an athlete elicits an immediate response, whether good or bad. In the non-athlete world, it might seem like very few of the decisions you make warrant any response at all.

The evaporation of the feedback loop we've relied on creates stressful ambiguity. Dropping into a less defined world after years of clearly defined goals is incredibly confusing and it feels as if you're spinning around space with no sense of where the ground might be. It feels shocking to the system, and even anxiety-inducing, to never feel like you fully know how you are doing, what is going well, what needs to be improved or how to improve it.

Decrease in Attention

Another big shift from the sports world to the regular world that bruises our precious, self-centered ego is the decrease in attention. In Chapter 8 we talked about how parents, coaches, trainers, friends, competitors, and fans make up our attention ecosphere. People care about our performance and what we're up to, so we get caught in the mode of thinking that it is all about us.

We garner much attention as an athlete because our Hero's Journey is exciting. It's epic. In our modern culture sports are sexy and athletes feel enormous pride participating in that world. How many times have you met someone for the first time, explained you were an athlete, and they responded with a statement or expression of being impressed? It's not quite the level of being an astronaut, but being an athlete is cool to the normal population. Jumping from that world of excitement, adrenaline, pride, and respect into your normal adult life feels abruptly dismal. In regular, adult life, when someone asks you what you do for a living the answer elicits a much different reaction.

Your life grows a lot quieter than the days you were an active competitor. The fans aren't cheering for you, the sponsors aren't calling your phone, the events don't want you and the prize money is being won by someone else. Attention you usually receive and love is diverted elsewhere, and it is a challenging shift for our ego to accept that it isn't all about us anymore. We're no longer wanted (according to the level of attention we receive), adding further sadness to an already confusing period.

Imagine a kid on Christmas morning opening two presents. The first present he opens with total excitement as he pulls out an action figure of an Olympic track star! Thanks, mom and dad! How cool! He runs around the house playing with his action figure and dreaming his own dreams. After he calms down he opens the second present, which is still another action figure but it is a middle-aged man in a business suit. The little boy looks confused and starts to cry, "I don't want this!" He throws the action figure down. The pursuit of being an athlete is cool, respectable, full of energy and exciting. Leaving that exciting world and entering the often attention-less, mundane life of being a regular adult can feel shocking to our system.

Additionally, our whole support system is upheaved. Teammates are no longer teammates. Coaches, nutritionists, trainers, and other supporting members become less prevalent or even obsolete. Our world grows quiet and there are less opportunities to confide in others and feel that sense of community. Athletes then find themselves alone and unrelated to, which grows feelings of isolation, frustration or even depression.

Similar to war veterans or prison inmates that experience a totally unique environment, athletes are then thrust to assimilate into regular society and struggle to find others with similar experiences. Not being able to relate to other people and feel understood must be one of the most infuriating feelings a human can feel. Couple this disconnection with feeling unsupported by those that made up your community and this creates one lonely and unful-filled ex-athlete.

Rationalization

Retirement is also challenging because, suddenly, we are forced to process the hard stuff of life we ignored or rationalized because we were so successful as an athlete. Remember how we talked about rationalizing inadequate aspects of our life with our gold medal wins? Our normal lives could be crumbling to pieces around us, but we always found validation in competing and winning. Family drama, friend drama, life drama? Who cares, you're leading the team in scored goals for the whole season. Because competition was an area of our life we were incredibly good at, we diverted our negative energy - anger, guilt, shame, embarrassment - into performing even better so we could still feel that sense of "being good" and feel less inferiority of being a bad friend, bad sibling or bad student. In retirement, we don't have our sport to lean on any longer and the relief that accompanies winning is nowhere to be found.

The "crutch" that diverted our attention from frustrating, embarrassing, or angering parts of our life has fallen to the ground and we are left to stand on our own two feet. No longer is there a pool to dive into, a field to run down or a court to conquer. What makes this an extremely difficult mindset to undo is that we have almost no experience handling the tougher situations of life without our sport patiently waiting for us as a safety net. When life hits us hard, we now feel the full effect of the blow like never before. We have no choice but to face the hard facts of life without our sport patiently backing us up.

Deep-seated mental habits of relying on our athlete identity to make us feel good despite life's challenges no longer work in our new, non-athlete world. It leaves us struggling to thrive in situations we have no experience how to handle. Everything we have lived through has had some glimmer of our sport overshadowing those events. Now, we must learn how to process uncomfortable situations head-on. We can no longer leverage our sports performance to soften the blow of inadequacies in our life, and this unfortunately intensifies those inadequacies.

Fear & Uncertainty

Our greatest fear stares us straight in the face – not being good at something. All of a sudden we find ourselves a master of none, our fear of being unskilled uncomfortably exposed. After years of achieving a level of mastery in your sport, life in retirement feels painfully average. We feel like just another body on the earth with no medals on our wall for "waking up" or "driving to work". Who is going to tell me "good job"? How am I going to constantly improve? Does anyone care what I'm doing? I was once an athlete! Hey! Listen! What if it's all downhill from here? Worse, what if I'm just mediocre for the rest of my life?

When the time comes, we have to actually let go of our athlete label. This is incredibly scary to us due to the unchartered territory of what's on the other side. We don't know who we are without sports. The future holds uncertainty and we may be scared to fully jump into a new chapter. Humans, in general, aren't great at embracing the unknown and entering a totally new life without our label is frightening. Our label gave us a place in the world and provided context so we could feel safe, categorized, and identified. Stripping that away and building "you" from ground zero feels daunting.

Because of our experience in sports, we will always have a part of us that will identify as an athlete. Where ex-athletes get into trouble is if they can never let go of that label as the sole label of themselves, preventing them from moving on into a new chapter. If an athlete retires and continues to lean on past accomplishments or the athlete identity of what once was without conscientiously building new pieces of what makes her "her" outside of being an athlete, not only is this person going to feel friction of trying to live in the present and plan for the future but this person is going to miss out majorly on discovering new, cool, fun parts of herself.

One More Thought. . .

Every athlete lives their own unique experience. While I believe these challenges are the core, affecting reasons of why athletes struggle in retirement, I'm sure individual athletes could further contribute to the list. Now that we've highlighted several reasons why it's so difficult to transition into a life post-sport, we can begin to forge a better path forward, adopting tactical mental strategies to thrive in our new season. Hint hint: perfectionism is out and being a human being is in.

Chapter 16 Endnotes

1. Vickers, E. (2019, September 11). *Life after sport: Depression in the retired athlete - BelievePerform - The UK's leading Sports Psychology Website.* BelievePerform - The UK's Leading Sports Psychology Website. https://believeperform.com/life-after-sport-depression-in-retired-athletes/

2. *Home - BelievePerform - The World's Leading Sports Psychology Website.* (2021, March 2). BelievePerform - The UK's Leading Sports Psychology Website. https://believeperform.com/

3. Bruce, D. F. (2008, May 30). *Exercise and Depression.* WebMD. https://www.webmd.com/depression/guide/exercise-depression#1

4. CommonLit™. (2013). *CommonLit | Life After Sport.* CommonLit. https://www.commonlit.org/es/texts/life-after-sport

5. Putukian, M. (2015). The psychological response to injury in student athletes: a narrative review with a focus on mental health. *British Journal of Sports Medicine, 50*(3), 145–148. https://doi.org/10.1136/bjsports-2015-095586

6. *Hero's Journey 101: Definition and Step-by-Step Guide (With Checklist!).* (2021, April 8). Reedsy. https://blog.reedsy.com/guide/story-structure/heros-journey/#:%7E:text=The%20Hero's%20Journey%20is%20a,and%20ultimately%20triumphs%20over%20adversity.

7. Gay-Rees, J., Martin, P., Todd, S. [Producers] 2019-2021. *Drive to Survive.* [Series] Netflix.

8. I. (n.d.). *Ric Flair quote: I've had more world championships than you've had women!* Inspiring Quotes. Retrieved May 28, 2021, from https://www.inspiringquotes.us/quotes/6HkY_iWFxIU9S

Chapter 17

How to Retire

For the longest time, I thought asking for help was a sign of weakness
because that's kind of what society teaches us. Well, you know what? If
someone wants to call me weak for asking for help, that's their problem.
Because I'm saving my own life.
—Michael Phelps, 23-time gold medal-winning USA Olympic swimmer

---

Let's look at some of the most effective tips, coping strategies and transition
guidelines to help navigate the unfamiliar ambiguity of entering a post-sport life.
Once you practice the exercises to reach acceptance and closure for your sports
career, it is incredibly beautiful and amazing to watch other parts of you flourish.
These parts of you were there all along; now, you simply have the time and energy
to open them up. It is amazing when you step away from time-consuming sports
and dabble into other parts of life you missed out on when actively competing.

Everyone Goes Through It

For athletes, "career transition trauma is a widespread phenomenon".[1] Every
athlete experiences retirement. Read that again. Every single athlete on the

face of the earth experiences retirement. Take comfort that the growing pains and uncomfortable moments you're feeling have also been felt by so many other athletes. We all go through it, just as you are going through it now.

During his time playing football and studying at Maryland, then later during his four years in the NFL, Phil Costa heard stories about athletes who struggled after their playing careers. But he was sure his experience would be different. He had goals: For one, he was determined to shed weight he no longer needed for football — and he did, dropping from 310 pounds to 250. He gave himself six months to figure out what he would pursue next. That's when feelings of depression crept in. "I was really looking for, what else am I passionate about? To try to find something I truly enjoyed doing," Costa says. So he searched. He spent a week with a lawyer to learn about his profession. He met with real estate agents and a politician. He shadowed staff at NFL Films. He wondered why he was struggling and confided in another former NFL player who had made the jump to his next pursuit look easy. "What's the trick?" Costa asked. "What am I not doing?" To Costa's surprise, the former player responded by admitting that he, too, struggled at the end of his playing career. "Just hearing somebody else, especially a guy like that, say that, it kind of took the weight off my back and made me feel better," Costa says.[2]

Biology & Stress

We know that when we retire from sport and drastically reduce exercise, our endorphins crash. Because there isn't much researched scientific evidence that has studied the effect of endorphin crashes in retired athletes, the best piece of advice is to simply be aware. It is helpful in and of itself, if you do start feeling depressive moods, to understand part of it is likely attributed to your physical biology.

One suggestion is to taper off your intense training schedule and commit to a doable weekly workout regimen. Go from 10 practices a week as an active athlete to 7 workouts, then 5 workouts, then maybe 2-3 workouts a week like a normal human. I'm not a medical doctor nor scientist, but my hypothesis is that tapering down your workout frequency rather than cutting cold turkey will help manage the chemical imbalance you experience when you suddenly depart from a world with flowing amounts of serotonin and dopamine to a world with much less of those hormones.

I would also consult with a doctor regarding additional supplements or nutrients that may help with low serotonin levels or hormonal imbalances. B-complex is great for overall brain function as "research shows that B vitamins support just about every aspect of brain health."[3] Other supplements such as GABA (Gamma aminobutyric acid) can also be helpful to support a healthy mind. "When GABA attaches to a protein in your brain known as a GABA receptor, it produces a calming effect. This can help with feelings of anxiety, stress, and fear."[4] Again, I am not a medical doctor, so consult a medical professional before adding new elements to your health routine.

I wish I could offer more concrete advice and evidence that looks into how our biology is affected with endorphin crashes after years if not decades in sport, but in writing this book I struggled to find credible scientific sources. But simply being aware that our moods are directly affected by chemical imbalances can help us make sense of why we might feel the way we do. (If you have supporting work or knowledge in this space, please reach out as I would love to hear from you).

A new exercise program and supplements will help replace the stress outlet of sport you've relied on for years, but be conscientious of how you plan to manage stress when stressful situations inevitably arise and you don't have your pool, field or mat to release daily tension. Do you journal? Do you light a candle? Yoga? Do you retreat by yourself or gravitate toward others? How else can you ensure you have a healthy outlet to relieve stress?

For me, two things I revert to always work to relieve stress. The first is to verbally process the situation and my feelings of stress about the situation. I've mentioned my use of the Voice Memos app on my smartphone, and you can try this for yourself as well. I open the app, press record and just word-dump everything in my head. "I'm stressed about…", "The worst thing that can happen is XYZ, which is highly unlikely and not that bad…", "I wonder if I do ABC how that might change the way I feel…", etc. I acknowledge the stress I'm feeling and I just talk to myself and verbally process what's going on. Doing this helps lighten the load I feel in my head and, for some reason, hearing myself talk out the situation helps open blind spots of things I may not have initially seen. Similar to journaling with pen and paper, voice memos are a great way to release the stress of a situation by getting it out of your head and looking at the situation as a whole.

The second thing I like to do is rather simple and understated. I like to walk or sit by a creek/river and envelop myself in nature. The first reason why I like to do this is because it engages my senses (sight - beautiful green trees and glimmering water, sound - rushing water & wind blowing, touch - barefoot in the grass, smell - clean air and scents from grass, trees, leaves, etc.) Engaging your senses with the sights, sounds, touch, and smell of nature has an incredibly calming effect that couldn't be more human on planet earth. It's simply human to respond to nature, and although our lives are overrun with endless electronic devices, metal, screens and sophisticated technology we are still made of flesh. We still have a heartbeat. We are still a species part of many ecosystems that make up the fire, water, air and earth that is our planet, and "time in nature results in a sense of belonging to the wider world that is vital for mental health."[5] If you haven't seen Zac Efron's documentary series on Netflix, *Down to Earth*, check out episode two where he and his film partner, Darin Olien (a health and wellness expert), take their shoes off and walk around barefoot in a field of grass in France.[6] Zac is reluctant at first.

Zac Efron: What are you doing? Are you barefoot?

Darin Olien: Yeah. I want to get my feet on the ground. It's a new country, all that travel. Don't you feel like you got to just get connected?

Zac: I'm very connected.

Darin: Dude, you're missing out I'm telling you. This feels so good. Take your bloody shoes off. I promise, if you take them off and it doesn't feel good you can put them back on.

Zac - *takes shoes off * How do you say poison oak in French?

Darin: You got to get the electromagnetic connection to the earth again. It will help your circadian rhythm. Tell me it doesn't feel good.

Zac, indeed, felt good. Something about feeling, seeing, touching, tasting and smelling the very planet to which we belong has a visceral, calming effect that we can't always describe in words. Tapping into nature's calming effect is so underestimated and therapeutic, not only for when we're feeling periods of stress but just for rooting ourselves in our basic human desire of being connected to the earth.

We will continue to dive deeper into self-discovery to better figure out what works best for you when it comes to relieving stress, but ask yourself - if I don't have my typical sports outlet to release stress from my life, how am I going to release that tension?

Celebrate

It is so important to take a breath and celebrate your journey. You poured so much of yourself into your sport and your sport returned the favor, gifting you life lessons, connecting you with lifelong friends and granting you amazing experiences that others simply cannot understand. You've also felt the lows - when you didn't make the team, when you sprained your ankle and were benched for a season and when you temporarily fell out of love with the sport, never wanting to go to practice again. Whatever your journey looks like for you, the wild ride filled with a rollercoaster of experiences will carry with you for the rest of your life. Don't take that for granted and celebrate your participation!

Sports take work. Training takes work. It is not easy to thrive in elite competition, and your soul deserves gratitude for the sheer amount of effort you've dedicated to your sport. Have you ever explained your training schedule to someone, and their jaw dropped when you started listing practice sessions and you weren't even halfway done? To us, that world seems normal. Relentless dedication is expected, and when we're going through it, we don't often realize exactly how dedicated and hard-working we really are. The level of effort required to not only compete at your optimal level but to compete with the optimal levels of everyone else requires time, focus and a whole bunch of effort, as you already know. So, even if you never lift a finger for the rest of your life, commend yourself for the full accumulation of all your attended practices, training sessions, meets or tournaments you participated in. While it may not faze us in the moment, retrospectively expressing gratitude for your effort opens your eyes to how much hard work you put forth and how much you deserve a pat on the back.

Celebrate how much you've grown. Thinking back to the very first day you stepped on the field (probably as a mere child) you covered a lot of ground both literally and figuratively to arrive where you are today. There is no sweeter journey in life than becoming a master at your craft, so congratulate yourself for how far you've come. Honestly, you can probably do things with your body that others would only dream of doing. Look at how much you grew, both on the court and in your heart. Look at everything sport gave you - the life lessons of persistence, gratitude, and sportsmanship. You did it all. Celebrate yourself and enjoy the tremendous amount of progress you have accomplished in your career.

For the first time in your life, there is no pressure to perform or "be someone". There is no practice you must attend. There are no strict dietary guidelines. There are no coaches breathing down your back. All the restrictions, requirements and forbidden behaviors have now lifted from your life. Ah, what a relief! Take a moment to enjoy the feeling of lighter shoulders and relaxation. Also take a moment to eat that chocolate cake or indulge in the fried chicken you had to avoid during training. It can be quite comforting to know your life will be a bit more relaxed here on out. Enjoy the calm.

At this point, it does not matter how your career ended. What matters is expressing well-deserved gratitude and appreciation of your journey. Celebrating the totality of your effort demonstrates self-love and self-kindness, ongoing practices to focus on in your new season. Heck, do I need to say more here? You've done the hard work for most of your life, and you deserve celebration.

Counseling

Every athlete who is new to retirement should consider attending counseling/therapy. Oh no, I said the word "therapy". You may have preconceived notions about counseling, you may totally resist the idea of finding a therapist, or you may think you don't really need it and can withstand the fluctuations that a totally new life brings you. I hate to break it to you, but you're probably wrong. Your sport has been part of who you are for years, if not decades. To think you are going to simply hang up your cleats and move on seamlessly into a new part of your life without any growing pains is naive. I apologize if this sounds patronizing or harsh, but I'm stating this strongly because I have seen the alternative of not tending to the retirement transition properly and, let me tell you, it is far from fun. To undergo such a paradigm shift that is retirement with no guardrails or guidance can easily spiral down to a despairingly lost and uncooperative mind. Eliciting the help of a counselor to navigate the moments you feel down, the moments you feel confusion, the moments you feel frustration or pain, will simply allow the transition into your new normal to be much easier and will leave you with a healthy foundation to write the next chapter of your life. It requires effort on your part to reach out and seek help and Erin Reifsteck, an Assistant Professor in the University of North Carolina Greensboro Department of Kinesiology and founder of the *Moving On! Foundation,* puts it perfectly when she states, "The research suggests that proactive coping is really important. So, not waiting until after you're experiencing the transition to deal with it, but to have some pre-retirement planning."[2]

A counselor is a coach for your mind with the ability to diagnose disorders such as anxiety, ADHD and depression, among others. Counselors offer suggestions, life frameworks, new perspectives and help you dig into your own life's questions to find meaningful conclusions and answers. Sitting down and speaking with a professionally trained counselor versed in the world of mental health and knowledgeable about many coping strategies is one of the best health investments you can do for yourself. In my experience, I've had counselors that were not athletes and were extremely unhelpful while others changed my life. You will vibe with certain counselors and will not vibe with others; that is okay. Depending on who is available to you, seeking out a sports psychologist may help expedite the understanding of your situation as someone focused on the sports world will understand the environments you've experienced. Or maybe you want to start with a blank slate, explaining your athlete life to someone who has no preconceived notions about what it means to be an athlete. Try, explore, and discover what feels right to you.

Books, podcasts, websites, and organizations can relate to your situation and offer insights that could really help you. But what these modes of communication lack is a specificity on what exactly it is *you* are feeling and what *you* are going through. Specificity is an unmatched benefit you can only find with a counselor, explaining the exact details of what weighs on your life, mind and soul. You can talk about a specific coach that pissed you off, you can talk about the exact race or game that ended your career or you can talk about how your family is not as supportive as you hoped during your retirement. A counselor is there to listen to exactly what it is you are experiencing and can offer tangible strategies to work through your internal and external struggles. Being able to talk about the details, dig into your specific situation, and uncover wisdom that is directly relevant to your life is an invaluable asset of seeing a counselor.

Counselors can be expensive, especially if you don't have insurance or your insurance plan doesn't cover those services. If you can't afford counseling, a free, easy, and surprisingly helpful way to connect with others and talk about what you're going through is voicing your experience to strangers on the internet. Yes, strangers on the internet. More specifically, on Reddit. If you're not familiar with Reddit, it is a discussion website with different forums (called subreddits) based on topics of interest. There are subreddits for almost everything - baking, personal finance, alcoholism, comedy, crypto-currency, the list goes on. The wonderful thing about Reddit is you can post anonymously to a subreddit and other users can chime in with their thoughts, opinions and advice. As an example, there is a particular subreddit called "Am-I-the-Asshole" in which users ask if they are the asshole in a particular situation to solicit third-party opinions. Am I the asshole for changing my Netflix password and not telling my roommate? Questions like that.

There are a number of subreddits for personal growth and seeking help during difficult times. /self-help /depression /off-my-chest /too-afraid-to-ask /self-improvement /un-sent-letters. You can search for yourself to see if there is a forum that exists for any particular topic you'd like to see. There really is an underrated and generally undiscovered benefit of soliciting advice or simply posting your experience to strangers on the internet. The nice thing about this is it is completely anonymous. No one knows who you are, where you live, or how much money you make. You can completely shed your emotional distress anonymously online and you might be pleasantly surprised at the feedback and responses you get. Someone may relate to exactly what you're going through and could offer extremely helpful advice on how they got through it. Someone may point you in the direction of a book or movie or podcast that talks about exactly what you posted. For these personal subreddits, there usually aren't trolls leaving rude comments, but alas it is the internet, and it can happen so be wary of the rare user posting a spiteful comment just to get attention.

However you seek guided help, through counseling or on the internet, ensure someone is on the other end hearing what you have to say. As humans, we crave being seen, heard, and understood. Imagine a situation where something crazy happened in your life and nobody understood what you were talking about. Maybe Muhammad Ali stopped you on the sidewalk, reincarnated, and told you the world was going to end in one year. You swore it was really him, and, for the purpose of this example, let's say it really was. But, when you ran and told your friends they laughed in your face or suggested you start medication. Then you ran to your family. They expressed concern and asked if everything was alright. No matter where you turned or who you desperately tried to tell, no one believed you or even listened to your full story. You were not heard. You were not understood. Inside, you were boiling with no way to release emotions, leaving you with maddening frustration and exasperated attempts to tell somebody. You can imagine how this could affect your mental health, your life perspective, and maybe even create lasting feelings of apathy. Don't suffer in silence. Create opportunities for yourself to express what you're going through and have that expression heard and understood. If this is not a common practice in your life, you will be amazed at how simple acknowledgement by others of your emotions can be so freeing.

Part of being heard and understood is our ability to express feelings with descriptive vocabulary. Imagine that the words "stress" or "depression" didn't exist. How would we communicate how we feel? Think back to our example about being diagnosed with the flu. We may feel a certain way but without accurate language or understanding to articulate those feelings, we would be stuck in frustration. It would be so incredibly difficult to define our emotional state, the first step we need to take to work our way through it. Take time and thought to think of what it is you're feeling and work with a counselor to support you throughout the transition into a life post-sport.

Volunteer

Right away, the very thing that gave us purpose - our sport - is gone. The fastest and healthiest way to root yourself in purpose is to help others. Depending on where you are in your own life journey, you may have already unlocked this life lesson long ago. Doing for others, serving others, making the lives of others easier is in a lot of ways a reason for being here on this earth. Take me for example. I find a tremendous amount of purpose in writing this book in the hopes that it may help another athlete struggling with the same challenges I struggled with.

In 1996 Agassi helped a friend's child attend college by paying his tuition with shares of Nike stock. His thoughts on helping his friend go as follows: "This is the only perfection there is, the perfection of helping others. This is the only thing we can do that has any lasting value or meaning. This is why we're here. To make each other feel safe." He goes on to explain another situation in which his trainer's daughter was suffering from an illness, writing:

A look of pure relief, and gratitude, and joy, washes over her face, and in this look, in this courageous little girl, I find the thing I've been seeking, the philosopher's stone that unites all the experiences, good and bad, of the last few years. Her suffering, her resilient smile in the face of that suffering, my part in easing her suffering - this, this is the reason for everything. How many times must I be shown? This is why we're here. To fight through the pain and, when possible, to relieve the pain of others. So simple. So hard to see. (Agassi, 2010).

As athletes, we get stuck in the importance of ourselves and our performance. To us, performing at an elite level is our whole world and most people in our ecosystem share the same view. When we aren't an athlete anymore and are taken out of that performance-first, self-centered mindset, we have an opportunity to see that there is so much more to life outside of sport. There is so much good that can be done for others, ways to make an impact greater than any first-place finish could ever do.

Adyashanti, a spirituality teacher, beautifully comments on the acts of service for others:

"One of the beautiful things about service is that we are simultaneously taking part in the well-being of ourselves. This points to something essential about service: when it comes from an overflow and a sharing of inner abundance, it is enriching and life affirming - not only for us, but for anybody involved in whatever we are trying to serve."[7]

Volunteering for others not only allows you to put life into perspective, but selfishly it's a great way to get out of your own head. Sometimes when we feel like we're struggling or down or experiencing depression, putting those emotions aside for a minute and serving others can ground you and show you what truly matters on this planet. If we are in that down moment or period of life, it's emotionally exhausting trying to work our way through it. It is simply not fun. Being able to shift our focus from our pain and struggle and pay attention to serving others and improving their lives removes the burden we feel from our own pain, even if temporarily, and fills our heart with compassion.

Don't let me preach it to you; try it for yourself. Check out local volunteer organizations, food banks, homeless shelters, schools, and many other opportunities. Sign up for one event. Serve the community. And soak in the relief of putting your ego aside, putting your pain aside, and changing people's lives. Go forth and volunteer.

Treat Retirement as a Form of Death

Retirement is a form of death. Although none of us wish for death, the unforeseen challenge of losing an identity - whether it be a professional athlete, a leading hedge fund manager in Wall Street, a top chef in Shanghai - is that you still exist in your body and must continue to live on finding a new 'you'. Objectively, one might say how liberating and freeing to be anyone you want to be. How cool. And, in a sense, that is true. But this is also incredibly overwhelming when your teeth have sunk so deep into a particular identity and all of a sudden your jaw is ripped away. How, then, do you build a new 'you' after you've contextualized everything in your life up until this point from the view of being 'the athlete'?

To process the death of your identity you must appropriately grieve the loss. Just as we grieve the death of others, we must also allow space to grieve the death of our athlete identity. This doesn't mean we will never self-identify as an athlete (we likely will for the rest of our lives) nor does it mean we totally wipe our brains of that part of our life. Not at all. We will always keep with us the memories of standing on the podium and we might even play a pick-up game here and there. Our medals will still be in our house and our grandchildren one day might ask us how in the world we beat that one person that one time.

You don't have to dress in black and sulk for a year. But, actively recognize that your identity is changing and you are evolving. According to an article in The Gazette, athlete retirement is "the psychological equivalent of losing a loved one, but very few know a healthy way to grieve it."[8] It doesn't matter if you were an Olympian, a collegiate player or a sophomore in high school that just decided to quit. You built an attachment to your sport, and you built an identity around that attachment. Undoing that identity attachment requires active mental effort and an acceptance that a part of you is now past tense. Glossing over or not fully processing this transition leaves heavy knots that sit inside you and can negatively permeate to other relationships and aspects of your life until they are resolved. So how can we process our grief?

According to experts, grief has 5 stages.[9] Take some time to think about these as they relate to your own retirement.

1. Denial - used to help us "minimize the overwhelming pain of loss"

Understand that not wanting to believe what happens is a coping mechanism that allows us to deal with the pain.

Example: We may still put on our team shirt every morning.

2. Anger - characterized by "extreme emotional discomfort"

Let it out in a healthy way by exercising, journaling, or talking about your feelings. Hire a coach, go to therapy, scream in a pillow, cry, blast music, etc.

Example: We may lash out at loved ones or self-criticize.

3. Bargaining - We might feel so "desperate that you are willing to do almost anything to alleviate or minimize the pain."

Reframe, use positive thinking. "I now have limitless options on what I can explore in my new life."

Example: We think about making a comeback.

4. Depression - The "emotional fog begins to clear and the loss feels more present and unavoidable"

Let it out in a healthy way, by exercising, journaling, or talking about your feelings. Again, hire a coach, go to therapy, scream in a pillow, cry, blast music, etc.

Example: We may want to lay in bed or avoid social events.

5. Acceptance - "We are no longer resisting the reality of our situation"

Example: Write a closure letter to your sport and root yourself in reality by saying affirmations or true statements - "I am no longer a swimmer" and "I am more than my athlete identity". Don't just highlight the good stuff.

In the final stage- acceptance - reminding yourself to not just remember the good story is critical to root yourself in reality. When something ends (a career, a relationship, etc.) our minds grasp for the good things we are missing because we know that we will no longer be able to experience those again. Have you ever gone through a breakup with someone where you notice you only miss the good parts about him/her as you're moving through the heartbreak? We often skip over the negative experiences out of our subconscious desire to feel sorry for ourselves. Read on to understand why we shouldn't just indulge the good parts about being an athlete, rooting yourself in the reality of the whole picture.

Stop Indulging Just the "Fun" Story

At first, the middle-aged business person action figure isn't too appealing. We don't want to go to work, we want to go to practice. We don't want to give a business presentation, we want a competition. Our minds are still stuck in the thick of being an athlete. We want to go back to those rewarding feelings of winning and beating the competition. We want to go back to the thrill of the journey of becoming the best. We want to go back to that life where we know exactly what to do and when to do it.

But when you retire, you aren't just walking away from the glory moments. You aren't just walking away from first place finishes. You're walking away from the heartbreaking moments, too. The times you puked on the pool deck, the resentment after your coach screams at you, the pain you feel in your legs after practice. The season you worked your butt off and didn't improve at all. The time you blew out your shoulder. The competition that ruined a friendship. I'm not saying you should focus on all the negative events in your journey, but be fair to your mind. Don't just indulge the podiums and medals and good times when that is only half the picture. Stop indulging just the "fun" story of your career. When you retire, you're also walking away from the darker moments that pain you.

Also, have you ever considered the opportunity cost of all those hours of training? Have you ever considered that you may have missed out on amazing lifelong friendships because you were always on the field? What would you be doing today if you never participated in sport in the first place? This is not an exercise in regret or "what if". This is simply a reality check - a reminder to calibrate your brain with the real story. Rather than allow your mind to run amok only grieving the good parts of sport, gently pull yourself back and find a bit of sweetness in the fact that you are also saying goodbye to the painful moments as well.

Closure

Playing our sport for years, we've built a relationship with the sport itself. There are things we love about it, hate about it, and things we wish were different. If we competed during some of our most transformative years during childhood, we probably associate monumental life events with our sport. When we first got our driver's license one of the first places we drove was practice. Maybe we remember practices that offered emotional release when something else was causing trouble in our lives, such as the death of a family member or a huge fight with a friend. Conversely, we probably associate positive highlights in our life with a particular tournament or game-winning point. When our sport is such a large, intertwined presence in our life we build an attachment to the actual sport itself.

Just as we seek closure when relationships end, people pass away or large transitions happen in our lives, during retirement we also seek closure when we close the competition chapter of our book. But how do you seek closure with your sport? It's not like you can sit down with "soccer" and have a conversation about how things are ending and thank "soccer" for all the lessons learned. No, but what you can do is personify the sport by writing a letter to express what you desire for your own closure. This is going to sound a little crazy, but you might be amazed at how light your mind feels after doing this exercise.

First, write a letter to your sport. Get out pen and paper or the keys on your keyboard and just let it flow. Tell your sport thank you. Tell your sport how it was there or wasn't there for you when you were a kid. Thank your sport for all the friends and people you've met along the journey. Express anything and everything you want to tell your sport now that you're in a transition of moving away from it. Doing this helps free up your emotional attachments to the sport by simply getting thoughts of your head and down on paper. Your letter can also highlight areas that may be more difficult for you to process. If you keep going back to a particular game or match that you should have won and you express frustration over how things played out, that is a moment in time you should probably reflect on and untangle. Writing a letter to your sport helps clear your mind and opens opportunities to move forward with clarity and acceptance.

After you've written a letter to your sport, I want you to get up and change seats. Now, you are going to assume the identity of your sport and write a letter back to yourself. Yes, your roommates or significant other or parents will think you are crazy. But it is amazing how doing this exercise offers an emotional release. You are being so kind to yourself and gifting yourself the words you wish you could hear. In the letter from your sport to yourself, write out everything you wish a personified version of your sport would tell you. When you do this, you will resolve emotional hang-ups, just as a masseuse presses on a knot in your back and after a few moments of pressure it loosens and disappears. Even though it's not real, the simple act of expression for things you want to say and things you want to hear resolves snags in your process of moving forward.

This exercise only works when you are 100% honest and transparent with yourself; don't hold anything back. No one is going to read these letters unless you choose to share them. Here are my letters to and from the sport of swimming, as examples:

Dear Swimming,

Thank you for being such a huge part of my life. I could have chosen soccer or softball, but I'm so glad I chose you. I am a strong and wildly capable person today because of all the experiences, both good and bad, you brought into my life. I genuinely view the rest of my life as smooth sailing because, man, training and competing and handling all the emotions of racing were enough to last me the rest of my life. I don't need any more!

I think what I am especially grateful for is how you allowed me to reach a potential and greatness in something to show me and others what I can really do. I have had so many races and practices where I pushed myself beyond my limits to reach the next level. I still remember that one morning practice we had a kick set with fins and my fins were too small. I pushed through the entire set and only when I finished did I notice the torn skin and blood around my ankles. I think I still have scars from that day. I swam times I never knew I could do, and I improved so much over the course of our 14-year relationship. When I started as a baby, five-year-old I was just doing what my parents told me to do, but as I got older I became one of the top swimmers and am grateful for that feeling of being accomplished in something. Thank you for allowing me the space to progress, grow and become good at something.

I am so grateful for the coaches you've brought into my life. My coaches have always looked out for me, both in and out of the pool, and you don't understand how safe that made me feel in my life. My one desire was to be the best swimmer I could be, and my coaches were dedicated to seeing me and my teammates reach those goals. I've had a good number of emotional breakdowns, whether it be performance anxiety or upset because I didn't make a certain team or swim a certain time. Many times I've sat in a folding chair on the pool deck after a race, towel wrapped around me and cried. And you know who was always by my side? My coach. Thank you for showing me how a mentor - a coach - can create such a lasting, positive impact on my heart and my life. My coaches are examples of how I want to help younger athletes achieve their potential.

I am so blessed that you brought teammates into my life. My teammates/ friends have such a strong bond, having to enter war every time we go to practice or swim at meets. Without saying a word, we understand the pain, the grind, the euphoria and all the other emotions on the spectrum of an athlete that we are going through. Nothing is quite like that effortless understanding. Without my friends, especially my friend Shannon, I probably would have quit the sport long ago. Thank you for bringing my amazing friends, and their amazing families, into my life.

Thank you for the crazy, indescribable meets I've competed at in my life. We train to compete and the swim meets are where the magic happens. I can't tell you how fun it was to travel to Savannah, GA for the state meet and wait on the pool deck for hours until it was time for my heat to swim. While waiting, my teammates and I played every card game under the sun, wrote sharpie on each other's skin, and snacked on cold pasta. We would go out to eat at Olive Garden or another carbo-load restaurant and then run up and down the halls of the hotel, pranking the other guests with a random knock and running away (sorry Holiday Inn). It was so fun to show off our hard work and jump off the starting blocks, swimming as fast as we could to show our parents, friends, and coaches just how fast we could go. One of my favorite, and biggest meets, I've swam in was the 2007 Southeastern Zone Championships in Houston, Texas. I made finals in my favorite event, the 50m free, and was standing behind the starting blocks waiting for the referee to blow her whistle. I have never been more nervous for something in my life. I wanted to win so bad. The whole Georgia team was standing on the side of the pool deck, cheering and watching as the race was about to begin and I wanted nothing more than to bring home the gold medal. I told myself to only breathe one time during the race to not slow me down. After the long whistle, all eight of us 14-year-old girls stepped up on the blocks and prepared for the 'beep'. "Swimmers, take your mark - BEEP!" We were off and I swam blindly all the way to the wall, immediately yanking my neck behind to look up at the scoreboard. I won. I won! I won by .01 seconds. I barely won. Lol. But I won. I remember just barely scraping by Megan Fonteno from Florida, who got second place by .01 seconds. Phew! That was close, but I was so happy to win. I looked over to my team and everyone was jumping up and down, cheering at the top of their lungs. That is one of my favorite moments you gave me. Thank you swimming.

While this short letter couldn't possibly encompass every experience, every moment, and every relationship that changed my life, I just want to say thank you for the ride. I've had some of the best moments in my life and some of the worst moments in my life because of you. Growing up in such an incredibly intense world of competition feels unique, as if you and I have this little secret of an alternate universe that not many others can relate to. I love that. It makes me, "me". Having experienced the highs and lows over the course of 14 years, I feel like you've given me a level of compassion and understanding that allows me to help others in impactful ways. You've put me through a lot, good gracious. Even though you've brought me to my knees at times, I wouldn't have my experience any other way because I am who I am today because of every moment.

Thank you, Swimming. I am forever grateful for everything we have been through.

Kim

Here is my letter from Swimming back to myself:

Dear Kim,

I am so proud of you. You have accomplished so much. You have grown so much. I know I threw some curveballs and tough moments your way, but you handled them and made it through - coming out even stronger on the other side. I am so impressed by your strength.

I know you might feel like you didn't reach your full potential. You might have wanted to go on to win at NCAAs or even make the Olympic team. Sure, those are nice milestones but they aren't what the journey is all about. As a human being, your goal on this earth is to maximize enjoyment, happiness and growth while you're here. Gold medals speak to a moment in time, not of the total journey of "becoming". It is okay if you didn't become world's number 1 - swimming for you is designed as an outlet to showcase progress and accumulate life lessons, not solely to win. Plus, I knew if I made your journey hard enough and pushed you to the edge, your experience in those moments would set you up for a blissful rest of your life. I know it was challenging to not make Olympic trials when all your friends did. I know it was challenging to not make the ACC team. I know it was challenging to work your entire life for something and then feel like you came up short. You hardly came up short, Kim. The wisdom you've accumulated, the friends you've made, and the opportunities you've been given because you were once a swimmer are far more valuable than any medal could offer. And, if this makes you feel any better there are a lot more losers than there are winners. Every heat, only 1 girl wins and 7 have to lose. So, just know that your journey was about teaching you, growing you, shaping you. It was never about being the all-time best.

Sometimes I hear you say that swimming isn't a fun sport and you wouldn't recommend it to kids if they had to choose. I wish you didn't have this view of me. I know I require a bit more time and attention than other sports. With me, you can't practice 6 times a week and be great; you need to practice 8-10 times a week plus dryland and additional weightlifting sessions. Additionally, there aren't many sports that require you to train and compete in a totally different earthly element - water - and because of that I understand I'm a bit more challenging than other sports. That being said, don't you think it is also pretty cool how good you became in swimming despite these challenges? If it were easy, anyone could do it. I know I'm not for everyone, but wouldn't you rather achieve great things in extenuating circumstances than be handed medals with little effort? I hope you appreciate your own dedication and sacrifice and understand that others might also enjoy the challenge and incredible reward of excelling in those challenging environments.

I have loved watching you grow, break records, smile and cry. I remember when your suit split right down your butt at a meet and you were so embarrassed and ran to the locker room. I remember when you got your period for the first time at practice and blood ran down your legs and all the guys laughed at you. I remember when you crushed everyone at practice, even when you outswam the distance swimmers as a sprinter. I remember when you relentlessly showed up to morning practice, put in the work, and then headed to school. I remember when you ate 6 bagels after practice because you worked that hard and were so hungry. I remember it all. The good, the bad, the ugly, the beautiful. Like a really good movie, your journey was beautiful - filled with turns of events, complete despair and total elation. Gosh, I am just so proud of your resilience and strength.

Kim - I know I am part of your past and you will go on to live a wonderful life without me. I hope you sometimes get back in the pool even if for a 500-yard swim. Remember that everything we did together made you the person you are today. Take the good parts of me with you and never forget the lessons you learned.

I am so proud of you and honored that you chose me.

Love,
Swimming

A secondary layer for writing letters and reflecting on your career is to practice forgiveness to reach total resolution. In your letters, certain moments in your career came up, so examine why they were the moments you highlighted. Which moments did you write down first? What about those moments holds you back? Take a moment to explore how you can practice forgiveness around those moments. This forgiveness doesn't have to be in response to something that is "wrong" or a bad thing someone did to you, it can simply be "replacing the negative emotions with positive attitudes".[10] For me, I might say I forgive the situation of not making the Olympic trial cut. It is normal to feel disappointment in that situation, and I understand that I achieved so many other goals and life milestones. I could hold internal grudges around all the reasons I should have swam faster and placed blame on others, but I don't hold that inside me and, instead, I forgive and take with me the positives - the strength and experience - it gave me.

After these exercises, how can you tell if you've reached closure? How can you tell if you still have blocks preventing you from living a new life after sport? When someone at a cookout asks "oh, you played [sport], wow! What was that like?" Your immediate thoughts and behaviors will tell you all you need to know. How do you answer them? Do you sigh and look at the ground? Do you perk up and smile? What's the first thing you say? Practice speaking your answer in the mirror and notice spots in your response that lean to the negative. Then, explore why. Dig into what is preventing you from untangling the knot. Most likely, it is a lack of acceptance of something, but pay attention to how you speak about your career to others to gauge how well you've reached closure on retirement.

Patience

No offense, but you might not be the greatest at normal life. You've spent years conditioning your body and mind to be a highly performing sports weapon. It will take time to undo those conditioned wires and rebuild different views of yourself outside of sport. Practice patience while you are rewiring because internal transformative work takes time. Going from such a unique, combat-like world of athletic competition to the ordinary and often mundane world of regular adult life can be unexpectedly shocking. Areas where you sought validation, such as practice and tournaments and games, suddenly vanish and there is discomfort in growing accustomed to a world with less concrete nods of approval. Suffering in retirement can sneak up on you, and many athletes struggle to shift their mindset to a healthy life-view and self-view after they finish sports for good.

Practicing patience with yourself through this identity transformation gives you the time and capacity to build a strong foundation for your new life. You might notice certain thoughts cross your mind such as "I'm not working out enough" or "I'm lazy" or "I don't have any goals anymore" or whatever it is you might be telling yourself. You might judge your behaviors, your conversations or even your own thoughts. Stop. Your life is in a transition period right now. There is enough going on to deal with on its own and your impatience and judgements will just slow down and impede your growth. Grant yourself kindness, patience and understanding that things won't be perfect and you may experience rough days, just as everyone does in this game called life. So, how do you best practice patience? Release and accept.

Release expectations. Release deadlines. Release unrealistic ideals. Contrary to popular belief, things actually don't have to be a certain way. We construct certain ideals and beliefs based on what society tells us is right, what our parents say is good and what everyone else is doing. That doesn't make those ideals and beliefs right, neither does it make those right for you. We don't have to be 23 years old with the perfect job right out of college. We don't have to be making six-figures by the time we're 30, 40 or ever. We don't have to suddenly wake up after we've retired and be totally resolved of our past life as a competition machine even if that is true for another athlete. There are no deadlines or precise protocols to follow in life; everyone is different, every journey is different, and everyone is at a different point along their journey. When you can release those preconceived beliefs that you need to be doing things a certain way right now (such as immediately and always feeling good and fine and successful and perfect) you automatically create acceptance in your life.

Acceptance, acceptance, acceptance. Accept things just how they are, as they are. Things aren't supposed to be better. Things aren't supposed to be worse. They are exactly as they should be right now. This concept derives from the Four Pillars that Buddhism is based upon. I highly suggest learning about Buddhism, not even from a religious perspective but from a practical, life view, existence perspective. Releasing your desire for your life to be different and accepting your life exactly as it is right now helps rid unnecessary stress, frustrations, and anxiety. It is the friction we feel in desiring our desires that creates dissatisfaction in our lives. I encourage you to lay in bed at night and think about what is going in your life that causes you tension or anxious thinking. Do you feel out-of-shape because you aren't doing 10 workouts a week? Do you feel out-of-the-loop because your friends are getting jobs or doing cool things and you're just at home? Are you looking back on your career and creating negative tension by wishing your career played out much differently?

One exercise to practice acceptance is through mirror work and daily affirmations. It may feel silly when you do it but stand in front of a mirror, look yourself in the eyes, and say your list of affirmations out loud in response to things you find harder to accept. Say: I am more than my athlete identity. I am strong. I am smart. I am healthy. I will practice patience with myself today. I'm a nice person. I am a good person. I have a healthy body. My future has so much to look forward to.

Create your own daily affirmations that make sense for you. Don't just write them down, look at yourself in the mirror and say them out loud. Why? The underlying psychology here is that your limbic system, the part of your brain responsible for creating memories and responding with fight or flight, does not know the difference between fake and real.[11] So, I can stand in front of the mirror, look at myself and say Kim you're worthless and stupid. My brain will take that at face value, seeing my lips move and hearing those words my brain will deem it as true. If I did that enough times to create that neural pathway I would believe that I was worthless and stupid. Your senses - taste, touch, smell, sight, sound - take in cues and signals from the environment to create a memory which is why actually looking at yourself and speaking your affirmations out loud helps rewire your brain with those positive affirmations accepting the things in your life that may feel harder to accept.

Patience is not only patience with yourself but with others in your life. Not many people are going to directly understand what you're going through as you navigate your retirement transition. Conversations may elicit remarks about your career that you may feel sensitive about. People who have always perceived you as "the athlete" may not understand you as a normal human. Plus, people that were staples in your life because of your role as "the athlete" won't be as available to you like they once were. Coaches, trainers, nutritionists, and other supporting members will shift their focus from you to another athlete. External events, comments and the actions of other people that may elicit an emotional response from you are out of your control, so remind yourself to practice patience when things upset you. When they do, slow down and let yourself feel everything you're feeling. Then, dive deep into what exactly it is that made you upset about the situation so you can take action to resolve those feelings.

A great exercise to reach the root of a problem, or why certain words or events make you feel a certain way, is a questioning technique developed by Sakichi Toyoda and was used within the Toyota Motor Corporation. This technique was initially developed to monitor quality control in Toyota's manufacturing plants to help identify the root cause of an issue. It is known as the 'Five Whys', and simply requires you to ask the question "why?" five times to uncover the underlying issue.[12]

Problem: I'm upset because my mom made a comment about how she wishes I was still competing.

Why? Because she loves watching me compete and win and I don't race anymore.

Why? Because she gets joy out of watching me race and likes celebrating my wins with me.

Why? Because she wants the best for me and now that I don't compete I'm afraid I won't be able to give her joy.

Why? Because my whole life I've been an athlete and have been able to give her that joy of watching me race and now I don't know how else I can make her proud.

Why? Because I don't know what else I'm good at that would bring her the same joy as my athlete competition did.

In this case, I would say I uncovered an insecurity about not being great at something that my mom deems worthy. I may have feelings of letting her down and being viewed as inadequate. I can't control what others say or do nor am I responsible for her feelings, but to resolve this internal tension I feel I might want to sit down with her and explain how it makes me feel when I hear comments about not competing any longer.

Sometimes, it may only require three "whys" to reach a meaningful conclusion, but practicing the technique illuminates what it is that is really driving your emotion. When you can understand the underlying driver, you can proactively work to unpack that emotion and uncover ways to reach a resolution. The Five Whys is all about understanding. Feel free to Google the Five Whys and learn more about the technique for your own practice in patience.

Restrict Social Media

This is easy to say and hard to do. If you have previously watched the Netflix documentary, *Social Dilemma,* you will understand the positive psychology behind every detail designed to keep us coming back for more, including the like button.[13] I strongly suggest limiting or eliminating social media for a period in retirement. Sometimes it's okay to be selfish and focus on ourselves when we need it.

I think a lot of us already know or have heard about the harmful effects social media has on our psyche. Everyone seems happy, everyone seems good, and seeing those images can further alienate you if you're not feeling happy and good. Especially as you retire, you have teammates and friends that may still be competing, or maybe they're getting jobs, or they're embarking on a new chapter of their journey, whatever that may be. When you're at a point in your life where you're just trying to figure out what comes next or what drives you or where you can derive meaning in your life, comparing yourself to other people is detrimental to seeking answers that are true to you.

Conduct your own social media inventory of which apps you use and how you feel when you're using those apps. As an example, if you scroll through Facebook and notice that you feel insecure or anxious after viewing everyone else's photos, take a concerted effort to reduce the time you spend on Facebook. You can remove the app altogether or if you know there are specific people or pages that create these same angsty feelings, each platform has a way to mute or unfollow. Pick what you think might work for you - it doesn't have to be permanent.

One thing to consider when using social media is how influential the images and videos you expose yourself are on your life. Did you know that when you dream your mind does not reinvent faces? In our dreams we see real faces of real people that we have seen during our life.[14] It can be that you met them in person, it can be an actor you saw in a movie, or it can be a TikTok star. That last one actually happened to me, I downloaded Tik Tok, began scrolling through videos and came across a funny comedian. I watched a few of her videos and then, one night, her face was in my dream. I have never met her before and probably spent a total of 30 seconds looking at her content. It seems like a silly, simple example but what you expose yourself to has a real & direct impact on your life.

Why do you think you speak the English language? How is it that you can even understand what I'm writing right now? You could have easily been born in France and grew up speaking French. Your parents could have exposed you to French words like *"oui"* and not until you got older would you start to learn the word "yes". Everything you know and learn are things you are exposed to. UFC fighter, Justin Wren, posted a video of himself volunteering in the Congo where a group of kids saw a white man for the first time in their lives.[15] The kids had never seen someone of a different skin color and were giddy with laughter, petting his arm to touch skin that was so different than theirs. It's not that the kids aren't intelligent because they don't know that other skin colors exist, their knowledge is simply a byproduct of the environment they are in and what they're exposed to.

Limit social media. Not only is it a healthy practice for any human being but especially now as you're going through a huge life transition it is healthy to be more cautious of what you expose yourself to when emotions are fragile.

Perfectionism Out; Compassion In; Self-Worth Up

Get rid of your fear of failure, your tensions about succeeding, you will be yourself. Relaxed. You wouldn't be driving with your brakes on.
—Anthony de Mello

I like to envision the trifecta of eliminating perfectionism, practicing self-compassion, and feeling a strong sense of self-worth as a one-leads-to-the-next-leads-to-the-next effect. When you eliminate perfectionist thinking, you open space for self-compassion which then grows roots for worthiness.

When you've won gold medals during your career, perfectionism was your best friend. Now that you're taken out of the context of elite competition, perfectionism will kill you. Perfectionism is not sustainable. Perfectionism is exhausting. Perfectionism does not translate to regular, adult life and will create an unsatisfactory existence day after day. If you fail to scrub your athlete brain of competitive, perfectionist standards, you will forever suffer in disappointment.

To undo our perfectionist thinking, it is helpful to know what our perfectionism satisfies (outside of just winning). "Simply identifying the underlying beliefs that drive your perfectionist habit is a good step toward changing them."[16] For athletes, perfectionism exudes one main thing we are running toward and one main thing we are running from. The thing we are running toward is acceptance. The thing we are running from is mediocrity.

Athletes, just like most humans, want to feel accepted. We want to feel like we belong. Others want us. External validation. Feeling accepted into a community. Feeling that sense of belonging. In the sports world, the way to indisputably be accepted is to be the very best. To win. Being extraordinarily skilled in sports means we are good, valuable, worthy, cool, prized, unique and accepted. There is a self-worth theory that "posits that an individual's main priority in life is to find self-acceptance and that self-acceptance is often found through achievement. In turn, achievement is often found through competition with others. Thus, the logical conclusion is that competing with others can help us feel like we have impressive achievements under our belt, which then makes us feel proud of ourselves and enhances our acceptance of ourselves."[17]

I have to agree. This could be for any part of life, not just sport. If you're valedictorian of your class you feel worthy because you're smarter than everyone else. If you're CEO of a company you feel worthy because you have the experience to run a business. If your cake wins at the bake-off you feel worthy because you made a better cake than every other baker. The medals we bring home and the records we break are the pillars of what our sports environment tells us is worthy and acceptable. We then adopt that philosophy and only accept ourselves when we acquire accolades.

Consider Olympic gymnast, Aly Raisman. She talks about her self-worth being based on her performance and how that affects her life:

> And so I think…gymnastics is so amazing but one of the things I've struggled with is worrying so much about what other people think of me and people-pleasing because that's really a lot of the sport. Even if I feel I did my absolute best routine, but the judges think it was my worst routine that's the result that I have. So, it's really hard to dig in and look inside myself and be happy with who I am without other people worrying about me. I think the people-pleasing got a little too much for me. I became obsessive over worrying about what other people thought.[18]

You can see how an athlete, over reliant on external validation to feel accepted and worthy, experiences so much friction post-sport when we are no longer validating our self-worth based on the athletic achievements we have. We continue to look to the people around us to tell us we are good and when that no longer happens simply because we aren't competing anymore, we can spiral down into our insecurities and unhealthily grasping for acceptance wherever we find it.

On the other side of the coin, the strive for perfection is a constant run away from the thing that scares us the most in the whole word - mediocrity. For athletes, being average is worse than death. Our worst-case scenario is to never win first place, never break a record, never be deemed "a great player" and to just simply be a bystander in sport. Perfectionism challenges us in all the extreme ways necessary to avoid those mediocre outcomes. It is a harsh way to live with a critical inner talk track, but it works. These mediocre outcomes, our biggest fears of just being average, are so scary to us because in our performance-based, results-based, doing-based sports culture being average tells us we are not valuable. We are not worthy. You are only worthy when you score points. When you make the 3-pointer. When you throw him out at first base. When you stick the landing. When you beat everyone else. If you do anything else, you don't receive the time or attention the first-place person does. You know the name Michael Phelps but do you know the name Erik Vendt?

This isn't wrong or bad; this is simply sports. But it is important to distinguish how we've spent years validating our self-worth based on the things we accomplish in sport so that when we enter retirement we can develop modified self-worth practices more fitting for regular life.

Knowing that perfectionism served us in sport to grant us feelings of acceptance and self-worth while avoiding our biggest fear of mediocrity, let's begin the journey of undoing perfectionism and building healthy thought patterns in a post-sport life. A good reminder and baseline safety net for finding satisfaction despite how we, or others, perceive ourselves draws from one of our advice tidbits in Chapter 13 - always do your best. When you do the best you can, no more and no less, by default there isn't much space for you to refute any performance outcome or decision. To reiterate a thought from Miguel Ruiz (2018) - "By always doing your best, you will break a big spell that you have been under."

Doing your best and accepting your best, perfect or imperfect, requires a decent bit of self-compassion, a difficult and almost foreign concept to a harsh, critical, perfectionist athlete. Growing your self-compassion is the way forward to loosen your perfectionist standards and strengthen healthier patterns of building your self-worth. Self-compassion is defined as "being warm and understanding toward ourselves when we suffer, fail, or feel inadequate, rather than ignoring our pain or flagellating ourselves with self-criticism."[19] The most notable behavior to gauge your own self-compassion is to monitor your inner self-talk. What do you say to yourself when you feel like you're not good enough? What do you say to yourself when you make a mistake? Are you stuck on it for weeks or does the mistake roll off your back? To practice self-compassion, shower your mediocre moments with kindness and you'll see it's like spraying weed killer on your perfectionist thoughts. The very things your perfectionist brain tells you are not okay are exactly the things you welcome and love now. As a silly example, I messed up cooking a meal and it tastes bad.

I'm glad I tried this new recipe.
It's okay that I'm not the best chef; this was my first time.
I did my best.

It may feel weird to accept the average parts of ourselves but, hey, that's non-athlete human nature, baby. If you're struggling being kind to yourself, I encourage you to read about Brene Brown's research, including her book, *Daring Greatly*, where she shares a list of guideposts for Wholehearted Living. Wholehearted living is "a way of engaging with the world from a place of worthiness"[20], healing neglected areas of our self-concept, such as our self-worth. With fewer opportunities, if any, to showcase our abilities in retirement, we often struggle to figure out how to live in this way because, again, our sports culture conditioned us to base worth on results. We literally do not know where to turn to feel worthy. While Brene Brown's 10 guideposts to Wholehearted Living are helpful, we are going to look at the first two that happen to top the list:

1. Cultivating authenticity - **letting go of what other people think**
2. Cultivating self-compassion - **letting go of perfectionism**

If we know that letting go of what others think (and thus eliminating our external reliance on acceptance) and letting go of our athlete perfectionism (and thus overcoming our fear of being average) are the keys to breaking our perfectionist athlete curse, HOW DO WE ACTUALLY DO THAT?

This exercise is going to be uncomfortable for you, but I can't wait for you to do it. Quite simply, I want you to do the 180 degree opposite of what a validation-seeking, perfectionist athlete would do. Pick a day. Pick one day in your life. On this day, you are going to do the bare minimum. You are not going to go the extra mile. You are not going to help your boss or friend. You are going to "forget to set your alarm" and wake up late. You aren't going to do your hair. (Still brush your teeth though, please). You won't text your family and friends back (unless it's an emergency). You're going to eat that unhealthy food you always avoided during training. Anything that comes up where you can choose to just scrape by or do the bare minimum, I want you to choose that. If you normally respond to co-workers in under a minute, take five minutes before you hit "send". For a single day, I want you to live the most average, poor-performing day that you have ever lived. This does not mean you are going to be a mean person. Being mean is not the opposite of perfection. But deliberately choose to not fulfill the self-inflicted, perfectionist expectations that you think others have of you - on purpose. It is going to be uncomfortable. It is going to break your brain. It is going to feel like you're letting someone down. Do it. Do the bare minimum. You can afford to lose one day and, worst case scenario, the following day you can explain to your friend/boss/etc. that you were doing a social experiment.

After this day is over, lay in bed and reflect. What was the worst thing that happened? Your greatest fear of mediocrity - was that exposed? Were you negatively impacted by the day? How did it feel to do a poor job? Did you care what others thought? Did you do the bare minimum but still survive? Can you see how you're basing so much of yourself on what others think of you? On a scale of 1-10 how uncomfortable were you? What did you notice was your default talk track to yourself when you were running late or didn't meet expectations? How did you treat yourself? What was the worst part of the day? What was the best part of the day?

To break the curse of perfectionism, confront your fear of mediocrity head-on by being mediocre. Be average. Notice how dialing back your effort and perfectionist ideals is not the end of the world. You still survived the day, no? When you realize it's not the end of the world to be average, you'll see just how dissatisfying a perfectionist life truly is. You'll see just how harsh your athlete conditioning has made you on your own self. You'll see how you place so much weight of your self-worth on what others think of you. Why do you care if they think you're bad at something? No one is having the extreme level of self-berating thoughts about you that you have about yourself. Do you think someone else is laying in bed at night thinking, "Oh my gosh I cannot believe he did those things. He is such an incapable person. I can't believe he could be so stupid and bad." No. So when you feel insecure and worried about what others think of you, if they think you are "good at your job" or "smart" or fill-in-the-blank, they most likely are not.

Because we are the main character of our own show, our own life, we feel like everyone is focused on us. We feel like everyone sees every single inch of mistake we make. They don't. For the most part, people tend to be way more compassionate with others than they are with themselves. Do you berate someone else for making a mistake? Do you tear them down because they didn't do something right? The small details you beat yourself up over do not matter. Frankly, no one cares either. You said something stupid in a conversation? That person has already forgotten about it. You messed up a project at work? Let me tell you something - you aren't the first person in the world to mess something up. There are so many mess-ups in this game called life outside of sport that I can't even ascribe a number. Humans are humans and your mess up is barely, *barely*, even a drop in the bucket. Root yourself in reality that others aren't thinking about you or criticizing you in the ways you've become accustomed to criticizing yourself.

I know being "good" and not "great" clashes with everything inside your bones, but what are the negative ramifications of being "good" and not "great"? Are there real-world implications or is it just your self-inflicted self-esteem taking a hit? I'll tell you now, only one of those is within your control. Ultimately, you'll see how much unnecessary self-torture you're putting yourself through by beating yourself up to be perfect when the consequences of being average aren't all that bad, if there are any at all.

You can still strive for improvement in life. You can still strive to be good at things. This is not an exercise to "become bad" or to be an unreliable friend. This is an exercise to break our athlete-inflicted curse of perfectionism, opening opportunities to practice compassion where we would normally practice self-berating. When your business project was average and not record-setting, when you forgot to do something your friend asked you to do, when you inevitably fulfill behaviors that make up the species you are born into, speak to yourself with kindness - "It is okay I'm not perfect at this. How long have I been doing this again? I tried my best and that's all I can ask for. I'm authentically myself, another human being on this planet, and I'm not the best at every single thing in life. It is not the end of the world if I don't do everything 100% perfect all the time. I'm perfectly human."

The bigger picture of you and your worth: Whether you know this or not, you are somebody despite any number of medals or records or athletic abilities you possess. This is a simple reminder that you have a personality and character traits that are totally unrelated and untied to being an athlete. You were somebody before you even started your sport and you will be someone after you end your sport. Being an athlete is part of your life journey and a component of who you are, it is not the total identity of you. So even if your self-worth is in the gutter about being a retired athlete, sports is just one faucet and there are so many others you can turn on.

Think about your entire life span for a minute. Let's say, best-case-scenario you live to be 90 or 100 years old. Suppose, for example, that you started initially playing your sport at 7 or 8 years of age and continued doing so until you completed college. Let's also assume that on average you played sports for 15 years of your life. That still leaves you 60, 70, 80 other years of your life where you're not playing a sport. That is a lot of years to live as a non-athlete! But right now, if you've recently retired, most of your years on the earth have been characterized by your sports participation so it feels very intense. For me, as an example, I started swimming when I was five and retired when I was 19. When I retired, roughly 75% of my life on this Earth was being an athlete. That is a rather large percentage to try and unravel. But when you turn 80 or 90 or God bless 100 years old, you will look back on your sports participation and say, "Man that was cool!" but it will be a small chapter of who you are. By then, you will have had so many other life experiences, met so many other people, seen so many other places and lived so much more life that your perspective on being an athlete will be entirely different.

When you've broken the curse, you can even take your self-compassion practice to the next level by expressing explicit love and gratitude for every one of your human behaviors (I'm not calling them mistakes). "I forgot to make the appointment for today. Well, I'm actually glad I didn't do it yet because XYZ…" or "I can't believe I said that stupid thing. Well, I'm actually glad I said that because XYZ…". Welcome your human moments with open arms and use these moments as your lifelong practice of self-kindness and self-compassion, making your existence that much more beautiful and easy.

Go break the curse! Have an average day. Welcome those mediocre moments. Shower yourself with kindness when you would normally analyze how to improve. Not everything needs to be measured. Love that you are human, good at some things and bad at others. Do your best but not more than your best. Don't be afraid to fail at something and when you do, practice self-compassion when your inner talk track wants to beat you up. Let go of your reliance on others to make you feel worthy and accepted. Give those gifts to yourself by affirming your own worth. Bippity boppity boo!

Unaffected

I want to add one more thought before the next section, which happens to be my favorite section. Although it's nice to think about a life where you're impervious to the thoughts and opinions of others, that is an impossibility as a human being. It is impossible to be wholly unaffected by what others think. To achieve that, you have to die. When someone tells you you're amazing and they love you, it is impossible not to feel good, even if just a little. When someone tells you you're terrible and an unreliable person, it is difficult to not feel hurt and try to understand why someone might say that to you. As humans, we are affected by our surroundings and while we can't block out everything to be an impervious wall to negativity, I do believe it is possible to drastically minimize the effect other's thoughts, opinions and feelings have on you. I believe it is possible to be so strongly rooted and content with who you are that when others say good things about you it is simply a cherry on top and when others say negative things about you it is simply an opinion you observe. You don't need either to feel your own sense of self-worth, but when they happen you can minimize their effect on you.

The way to do this is grow really, really, really secure in who you are, which sounds simple but as retired athletes with foreclosed identities and little exploration fleshing out the full picture of us it is rather hard. Are you a kind person? Are you good at making friends? Are you impulsive? Are you honest?

Are you detail-oriented or do you see the big picture? There are so many other questions you need to flesh out about yourself (which we talk about in our self-discovery section coming up) to build a stable, rooted picture of you. When you do this, when you *really know* who you are as a person, you're not as easily swayed or influenced by your environment. You're you. Perfectly you. When you know who you are and are confident in knowing who you are, what others think about you drastically loses its effect on you. If you know you're a fast communicator and you text back within a couple minutes, someone saying you take forever to respond is going to seem silly to you. You know it's not true because you know your behavior patterns of texting. They could say whatever they want about your texting, but when you know how you operate and what makes you "you" it doesn't matter what someone else could say about you.

There is one person I know in my life that has this nailed down, and it is amazing to watch external feedback, opinions, and actions of others roll off his back in the most effortless way. Watching his behavior, he truly does not place merit on what others think of him because he is so secure and self-confident in himself. He rarely, if ever, experiences anxiety or rumination on the thoughts or opinions of others. When he loses a deal at work, which rarely happens, he doesn't think "Oh no, they didn't pick me. They must not like me. I'm not good enough. I did a bad job with my pitch." No. Knowing him it is almost laughable to picture him thinking this. Rather, he thinks "They made a mistake by not picking me. Their loss." It isn't an outwardly boastful attitude, but it is the strongest form of self-confidence, self-worth and security about knowing who you are. Because he is so strongly rooted in himself, he knows his strengths, weaknesses, preferences, priorities, beliefs, values, everything. Knowing all these pillars of what makes him "him", he lives a rooted, aligned life with minimal internal effects of external factors. Acutely tuning your self-view with a secure, rooted identity of "you" automatically creates the byproduct of caring less what others think. Now, let's get to know ourselves.

Self-Discovery

This is the best part! The fun part of tending to the less nourished parts of the garden of your identity is that you can watch old plants grow back to life and plant new seeds at the same time. Now that sports aren't taking up all the space in your soul, you can spend time doing hobbies you enjoyed when you were younger or begin to learn a new skill. Maybe you want to explore art, learn more about finance, or find a job in a field that interests you. The possibilities are truly endless, which is an amazing and fun advantage about our modern life. There are so many activities, people, and projects to get involved with, you can explore so many new things and find what makes you happy. The internet alone can change your life.

One crucial question to ask yourself during this time is what is important to you? I struggled to answer this question when I was going through retirement. I saw groups of people protesting life causes such as animal rights, others studied overnight to pass the business school exam, while others religiously worked out at the gym every day. It seemed everyone had that special calling inside them, pulling them through life. Everyone had something that was important to them. I didn't have that, and I didn't know what that was for me. I didn't feel strongly enough about any one thing to cause me to move in a single direction. I really was lost - everything felt bland and unimportant.

This felt weird to me, that I didn't even know what I cared about. So, every day I forcefully paid attention to what made me feel good and what did not. Being around a group of people for an extended period of time? More draining than energizing. Working out and exercising? Yes! Eating a healthy meal and fueling my body with proper nutrition? Yes. Doing similar tasks every day at work? Not so much, I seek change. Playing video games for hours? Sometimes, but I'd rather be outside. These don't sound like groundbreaking insights, but when my entire life focused on being one person I didn't have a foundation to truly know who I was at my core. I pieced together small characteristics of what I like, what I didn't like, and what made me feel good, so I could reflect my behavior around what made me, "me".

If you want to build a longer storyline of you, look back at your behaviors, for behaviors tell you so much more about who you are than your thoughts ever could. Do you follow through when people ask a favor? Are you an avid communicator? Do you plan the parties or attend the parties? Look at the things you have deliberately chosen or deliberately avoided to get a sense of what you prioritize. A simple example where I use my behaviors to indicate things about who I am is my avoidance of going to concerts. I absolutely love listening to music, but I'm not a huge fan of buying a ticket and going to a crowded concert. It isn't as appealing to me (both pre/post-Covid-19) to stand in a group of people for hours and watch someone on stage. I've certainly enjoyed concerts I've attended but going to a concert is low on my list of weekend activities. Looking at my behavior of choosing not to attend concerts, I can probably derive that I'm someone not comfortable in a large group of strangers. Which is true. Some people want to live in a high-rise in the middle of the city where all the action takes place, and some people want to live in the suburbs with peace, quiet and space. I'm the latter. Although a small example, you can review some of the decisions you've made in your own life to determine what is important to you, building a foundational picture of who you are as a person.

Take the time to find a role model. This could be a family member, a celebrity, an expert in their field, your nice neighbor or even yourself in five years. Who is someone in your life you admire? Why do you admire them? Examples of people you want to emulate are great indicators of what is important to you. Uncovering importance is a critical component to knowing who you truly are.

I highly suggest taking a professional personality assessment(s). There is the classic Myers-Briggs, but you can also conduct a quick Google search for personality tests and pick two or three to complete. See what the results say. You may think you know yourself and you probably have most things right, but there are things tests will tell you about yourself that may surprise you. Understanding which traits allow you to work effectively and grow internally dictate where you should focus your attention. If you are a person that thrives on change and innovation, you probably will find greater satisfaction working in a fast-moving startup company than in a large corporation with slow-moving bureaucracy. If you are a person that thrives on interpersonal relationships, you probably shouldn't become a software engineer. Becoming aware of who you are and what drives you helps you make decisions in your best interest, ultimately leading to greater life enjoyment and happiness. Now, without sports draining most of your time, you can do the work to understand more about who you are regardless of your "athlete" label. Plus, it can be totally fun getting to know yourself deeper and uncovering parts of you that you may not have ever known were there.

Every time I signed an offer letter with a corporation I cried. They weren't tears of joy. Deep down, I knew I thrive on change, innovation, new ideas and creativity - traits that are rare in large companies. Entering the "corporate world" of repeated tasks and predictability killed part of me inside. I did the jobs, but I could have listened to my physical responses of literal tears streaming down my face when committing to something totally misaligned with who I am. My jobs paid the bills, but after the newness of my job wore off my unfulfilled heart reared its ugly head and created tension in finding my purpose. The moral of the story is to listen to yourself, take note when things don't feel right, and take note when things do. Specify the personality traits that make you "you" and allow those to drive your actions whether it be in a career, with family, or with friends.

Whether you are a spiritual person or not, dive into the beliefs that make order in the world around you. How do you know right from wrong? Can you name the 12 laws of the universe? Do you understand the law of gravity that keeps you here on Earth? Human existence has such a cosmic and fascinating nature, and it's fun to further your understanding of the way things are. What do you believe in? Are you religious? What guides your moral compass? The answers to these questions may not be black & white, and they'll evolve for you over time, but these questions can help you begin to structure your own belief system that will serve as the core of your life. Also, stay curious with a "beginner mindset" when approaching these questions as they can get deep and daunting. It is okay if you don't know the answers or aren't sure where to begin when thinking about these topics. I certainly don't have all the answers, but I enjoy exploring. I love discussing with others, reading the lengthy forums on Reddit, watching documentaries and YouTube videos to simply learn. There are PhD's, Buddhist monks and astrologists that spend their entire lives deciphering meaning, purpose and what makes us human and even they don't have all the answers. But ask yourself some of these deeper questions and continue to engage in your world.

Another question worth pondering is what gets you excited? Does a weekend alone with nothing to do get you excited? Does a family gathering get you excited? Does booking a trip to a new destination get you excited? Spending time to think about what creates feelings of hopefulness and excitement also helps guide your attention. If you love doing puzzles with your niece, try and make more time on your calendar for family. If you loathe being indoors, seek hiking clubs or nature organizations that help get you outside. What do you look forward to? Imagine that your best friend or significant other walked into the room super excited and said "hey, we're going to ____!" How would you fill in that blank?

When you start to uncover who you really are, practice prioritization. Figuring out what brings you joy and where you place importance determines where you should focus your energy. If family is first on your list, you'll probably want to make a weekly family dinner night. If friends are first on your list, you might be an active texter to stay connected with them. Prioritization isn't set in stone and can certainly fluctuate depending on the situation but adding a bit of a prioritization structure helps give you a baseline on where to spend your time and attention first.

Self-discovery may feel daunting. It may feel like you're starting from zero once you've been plucked out of your athlete world and dropped into normal life. You may have hesitation about digging into yourself and figuring out who you are, but once you've done the work to guide you on "you", you'll realize with this understanding it is easier to live your days with satisfaction and fulfillment because you know what behaviors access those feelings. Little by little, you uncover what brings you joy, what doesn't bring you joy, and what drives meaning to your life. This is a process all human beings find themselves in for the duration of their lives - is it not the impending existential question to ask, 'Who am I'? The journey of discovering more of who you are is so rewarding and fulfilling. The more you practice behaviors that suit you, the more happiness you open yourself up to in life.

And, when we experience the inevitable downs that accompany the journey of life for every single human, think of your five-year-in-the-future self. What would your future self tell you right now? What would he/she want you to know? Whether you know it or not, reading this book and doing the inner work you're doing is making your future self so proud and happy. Think about that person. Who are they? What do they look like? Are they happy? When you do the hard, uncomfortable work now, you're making your own life easier and more open down the road.

The best way to think about this is as if you were an employee at a company you love versus at a company you hate. If you hate your company, you might kick the trash can to knock it over or purposefully jam paper in the printer. A couple days later when you need to print something or throw something away, your life is even more frustrating because you must pick up the trash can and take apart the printer to fix the problem. This is unnecessary work that multiplies your negative experience at the company. But, if you love the company you might bring in new coffee flavors for the break room or take the time to organize and wipe down your desk space. Then, every morning you come in and notice your happiness boosts because you have a pleasant morning brew experience, and you feel refreshed that you're starting your day with a clean desk. Because of your previous investment into the coffee and desk, your positive experience at the company is multiplied. Think of yourself in five years; what investments can you make now to make your future life easier? Keep fighting for the future you.

As you continue to build the picture of who you are, also take some time to reflect on who you are not. It's okay if you aren't a person that knows exactly what to say to a friend that's having some trouble. It's okay if you're not the most compassionate person. It's okay if you're not an introvert. It's okay if you aren't incredibly friendly and rather shy. It's also okay if you aren't shy and are incredibly friendly. Process of elimination helps as you ride along on your journey of self-discovery. Knowing you are not a certain archetype also helps you uncover more about what you are.

When you start to build a sense of who you are, your preferences, where you get energy, and what makes you unique, welcome the total being of you with open arms. Love yourself. Self-compassion, self-kindness and self-love are practices that will take some time to get used to because, as athletes, we've been so critical for so long. Get to know you and accept you. All your flaws and every unique trait that makes you "you" regardless of what any other person might think. Serenade yourself when love songs play on the radio. Yes, you will get strange looks. But, think of who you might be in five years and practice loving that version of you. Show your future self you are committed and excited to grow into him/her. Truly fall in love with yourself because you've likely missed out on showering yourself with kindness and love for a large chunk of your life being the critical athlete. See how it feels to love yourself. And yes, you deserve it.

Self-discovery is gratifying, fun but also a lifelong journey. As you meet new people, experience different environments, and make decisions you'll further collect data about your behaviors that will indicate who you are. This won't happen overnight. Enjoy the process of getting to know yourself outside of the sports arena and revel in watching new, beautiful flowers pop up in the garden of "you". No matter what the flowers look like, what colors they are or what they smell like, love anything and everything that comes up. After all, it is you.

Undoing Rationalization

After I retired from competitive sports in college, I struggled to deal with basic situations not having my sport constantly backing me up. I couldn't defer and had to face tough moments head on, which was incredibly uncomfortable and difficult to learn. If I got a bad score on an exam, I couldn't tell myself like I had for so many years, "oh well, it's not a big deal I'll just race even harder this weekend to break a record and I won't even remember this class in a year", which is how I dealt with much of my life that didn't occur in the pool. I avoided facing the painful facts and instead doubled down on the area of my life that was skyrocketing above everything else.

Out of survival and because I had no other choice, I learned to accept and handle life's situations with these three mindset practices practiced in this order:

1. Accept that I'm human and make mistakes
2. View situations objectively
3. Take responsibility for myself

We've already dissected perfectionism, making it difficult for our ego to accept fault, admit error or blatantly claim that we did something imperfect (or wrong). Boy, it is not easy. Referencing our previous section about acceptance, accepting that we are indeed a human being that will make errors tomorrow and the next and the next is simply part of life. Learning to accept the physical laws of the species that I was born into, like the inevitability of mistakes, eliminated resistance in my attempts to rationalize or overcompensate. I accept and expect a human, not a perfectionist robot.

A byproduct of this new perspective was the ability to view situations objectively. If I failed a statistics exam (which I did many times), I viewed the situation with an objective lens. Yes, the professor doesn't speak English that well, but I also didn't study enough. Owning up to areas where I wasn't necessarily "perfect" became easier to do once I learned how to accept the human being in me. It was safe to do so. I didn't avoid admitting my faults and was able to remove biases and charged emotions about any situation. I ended up removing an often-felt burden of victimization and feeling wronged that amplified negative feelings. I could have resented my statistics professor for making the class so challenging and walked around placing the blame on him. I could have held my rose-colored self-view as a perfectionist and refused to admit the human being in me. But, in learning to truly look at the events in my life objectively any ill-will or feelings of being a victim evaporate.

Once I accepted that I was an error-prone human being and practiced looking at all sides of a situation, I was then able to accept total responsibility for me. I could see areas where I didn't do my best and could step up to the plate and admit that my shortcomings were my responsibility. I couldn't delay, defer or avoid responsibility because I didn't have an area of my life to use for overcompensation. Swimming was gone, and whatever happened to me (within my control), happened because of me.

This shift in the way I viewed myself and the events in my life lifted an enormous weight off my shoulders. I had lived with the rooted mindset that I was always perfect and it was never my fault because, being an athlete, I was conditioned from both internal and external cues that I was good, strong, perfect and smart. So, when negative experiences inevitably happened it would always crush me because I couldn't get past that mindset of "how could THIS happen to ME?" I often felt victimized which was even more confusing and painful. I never had the wisdom to view myself as part of the problem. And, I want to clearly state I'm not saying this to shame myself or guilt myself. I am expressing this from a kind, objective eye about what I've noticed in my own life behavior.

Now, with a humanistic, objective view, I felt safe to accept my faults. I was able to not only resolve myself in situations that didn't pan out in my favor, but I actively engaged in my shortcomings, as uncomfortable as it was for me, to work through the problems life threw my way. If I didn't take an active role in changing my mindset around rationalizing difficulties, my frustrations would fester inside myself ultimately creating a bitter human being. Rather than practicing an avoidant conflict style with issues that arose outside of my sport, I learned to accept the human in me, observe objectively, and take responsibility for my life without my athlete identity backing me up.

Attention

Once your final match ends and you walk off the field for the last time how do you navigate the psychological shift of going from being the star to being just another person? Simply seeing bleachers full of supporting fans to no bleachers at all influences how we perceive ourselves. Am I not good enough anymore? Am I not worthy of the attention anymore? These questions may be subconscious, but it is normal to ask these questions once the attention shifts away from us once we retire.

At first, it can feel humiliating to your ego to let go of its own importance. For so long you've been the center of attention. All the sacrifices your family and coach have made have been for you. You. There will be an internal struggle and denial of accepting that you're no longer the shit that everyone else thinks you are. Your ego craves accomplishments, recognition, and applause - things that practically vanish when you retire.

To smooth over the new decrease in attention, it is critical to understand the attention you've garnered focuses on what you've done and not who you are. In the sports world, no one can fill up a stadium of fans for "being the kindest" or "being the funniest". You've achieved medals because of your strength or speed, not because you were kind enough to pay for the coffee for the next person in line. Sports are a concrete, surface level, black & white results world based on what you can do. The attention you receive reflects your capabilities, and when you retire and the attention is gone it is never a reflection on who you are. It is simply a reflection on the impossibility of showcasing your capabilities anymore. I know you know this is true because you can probably name an experience or two where you had a kickass season or stellar routine and someone whom you did not know or weren't friends with came up to you afterward to say, "Nice job". They don't know who you are, your favorite color, what books you like to read or your skincare routine. They simply gave you attention for the things you did on the field. Attention as an athlete, whether we have all of it or none of it, has nothing to do with you.

Referring back to The Four Agreements, one of the four agreements is to never take things personally. This is one of the great pillars to live life by, removing the unnecessary stress and burden of taking things so close to heart.

> Even when a situation seems so personal, even if others insult you directly, it has nothing to do with you. What they say, what they do, and the opinions they give are according to the agreements they have in their own minds…Taking things personally makes you easy prey for these predators, the black magicians. They can hook you easily with one little opinion and feed you whatever poison they want, and because you take it personally, you eat it up… (Ruiz, 2018).

Remember, after you retire and the bleachers are empty it is simply because you're not actively competing anymore. It's not an outward showcase that people don't like you or don't love you anymore.

Support From Others (and making new friends)

Human beings are innately social creatures, desiring belonging and community. In an article about retirement, Scott Tinley, two-time Ironman World Champion, claims that "social support is the most significant factor in an elite athlete's successful transition into retirement."[21] While you've had a team with you your entire sports journey, supporting your wins and comforting your losses, a post-sport life doesn't offer the level of entrenched team support that sport offers. It may suddenly feel like you're unrelated to, you feel less important, and you lack the basic human need for connection. The disconnect and lack of social support can drive you further into isolation.

If you have understanding family members, reach out to them. If your teammates are also entering a post-sport life, commit to supporting each other. As the world of sports psychology and mental health awareness grows, the number of community resources available to retired athletes is also growing. Connect to others via online groups or platforms such as Reddit, Facebook or communities offered by independent organizations. The internet can serve as an open door for you to discover like-minded people that share the same life experiences and truly "get it". How relieving it is to talk to someone who knows exactly how you feel. Lean on community groups, lean on the human connections you have, or can create, and recognize that the strength of the social support in your life is a critical factor in successfully realizing a healthy transition.

Learn how to make new friends, too. This can be a seemingly simple yet challenging task for ex-athletes to do considering we haven't always practiced the social norms non-athletes are so used to when making new friends. We talked about how our friends may have started as our teammates who were given to us by our environment and we may ask "would we even be friends with them if we weren't on the same team?" We may not know or have the courage to walk up to someone new and strike up a conversation on our own. Maybe we're always used to being approached, so it feels different to us to have to do the legwork of conversing with another human. To brush up our social skills of making new friends, learn by example and practice, practice, practice.

You know who the sociable people are in your circles. You know who seems to glide through conversations with ease and charisma. Spend some time with those people and watch how they interact with others. What do they say? Are they talking more or listening more? Observe how they converse and interact. If you don't have access to a friendship-making guru, set aside some time to sit at a coffee shop and eavesdrop on other tables. Weird, yes. But helpful, yes. Sit on a park bench and watch how people interact with each other. People-watching is so entertaining. Watch, listen and learn what others do and say and decide for yourself what you like, what you don't like and what aligns with something you yourself might say or do. Expose yourself to a number of different people in different situations and practice what you've observed. You can access new groups of people with common interests on websites such as Meetup.com, Facebook groups for people with same interests, online book clubs, and more.

Show up to the same events or places on a habitual basis. How did you become close with classmates and friends in middle school and high school? You all went to the same classroom every day or engaged in the same activities. Over time, those faces became familiar and before you knew it you had a new friend. Go to the same coffee shop. Join a new team. Join a new club. Repeat social environments to increase your chances of making a new friend.

Say "yes" more than "no". If you're invited to go somewhere or do something say "yes". Just go. It doesn't have to be a huge ordeal. It doesn't have to be intricately planned and laid out on your calendar. There doesn't have to be some ulterior motive or meaning behind hanging out other than, quite simply, just hanging out. After all, humans are wired for connection. If you have a bit of free time, go. Just go. This is a bit more of my tough Irish love. Just go.

Diversify Your Life

As an athlete, we've pursued our dreams as a singular pursuit. Hopefully by now you understand the role of Identity Foreclosure in closing off other parts of ourselves and our lives to give 100% committed dedication to be the best athlete we could be. Now, explore your life by diversifying your pursuits and activities. Not only does this remove the intense pressure that accompanies an over-reliance on one area of our life to meet our needs, but it creates a well-balanced individual.

The perfect analogy to this is the stock market. As an athlete, we dumped our entire cash into a single stock. That single stock made up 100% of our portfolio. When that stock performed poorly, we felt the pain of our price dropping. But, when the stock hit a stride we smiled and reveled in making a hugely profitable return. It makes sense why, as an athlete, the highs feel so high and the lows feel so low because we are totally invested into the single pursuit of playing our sport.

All the finance experts recommend diversifying your portfolio as to not give too much weight to any one investment. Don't just invest in a single stock, such as Coca-Cola, invest in multiple stocks. Not just large cap stocks but small cap stocks, invest a bit in bonds, international markets and maybe even cryptocurrency. Why? To decrease risk. If any one of them performs poorly you have others to help counteract the difference. It is the same philosophy to live a balanced, healthy life. If you want to go "all in" on another pursuit in life such as your job, that is fine, but expect similar intensity of the highs and lows that made up your athlete career.

My advice would be to not throw all your eggs in one basket. Pick up a new sport, establish a new friend group, if you have a job that allows enough time for a side hustle explore that option, read different genres of books, anything you can do to expand your activities and explore several pursuits to decrease risk of over-reliance on one activity to meet your needs is encouraged. Decrease risk, expose yourself to several different people and activities, and diversify.

You Don't Know Everything

As an athlete, you were an expert. You knew the ins and outs. You knew what worked for you and what did not. You knew everything. Entering a post-sport life, you will not be an expert. You're not an expert at life (is anyone?). You are a student of life. You can learn so much. At first, this may feel insulting, but it is actually rather relieving. Instead of being the teacher, constantly performing under pressure, you get to sit back and be the student. You can watch, listen, learn, and revel in a bit of comfort that you aren't expected to have all the answers. You're allowed to figure it out as you go.

You've always been the star of the show, carrying the burden to 'ooh' and 'aah' the crowds. You've always been in control. Maybe in conversation you notice you're always thinking of what to say next rather than listening to the other person speak. Do you often find yourself in control, composed? Or do you find yourself laughing in conversation, letting yourself be ebbed and flowed? Athletes have a hard time letting themselves be "affected", letting go of control. Do you ever drop your guard and let yourself be 'oohed' and 'aahed' by others, by the world, so for once you can be the person reacting to your environment? Try it sometime. Drop your guard that you have to know everything, control everything, and let yourself react. Enjoy the relief of taking a seat and letting the world perform for you for once.

Create a Plan

Last but certainly not least, create a plan. Before you actually conduct any action, outline potential steps even it is just one. Think about a game or a match where you created a plan to effectively compete. Maybe you had a tennis match, and you love to play with two different rackets with different styles. You want to play the first set with one racket and see how it goes. In case things go wrong or the racket isn't working for you, in the second set you can always reach in your bag and play with your second racket. Albeit a super small example, this simple plan of potentially switching rackets offers relief and comfort before you play considering the uncertainty of how you might compete in the first set.

This is especially true when we are feeling overwhelmed, it may feel like we have no control over the situation. Especially when we're new to retirement and feel like there's a long road ahead of growing contentment and satisfaction in our new life, creating a plan helps us visualize what we can do and how we can make progress. When we create a plan, or just the first step of action, we take back a little bit of control and create our own hope. The best analogy to explain creating a plan is the simple metaphor that it provides a light at the end of the tunnel. Without a plan, you're stuck in the dark not knowing where to begin, which direction to go or what's involved to get you there. You roam around in a dark tunnel feeling lost and helpless. A plan offers actionable guidance, relieving uncertainty and shifting your energy to your desired direction. Your plan can include daily, weekly, or monthly steps to help guide you. In your plan, a few examples could be…

- Plan celebratory dinner or event with your friends/parents
- Daily mirror work with affirmations
- Exercise 2-3x a week
- Read 1 book a month
- Build a Saturday morning self-care routine
- Set up a weekly call with a teammate/mentor to check-in
- Write closure letters to your sport & from your sport
- Counseling/therapy 1x a week
- Allow space for grief and sensitivity about not actively competing
- Sign up for one volunteer event
- Write out a list of things that characterize you
- Write out a list of things that are important to you
- Start a small project around your living space (DIY)
- Attend one new social event

Whatever your plan happens to look like for you, lay out the steps to help guide your attention and effort. You'll see, before any action on your part has taken place, you'll feel lighter, hopeful, and ready to simply take the first step in your new life.

Chapter 17 Endnotes

1. Taylor, J. (2014, May 15). *Book Chapters*. Dr. Jim Taylor. https://www.drjimtaylor. com/4.0/writing/book-chapters/
2. *When the Playing Days End | An NCAA Champion Feature | NCAA.org*. (n.d.). NCAA. Retrieved May 28, 2021, from https://www.ncaa.org/static/champion/when-the-playing-days-end/
3. *Why Vitamin B Complex Is Important to Your Health*. (2021, May 5). Verywell Fit. https:// www.verywellfit.com/b-complex-vitamins-89411
4. the Healthline Medical Network. (2019, March 8). *What Does Gamma Aminobutyric Acid (GABA) Do?* Healthline. https://www.healthline.com/health/gamma-aminobutyric-acid
5. *Spend Time in Nature to Reduce Stress and Anxiety*. (2018). Www.Heart.Org. https:// www.heart.org/en/healthy-living/healthy-lifestyle/stress-management/spend-time-in-nature-to-reduce-stress-and-anxiety#:%7E:text=Time%20in%20nature%20 results%20in,is%20vital%20for%20mental%20health.&text=Angsty%3A%20At%20 times%2C%20you%20might,how%20wondrous%20the%20world%20is.
6. Efron, Z., Olien, D., Barrett, J., Gmelich, G., Henson, C., Simpkin, M., Volk-Weiss, B. (Executive Producers). (2020). *Down to Earth* [TV series]. The Nacelle Company. Netflix.
7. Pawula, S. (2019, September 17). *How to Let Go of Self-Attachment (And Why It's Important)*. Always Well Within. https://www.alwayswellwithin.com/blog/let-go-self-attachment
8. LIZ HENDERSON liz.henderson@gazette.com. (2021, February 8). *Athletes struggle to find purpose, identity after sports | Special Report*. Colorado Springs Gazette. https:// gazette.com/news/athletes-struggle-to-find-purpose-identity-after-sports-special-report/article_ea000d90-220f-11ea-b1ac-9f79e1310dd8.html#:%7E:text=Experts%20 say%20the%20dynamics%20of,term%20physical%20and%20psychological%20 health.&text=The%20pressure%20to%20recover%20leads,them%20especially%20 susceptible%20to%20depression.
9. Grief.com. (2021, March 31). *Five Stages of Grief by Elisabeth Kubler Ross & David Kessler*. https://grief.com/the-five-stages-of-grief/#:%7E:text=The%20five%20stages%2C%20 denial%2C%20anger,some%20linear%20timeline%20in%20grief.
10. Wikipedia contributors. (2021b, July 30). *Forgiveness*. Wikipedia. https://en.wikipedia. org/wiki/Forgiveness
11. M. (2021b, May 19). *Negative Thinking – What your poor brain doesn't know. . . .* Mi-Psych | Mindfulness & Clinical Psychology Solutions. https://mi-psych.com.au/what-your-brain-doesnt-know/
12. Davies, S. T. (2021, June 13). *How to Overcome Obstacles by Using Toyota's Five Whys Technique*. Sam Thomas Davies. https://www.samuelthomasdavies.com/five-whys/
13. Orlowski, J. (Director). (2020). *The Social Dilemma* [Documentary]. Exposure Labs, Argent Pictures, The Space Program. Netflix.
14. D., L. (2019, March 15). *15 Interesting Facts about Dreams*. Bored Panda. https://www. boredpanda.com/15-interesting-facts-about-dreams-dreaming/?utm_source=editor. reedsy&utm_medium=referral&utm_campaign=organic
15. *Justin Wren: First time kiddo's of Congo see white dude! Fight For The Forgotten*. (2012, September 27). [Video]. YouTube. https://www.youtube.com/watch?v=ide5YjD6AhI
16. Busch, M. (2019, May 26). *8 Ways to Stop Being a Perfectionist*. May Busch. https:// maybusch.com/8-ways-stop-being-perfectionist/

17. Ackerman, C. E., MA. (2021b, April 15). *What is Self-Worth and How Do We Increase it? (Incl. 4 Worksheets)*. PositivePsychology.Com. https://positivepsychology.com/self-worth/

18. Dokoupil, T., King, G. (2021, May 1st). Olympic Gymnast on Importance of Mental Health, "World Wellness Break". *CBS News*. https://www.facebook.com/watch/?v=2916426025244842

19. *Definition and Three Elements of Self Compassion | Kristin Neff*. (2020, July 9). Self-Compassion. https://self-compassion.org/the-three-elements-of-self-compassion-2/

20. Brown, B., PhD. (2021). *BY Brown, Brene, Ph.D. (Author) [Daring Greatly] 04–2015 Paperback*. Avery Publishing Group 2015–04-07.

21. West, G. (2012, July 13). *Why is it so difficult for athletes to retire?* Fort Worth Star-Telegram. https://www.star-telegram.com/sports/article3831989.html

Post-Game

"Pleasant experiences make life delightful.
Painful experiences lead to growth.
Suffering points up an area in you where you have not grown,
where you need to grow,
and be transformed and change."
—*Anthony De Mello*

Chapter 18

The Locker Room

Our athlete identity as the core of who we are deeply affects all aspects of our lives, subconsciously and consciously. Reflecting on the who, why and what of being an athlete, we take the squeegee to fogged glass helping us see clearer, draw accurate conclusions, derive meaning and act wisely in ways that best serve ourselves. We can resolve past tensions that grip deeper parts of us while making informed decisions in our current lives. We can practice healthy mindsets that prevent us from succumbing to extreme pitfalls. We become more in touch with the athlete inside us, taking care of that competitor with an attentive, proactive approach. We're then able to reach milestones of clarity we never thought existed.

Because of an athlete's perfectionist attitude, it is a simple yet powerful reminder that growing mental strength isn't about becoming a perfect you. It isn't about highlighting flaws and "fixing them". Athletes often want the technical remedy that will heal the problem. But, with more fluid, deeper, intangible practices like shifting perspectives, the focus is on perfecting the practice and not the person. Become really good at acceptance. Become really good at managing expectations. Become really good at objective thinking and forgiveness. Devote yourself to growing your method. Hopefully, by the end of this book you've realized insights or messages that resonate with your own experiences. Use what clicked with you as opportunities to build the pillars that will set you up for the rest of your life. These mindsets aren't restricted to the athlete's environment, although highly applicable, and can build your tolerance for whatever waves crash on your shore. Like pouring concrete into a new sidewalk frame, what ingredients are you going to mix to create the foundation that will make it easy to walk the rest of your life?

One Final Thought

In 1996, Gymnast Kerri Strug secured the Gold for USA by performing her vault routine on an injured ankle. She injured herself after her landing on the previous vault but the coaches urged (forced) her to continue, for the gold was dependent upon the score of her vault. If you watch the video, she runs, vaults, lands, and immediately bends her knee to lift her injured ankle off the floor. She falls to her knees, wincing in pain and is carried off the mat by the coach because she could not walk. Her effort to continue to vault was applauded and heralded as a heroic act. Sure, she won the gold for the team, but I can't help but cringe watching her agonizing facial expressions after falling to the mat.

If this is how physical injuries were treated in 1996, imagine how mental injuries were treated (or totally and completely ignored). That era of sport is what I characterize as young, naive, and unknowledgeable about prioritizing the health of an athlete. Winning came before above all else and Strug's vault showcases the historical, harmful approach of neglecting the health of athletes. It makes sense why there are dismal statistics of athlete's suffering, such as the fact that "35% of elite athletes suffer from a mental health crisis."[1]

The new, burgeoning era of sport is here, and I characterize athletes in this era as mature, responsible and mindful. Athletes recognize the few seconds or minutes of competition are not worth the sacrifice of suffering off the field. Athletes recognize there is more to who they are than being "the track star".

Olympic gold medalist and world-famous gymnast, Simone Biles, surprisingly withdrew from the team and individual competitions in the 2020 Tokyo Olympics and posted on her social media, saying, "the outpouring of love & support I've received has made me realize I'm more than my accomplishments and gymnastics which I never truly believed before."[2] Athletes recognize that while winning is the goal, it doesn't trump the negative ramifications of mental health neglect. Is that gold medal worth a year-long bout with Major Depression? It is inspiring to see athletes stand up for themselves, for their minds, and set the new precedent that health is wealth and more valuable than another trophy on the shelf.

My hope for athletes in this new era is that elite competition becomes fun again. My hope for athletes is that no matter what emotional road bumps or hardships you encounter on your journey, you can process and thrive through it. My hope is that the heartbreaking statistics in sport decrease. My hope is that this book further cracks open the ceiling to shed light on what athletes can start practicing today to build a stronger mind. My hope is that athletes better understand themselves as competitors and use that knowledge to make aligned decisions. My hope is that athletes take advantage of the knowledge being put out there about mental health in sport to compete your best, support other athletes and, most importantly, grow an even stronger, healthier mind.

Don't indulge the victim story that is easy to lose yourself in considering the complexities of being an athlete. Don't allow your mind to suffer because the sports culture conditioned you to not tap into your emotions. Don't give up and slide through life wishing you could live with more clarity and ease. Because you can. You can sift through your identity and align yourself so sharply with who you are. You can clear emotional hang ups from your athlete journey to open up space for exploration and joy in a new chapter of life. You can compete at insanely elite levels with a near perfect physical body while also maintaining a never-before-felt level of strength for your mind. Now, maybe you can answer this question for your own life. What if you took care of your mind just as much as you did your body?

Chapter 18 Endnotes

1. McMillan, B. (2019, May 16). *Mental Health and Athletes*. Athletes for Hope. https://www.athletesforhope.org/2019/05/mental-health-and-athletes/#:%7E:text=But%20of%20college%20athletes%20with,burnout%2C%20or%20depression%20and%20anxiety.
2. Biles, S. [@simonebiles]. (2021, July 29). the outpouring love & support I've received has made me realize I'm more than my accomplishments and gymnastics which I never truly believed before. [Instagram photo]. Retrieved from https://www.instagram.com/p/CR5oCyRhfS3/.

Acknowledgements

My first thanks go to my parents, for putting me in sports in the first place. For the endless swim meets, expensive swimsuits and cleats, and the rollercoaster of emotions experienced along the way, I thank you for your unconditional support of your athlete daughter.

To my coaches, helping me realize my own successes and being some of my favorite role models. Ian Goss, Michael Soderlund, Eric Stefanski, Paul Naruse and Glenn Meeden. Words don't describe the impact you have on me. To my teammates, especially Shannon O'Malley, thank you for keeping me sane and being a rock of support during my toughest high school moments.

To my therapist, thank you for sticking with me through one of the most hectic years of my life. Thank you for guiding me on the gratifying journey of figuring out my own self and being one of my biggest supporters when I came up with this crazy idea to quit my job and write a book.

I am indefinitely indebted to the people who have helped with the actual creation of the book. My editor, Mohamad Al-Hakim, thank you for reading the nonsense of my thoughts and applying a method to the madness. My book designer, Matthew Revert, thank you for creating a polished final product.

To the early supporters who took a chance reading a manuscript from a first-time author. Thank you, Dr. Markus Rogan, Dr. Jim Taylor, Mariana Flores, Haley Perry and Sarah (@sarahijaved). Your thoughts, feedback and positive reviews further inspired me to bring this project to light.

Endless thanks to those who lent their ear to a Georgia girl with a simple idea of helping other athletes. Your advice and connections in getting this project out into the world has been invaluably helpful: John Acunto, Eric Nemeth, Chasity Edwards, Joe Nahra, Eric Kussin, Shante Bacon, Lia Head-Rigby, Kelly Whitehart, Billy Ching, Nate Malek and Stefon Walters.

To the athletes that read this book. I hope you find some benefit so that when you're navigating the bumps along your own journey, the hurt hurts less.

About the Author

Kimberly Carducci is a former D1 Swimmer, Author, Podcaster, Sports Researcher and Mental Health Advocate. She was a 4-time State Champion, 4-time Scholastic All-American, 4-time All-State Selection and an 8-time All-American Honoree. She was a member of the 2005 Georgia Zone Team and was a member and individual champion on the 2007 Georgia Zone Team. Recruited to compete at The University of North Carolina, Carducci garnered accolades including National College Swimmer of the Week.

Her personal journey of overcoming severe depression after retiring from sport drives her to educate athlete's on how best to manage the toughest moments of elite competition.

Her organization, Everything Athletes, serves as an online refuge supporting athlete's mental health struggles and offers practical wisdom to thrive in sport. In addition to her website, podcast, online courses, and blog, *The I of the Tiger* is her first published book. She's an avid reader and loves to dive into athlete memoirs and personal growth topics.

Carducci currently resides in Atlanta and has since picked up recreational tennis as her new sports endeavor. Follow her social media accounts to stay up-to-date with future content, @everythingathletesdotcom.